FINDING THEIR VOICE

Northeastern Villagers and the Thai State

Charles Keyes

Silkworm Books

ISBN: 978-616-215-074-6

First Published in 2014 by

Silkworm Books
6 Sukkasem Road, T. Suthep
Chiang Mai 50200 Thailand
info@silkwormbooks.com
http://www.silkwormbooks.com

Typeset in Arno Pro 11 pt. by Silk Type
Printed in Thailand by O. S. Printing House, Bangkok

5 4 3 2 1

CONTENTS

PREFACE

This book is the product of my long engagement of over a half-century with the study of rural northeastern Thailand, the region better known in Thailand as Isan. I first encountered the region through various publications that I consulted while I was a graduate student at Cornell, but although I decided I would focus my research on this region it was not until 1962 that it became a reality to me. Even before Jane, my wife, and I first went there in mid-November 1962, we learned how the region was viewed by the employees of the United States Operations Mission to Thailand (USOM) under the United States Agency for International Development (USAID), by a number of Thai officials, by our Thai teachers, and by friends we made in Bangkok where we lived from mid-August to mid-November 1962. We became aware that the Northeast was considered to be a political problem (*panha Isan*) not only because of the linguistic and cultural connections of the vast majority of the people of the region to the Lao, and the presumed connections between some northeastern political leaders and Communist parties in Laos, Vietnam, and China, but also because of the economic underdevelopment (*doi patthana*) of the region. From the beginning my research was inevitably as much concerned with the politics of the region as it was with the theoretical issues about peasant society and modernity—or, to use more contemporary terms, agrarian transformations—that I had focused on as a graduate student in anthropology.

Between late 1962 and April 1964 Jane and I carried out research in Ban Nong Tuen, a village in Tambon Khwao, Muang District, Maha Sarakham Province in the center of the northeastern region.[1] We have returned to this village many times, and we made extended restudies there in the early 1980s and in 2004–5. As I said in my thank you speech when I was awarded an honorary PhD by Maha Sarakham University in 2004, this village has become over the years my "reality check" on what I know about Thailand (Keyes 2004). Even though I have also spent a long period engaged in research and teaching in northern Thailand and have lived for some time in Bangkok, I have continued to turn to Ban Nong Tuen and to the rural Northeast to make sense of the transformations Thai society has gone through in the past half century. This village will have a prominent role in this book.

I have also drawn on many of my writings about northeastern Thailand over the years, attempting here to go beyond those works and, as I discuss in the prologue, *rethink* what I had thought I understood about the region and especially about those who identify as "villagers" (*chao ban*) even when they have long lived outside their natal communities. As I hope I show in this book, understanding the transformed "rural" northeastern region is essential to understanding how the Thai nation-state is being reshaped in the early twenty-first century.

I am deeply grateful to many people for their reactions, comments, criticisms, and sometimes perplexed responses to what I have written and discussed about Thailand's rural Northeast. Foremost among my debts is that which I owe to Jane, who agreed to go to Thailand immediately after we were married and live in a village without any modern conveniences. She has been my partner in research, my best critic, my editor, and my collaborator.

Although I am now a retired professor rather than the graduate student I was when I first became interested in northeastern Thailand, I recognize that many of my ideas were first shaped by my major professors at Cornell. I am indebted to the late Lauriston Sharp, who was responsible for my taking an abiding interest in the transformation of rural Thailand. I am indebted to the late G. William Skinner for guiding me to take a regional as well as a village-based approach to the study of sociopolitical change. I owe a debt to the late George McT. Kahin, who, although not a member of my PhD committee, still influenced me strongly by showing me how political engagement can be joined with good scholarship.

I also owe a significant debt to the late Ngao Khamwicha (1935–91) who became a close friend as well as my mentor on rural northeastern Thailand when we shared a house in Ban Nong Tuen during our first period of fieldwork. His wife, Nuan, and their children and grandchildren have remained Jane's and my family in the village. When we were engaged in our first research in northeastern Thailand, A. Thomas Kirsch (1930–99), then a graduate student at Harvard and later professor of anthropology at Cornell, was also undertaking fieldwork in another part of the rural Northeast. I truly miss the exchanges by letter, and later by email and phone, as well as in person, that I had with Tom about our experiences in Isan. I wish he could have given me feedback on this book.

During our first time in Bangkok, we met Bill Klausner, then with the Asia Foundation, and benefitted from his advice as one of the first researchers to carry out a study in rural northeastern Thailand. Over the years I have often turned to Bill, who most recently has been the president of the James H. W. Thompson Foundation and an affiliate of the Institute of Security and International Studies at Chulalongkorn University, to get his reaction to what I have written about northeastern Thailand and Thai society and politics more generally. I am very grateful that he has continued to offer me insightful reactions to my interpretations.

I have myself served as a mentor to a number of students from Thailand and several of these have assisted me in our research while going on to forge significant careers of their own. Amara Pongsapich, my first student from Thailand, who would go on to have a distinguished career at Chulalongkorn University and more recently as the head of the Thailand Human Rights Commission, helped me when she was a student to work through a number of works in Thai about Isan. Paitoon Mikusol, now retired after holding academic positions at Srinakarinwirot University in Maha Sarakham and Walailak University in Nakhon Si Thammarat, assisted us in our fieldwork in the early 1980s. Ratana Tosakul, now at Thammasat University, and Pattana Kitiarsa, who taught at the National

A NOTE ON TRANSLITERATION

In this work, I have based my romanization of Thai words upon the 1999 version of the Royal Thai General System of Transcription, as devised by the Royal Institute of Thailand. In this system, neither tone nor vowel length is indicated. My use of *muang* rather than *mueang*, in accordance with the convention among Thai studies scholars, is an exception to the Royal Thai system. I have used standard English versions of Thai proper names and place-names rather than transliterated forms. When standardized names do not exist or are uncommon, I have used the transliterated forms.

PROLOGUE

On May 19, 2010, beginning at about four o'clock in the morning (I know the time because I was in Bangkok and already on-line watching the tweets), Thai military forces began to position themselves around the Ratchaprasong/Lumpini/Silom area of central Bangkok where protestors known as the Red Shirts (*Suea daeng*) had been rallying since April 3. As the troops tightened the noose, the leaders of the protestors—who now numbered about three thousand—decided to surrender in order to limit the loss of lives that further opposition would likely incur. Thus ended, for the time being, the two-month public protest (which began first in another part of the city) organized by the United Front for Democracy against Dictatorship (UDD, *Naeo ruam prachathipatai totan phadetkan haeng chat*), better known as the Red Shirts. The protestors sought the resignation of the government led by Abhisit Vejjajiva and the Democrat Party, a government that the UDD considered had come to power through political machinations rather than by election.

On the night of the nineteenth, I was in a hotel in Thonburi, where I was attending an academic workshop at the nearby Princess Maha Chakri Sirindhorn Anthropology Centre. I was surprised when I received a phone call from Seth Mydans, the senior *New York Times* correspondent in Bangkok, who told me he wanted to write something reflective about the crisis. It took me a moment to shift from my preoccupation with the events of the day that I had been discussing with colleagues to try to formulate a brief perspective based on my nearly half-century research and experience in Thailand, much of it focused on the rural part of northeastern Thailand. What I said was summarized in a quote that ends the article Mydans published the next day (Mydans 2010): "My understanding of what I have learned over the years has really come into question. . . . I question all the things I've learned about this country."

As I reflected on what I meant by this statement, I realized I had a number of questions about the rise of the Red Shirt movement. For one, I wondered why the protestors, who although they were overwhelmingly people with roots in rural northeastern Thailand, should identify as *phrai*, a term that historically had meant peasants that were bonded to members of the elite, when I knew from my own research that rural northeasterners had long since ceased to be traditional peasants. I also questioned why the protestors had made red the symbol of their identity, a color widely seen in Thailand as associated with communists, when I knew that rural northeasterners had been deeply skeptical about communism and that this skepticism had contributed to the failure of a communist-led revolution between the 1960s and the early 1980s. I had yet another question: Why were the protestors so insistent that new elections be held rather than seeking to take over the government directly? Why, in other words, did the protestors put so much faith in democracy?

The rethinking that I felt compelled to do led me back to my book, *Isan: Regionalism in Northeastern Thailand,* published in 1967. That book had been written at a time when the Thai government confronted what was termed the "northeastern problem" (*panha Isan*). The problem, as it was then understood, derived from official concerns that the people of the region, most of whom share a linguistic and cultural heritage with the Lao (the dominant people of Laos), might seek to separate their region and join it to Laos. At the time, the Thai government, abetted by the United States, had become engaged in a war in neighboring Vietnam, Laos, and Cambodia. The government also feared that the northeasterners, in questioning their status within Thailand, might look for guidance from communists in those countries as well as in China. A half-century later, many in the Thai elite are still concerned that the people in the region have a problematic relationship to the Thai nation-state.

It seemed puzzling to me that there should still be a "northeastern problem," despite the fact that today Thailand enjoys friendly relations with Laos even though it has a communist-led government; despite the fact that rural northeasterners have clearly gained from the dramatic growth in the Thai economy over the past half century even if not nearly as much as has the elite and urban middle class; and despite the fact that people with roots in the Northeast today have long since come to accept and understand that they are "Thai" even if they also retain strong attachment to their rural Lao traditions. The problem today should be seen, I now maintain, as lying not with the questionable loyalty of the rural people of northeastern Thailand but with an inadequate appreciation by the elite and urban middle class of the legitimate desire of northeasterners to have a significant voice in national politics. The ethnoregionalism of the Thai-Lao of northeastern Thailand that I first traced in *Isan* and again here must be seen today as a manifestation of pressures also exerted by others in Thailand—by the Malay-speaking people of southern Thailand, by the Khon Muang of northern Thailand, by the Khon Pak Tai or southern Thai, and by the hill peoples of northern Thailand—to forge a new national consensus that allows for greater recognition of the diversity of the citizenry. This is a long-needed replacement for the internal-colonialist Siamese elite–centered nation that was first envisioned in the late nineteenth century and has been the basis of Thai government policy ever since. In other words, Isan is not the problem today; the problem lies in a political system that remains defined by assumptions that the Thailand of the early twenty-first century is the same as the Thailand that emerged from the Siamese empire in the late nineteenth century.

Map of Northeast Thailand

Main roads and highways
Railroads
Commercial airports
United States air bases

1

RURAL ISAN

FROM LAO TO ISAN

The peoples living in the northern part of the Siamese empire at the end of the nineteenth century were generally referred to as "Lao" by the people of Siam and by the members of the Bangkok court in particular. This appellation designated speakers of dialects related to the dialects spoken today in Laos and northeastern Thailand, as well as in northern Thailand, in northern Laos, in Kengtung in the southern Shan states, and in the southernmost part of Yunnan in China. Together, the peoples considered "Lao" constituted well over half of the population of the Siamese empire, whereas those considered "Thai," meaning the people of central Thailand and the upper southern peninsula, constituted no more than a quarter of the population.[1] Even after the Siamese court was compelled, in a series of treaties with the French, to recognize areas that today are in central and southern Laos and northwestern Cambodia as belonging to French Indochina, the "Lao" population of Siam still constituted approximately half the population.

The French claimed the "Lao" as belonging to their Indochinese empire. In response, the Siamese court set out to redefine the majority peoples living in northern and northeastern Thailand as "Thai" rather than "Lao" (chapter 2). This was part of an effort begun in 1892 to refashion what had been the empire of Siam into a modern nation-state that could withstand threats from the expanding British and French empires. The nationalizing task was taken up by Prince Damrong Rajanubhab, a man who served as both minister of interior and minister of education under his brother, King Chulalongkorn, and who became the "father" of Thai national history. Writing after the events, Prince Damrong observed, "People in Bangkok have long called [the peoples of northern Siam] Lao. Today, however, we know they are Thai, not Lao" (Damrong 1961 [1935], 318, my translation).

As minister of interior, Prince Damrong was responsible for instituting new political divisions for the previously rather autonomous vassals and domains (*hua muang*) in the Lao areas. These divisions, called *monthon* ("circles," a word derived from the Sanskrit mandala[2]) were given new names to indicate that they were regional components of the Thai state. Prince Damrong turned to Sanskrit, the classical language that had long been used as the source for administrative terms in Thai, for the new names for the Lao *monthon*. Although the *monthon* system would later be abolished in favor of division of the country into provinces (*changwat*), Isan, whose root meaning is "northeast," was chosen for one of the *monthon* in northeastern Thailand and subsequently remained in use to refer to the whole of the region.[3] Whereas the other regions of Thailand are sometimes identified with a major political-cultural center, (i.e., Bangkok with the central plains, Chiang Mai with the North, and Nakhon Si Thammarat with the Tai-speaking South), the Northeast has no single political center and Isan is, thus, a more collective designation.[4]

Despite the Siamese authorities' attempt to suppress the identity of people in the Northeast as Lao and resituate them as regional Thai, the northeasterners continued to call themselves Lao.[5] In the Buddhist millennialist (*phu mi bun*) uprising of the early twentieth century, which was the first mass resistance to integration into the Thai nation-state, the Lao sought to restore the premodern order in which Lao-ness was represented by traditional *chao* or lords (chapter 3).

The vision of belonging to autonomous Lao domains finally began to fade with the establishment of a parliamentary system in 1932. As I recounted in my Isan monograph and which now has been told in greater detail by Dararat Mettarikanon (2003), after 1932 the people of the region came to recognize that democracy afforded them an opportunity, through their elected representatives, to have their voices and interests heard on a national stage. It was this first democratic moment in Thai history in the 1930s that proved to be the midwife to Isan ethnoregionalism. From this time on, more and more northeasterners began to understand themselves as *khon Isan*, that is, as Lao within a Thai nation-state. When this moment ended in the late 1940s with the assassination of a number of northeastern MPs, it became apparent to many in the region that gaining a voice in the processes that produced policies directly affecting their lives was something they would have to struggle for.

THE VILLAGE: THE BASIS OF ISAN IDENTITY

Most people born in northeastern Thailand trace their origins to villages in the rural areas of the country. The village remains to this day the bedrock of Isan identity and has shaped the moral basis of that identity. The village, as vividly remembered in the autobiographical novel *Luk Isan* by Kampoon Boontawee (1976), was a place in which relatives and neighbors came together to help each other in confronting the vicissitudes of the environment—poor soils, drought alternating with floods, and, in the twentieth century, rapid growth in population.[6] In 1982 a film directed by Wichit Khunawuthi was made of this book. The film never became popular among Thai middle-class filmgoers, but it contributed, nonetheless, to the image held by the urban middle class of northeasterners as poor unsophisticated peasants.[7] The patterns of life described by Kampoon as existing prior to World War II persisted throughout much of rural northeastern Thailand into the 1950s and 1960s, as is evident from autobiographical accounts by Prajuab Tirabutana and a number of anthropological and sociological studies.[8]

In 1963–64 when my wife, Jane, and I first carried out ethnographic research in Ban Nong Tuen in Maha Sarakham Province in central northeastern Thailand, we found a village very similar to that portrayed by Kampoon. Not only was there an exchange of labor among related households, but all households joined together to support the *wat*, the

Poster for the 1979 film *Luk Isan*, which was based on the autobiographical novel by
Kampoon Boontawee (courtesy National Film Archives)

Buddhist temple-monastery, and worshipped together at the shrines of
village spirits.[9] The *wat* served not only as the moral gyroscope for the
village, but was also the venue of village festivals including performances
of *molam mu*, the distinctive folk opera of Isan in which performers
singing in the local language enact a legendary tale to the accompaniment
of the *khaen*, the reed mouth organ that is the iconic symbol of Isan
identity. At the *wat* rituals followed the Lao tradition of *hit sipsong*,
the rites of the twelve months.[10] These rites were articulated with the
rice cycle, and with the rice cycle they created a temporal framework
for village life. The *wat* was also the center of the rural community's
social space not only because it comprised the physical space in which
communal activities took place but also because it contained the
reliquaries (*that*) holding the cremated remains of deceased villagers.
These reliquaries, located around the perimeter of the *wat*, formed the
boundary between sacred and secular space and linked the village of
the past with the village of the present. Most village men were ordained

as Buddhist monks (*phra/phikkhu*) for a period of not less than three months.[11] Former monks became lay leaders and held other important roles in village society.

Prior to the late 1960s when the land frontier essentially became closed, villagers who did not inherit sufficient land from their parents to make a living would move elsewhere where they could homestead. In this way satellite or descendant villages were established and these would eventually replicate the same social and cultural patterns as the original community (see Keyes 1976). By the 1960s, however, some villagers—mostly males—had begun to seek new types of economic opportunity, namely by working in non-farm jobs mainly in Bangkok and the surrounding area. Households that had expanded their commercial agricultural production in the 1970s and 1980s increasingly found that the earnings of family members who worked in the industrial and service sectors of the economy brought much higher incomes than did commercial agriculture. By the 1990s there had been a marked shift in the economy of rural northeastern Thailand. Rigg and Salamanca (2009, 263–64) concluded, based in part on their own re-study of other villages in Maha Sarakham Province, that "migration and mobility have come to be defining features of life and living in Northeast Thailand."

While it is the case, as they observe, that throughout rural northeastern Thailand "the household is increasingly defined by its spatial disaggregation," it does not follow that "the village covenant has been fractured." The world of the northeastern village continues both in the attraction that village *wat*-centered festivals have for those living and working away from their homes and, more significantly, in the substitution of the physical village for a virtual one whose members share an ethnoregional identity. Rigg and Salamanca (2009, 268), in support of their position, associate themselves with the argument of Samuel Popkin (1979) in *The Rational Peasant* as against the "moral economy" argument advanced by James Scott (1976) in *The Moral Economy of the Peasant*. In my own consideration of what became known as the Scott-Popkin debate, I argued (Keyes 1983b, 865) that "although [northeastern Thai] peasants do seek through rational calculation to maximize the well being of themselves and their families, they are constrained in so doing by the particular political-economic conditions within which they live and also by the particular world of meaning in which their actions make sense. This world is a moral universe in which individual desires, to employ Buddhist language, are to be brought under control by moral reflection on whether one's actions cause suffering to others." This moral universe is manifest not only in the traditional village, but also in the protest movements that northeasterners have joined. In other words, these movements, while seeking practical political-economic ends, have also entailed a moral critique of how government imposes on villagers an elitist and urban-centered approach to development.

EVOLUTION OF RURAL NORTHEASTERNERS' RELATIONS WITH THE THAI STATE

As I show in this book, the confrontation of the Red Shirts and the government in March–May 2010 was the most recent in a long history of confrontations between rural northeasterners and the Thai state. This recent crisis came almost a century after another crisis of authority that took place primarily in northeastern Thailand, although it was also manifest in northern Thailand at the beginning of the twentieth century. In northeastern Thailand in 1901–2 large numbers of villagers followed local men they considered to have the moral charismatic authority based on Buddhist ideas to contest the authority asserted by the Thai monarchy. The uprising known as the *phu mi bun*, or "men with [Buddhist] merit" movement, occurred in response to the efforts of the modernizing government of Siam, as Thailand was then known, to institute centralized administrative control at the expense of traditional local lords and princes. Although Siam was not formally brought under Western colonial rule, there was a strong similarity between the new centralized state system instituted in formerly relatively autonomous areas of the Siamese empire and the colonial systems instituted in such areas as neighboring British-controlled Burma and French-controlled Indochina. Like many of the movements elsewhere in the world being transformed by colonialism (cf. Adas 1979), the *phu mi bun* uprising was millenarian in character—that is, followers believed that through engaging in certain ritual acts, their leaders could institute a more just order.

An earlier generation of scholars, following Marxist thought, argued that once the political consciousness of peasants was raised or reshaped by leaders having more objective understandings of the situation, they would turn from millenarian movements to truly revolutionary ones (see, especially, B. Moore 1966, Worsley 1968, and Wolf 1969). Despite the expectations of some, based in part on interpretations of the Russian, Chinese, and Vietnamese revolutions, that peasants would become the base for revolutions led by communist parties, communist-led revolutions rarely, if ever, advanced the interests of peasants (see Keyes 2011b). Nonetheless, the conditions for the mobilization of peasants that were identified by Migdal (1975, 237) remain true for any movement that depends on the support of rural people: "(1) a peasantry that has been driven to increased political participation, (2) in an economic network full of shortcomings and injustice, and (3) an outside revolutionary leadership willing and able to invest organizational effort to build new institutions by mobilizing the peasantry (and perhaps other formerly dormant groups) into politics and then use these institutions to destroy the existing political institutions."

At the beginning of the twentieth century when people living in what became northeastern Thailand first became subjects of the modernizing state of Siam, they were "peasants" in the classic sense. That is, they were agriculturalists who consumed most of what they produced or collected in the forests, but who still generated some surplus from their production. Although this surplus was used primarily for religious purposes—in the case of the Thai-Lao, for support of the local temple-monastery—some was also appropriated by local "lords" as taxes or in the form of labor.[12] As Wolf observes, it is such payments in kind or labor to those who exercise "superior power, or *domain*, over a cultivator" that distinguished the *peasant* from *primitive* cultivators (Wolf 1966, 10, emphasis in original). This *domain* is based not simply on the use of coercive power, but on the acceptance by peasants of the moral authority of those who exercise domain over them.

In premodern Siam, peasants who were subject to the authority of the king or of those who drew their authority from the king were known as *phrai*. As this term re-emerges in the early twenty-first century as a label adopted by protestors who mostly have roots in rural northeastern

Thailand, it is important to understand the historical meaning of the term. The best source for beginning this understanding is a monograph by Akin Rabibhadana (1969) who drew primarily on premodern Siamese legal sources (also see Terwiel 1983, 1984).

In the first instance *phrai* were distinguished from *that*, this latter term usually being translated as "slave." Although the word *that* does not have quite the same connotation as the English word, the translation still points to a basic distinction between those who were permanently at beck and call to do their masters' work and those who primarily produced for the support of their families but still had obligations to an overlord.

Whereas in Siam proper—that is, in the capital and the areas under direct control of the king—*phrai* were bound to superiors (*nai*) who were themselves directly subservient to the king, in the area of what is today northeastern as well as northern Thailand *phrai* were subservient to local lords (*chao*). A major cause of the uprising of 1902 was the Siamese court's move to replace these lords by officials appointed by the Siamese king.

King Chulalongkorn (r. 1868–1910) and his associates undertook to transform the empire of Siam into a nation-state not only by imposing a uniform system of provincial administration on the whole country— thereby displacing local lords—but also by transforming the king's subjects into citizens. King Chulalongkorn is remembered for having abolished slavery beginning in 1874, but the elimination in 1905 of the corvée system to which *phrai* were subject (along with the final elimination of slavery) brought to fruition a process of "freeing" labor that had begun with the Bowring Treaty between Siam and Great Britain in 1865 (see Baker and Pasuk 2005, 42–43, 61). By the beginning of the twentieth century, *phrai*, "bondsmen," had been transformed into *chao ban*, "villagers," who were now subservient not to hereditary superiors but to the Thai state.

The rural people of northeastern Thailand, with rare exceptions, were never slaves nor bondsmen tied to members of the Siamese elite. With the elimination of the *chao*, or local lords, these people now found themselves subject to new relationships with representatives of the Siamese court. They were required to pay taxes on their productive land and men were subject to an annual draft. Neither taxes nor the draft were particularly onerous as land taxes were always quite low and the draft was run as a lottery with only a few eligible men being chosen from any one village.

By the 1930s the Thai state had fully replaced traditional lords as the holder of ultimate authority over all who lived within the boundaries of the kingdom. In 1932 the character of the Thai state changed radically when a group of non-royal military officers and bureaucrats compelled King Prajadhipok to accept a constitutional monarchy. While most rural northeasterners still encountered the state primarily in the guise of the government officials appointed to administer districts and provinces, they now found themselves invested with the right to elect their own representatives to the national parliament (chapter 4). Rural northeasterners found parliamentary democracy to be a means whereby their local interests could be voiced in a forum where national policy was at least discussed. Even though the 1932 coup led in fact to the military assuming the dominant role in the Thai polity, a role that ever since it has only reluctantly shared from time to time with an elected parliament, nonetheless, the memory of a democratic society remained strong among many northeasterners.

Insofar as villagers continued to engage in what was primarily a subsistence-based agriculture, and while the intrusion of the Thai state remained quite limited, villagers were able to continue leading a more or less traditional peasant way of life. Beginning in the early and mid-1930s, however, the state began to have a more profound influence on rural society as government schools were established in villages. The school served to inculcate in villagers basic competence in the national language (standard Thai) and to make them aware of being situated within a nation dominated by the Thai state. It is striking that although traditionally the education many male villagers had received was provided by Buddhist monks in village temple-monasteries, there was no significant resistance to the establishment of state-mandated compulsory primary education. In part this was a consequence of the success the Thai government had in recruiting local people—at first monks, and subsequently often ex-monks—to become village school teachers. By the onset of World War II, most village children in northeastern Thailand had spent three to four years studying at the local government school.

During World War II the Free Thai Movement that challenged the Phibun government's alliance with Japan attracted the active participation of a number of northeastern Thai politicians. Several of these politicians had significant support among rural people of the region. The fact that the Free Thai Movement was linked with the Free Lao Movement would subsequently be interpreted as indicating that northeasterners harbored separatist inclinations.

In the postwar period the Thai economy began to expand, and this led to a marked increase in the demand of labor. As the government ended the migration of Chinese to Thailand, an increasing number of northeasterners, first primarily male and by the 1970s female as well, began to migrate to the Greater Bangkok metropolitan area to take up wage labor (chapter 5). Most migrants in the early period went only for temporary work and then returned home to resume lives as farmers. Their experiences, however, made them aware of the significant difference in their incomes from both farm and non-farm work as compared to those enjoyed by the expanding middle class in Bangkok. They also returned with the recognition that they were looked down on as *khon bannok*, rural people, whose Lao customs—notably, their preference for glutinous rice (*khao niao*) and fermented fish (*pa daek*; standard Thai, *pla ra*)—and accents were seen by Bangkokians as being uncouth.

At the same time, northeastern villagers were also affected by the reemergence of the monarchy after King Bhumibol's return to Thailand in the early 1950s. While the governments of a succession of Field Marshals—Phibun Songkram (1946–56), Sarit Thanarat (1957–63), and Thanom Kittikachorn (1963–73)—established the dominance of the military in the Thai polity, the increasingly prominent role played by the king made villagers aware of a distinction between those who exercised power (*amnat*) and the king who provided legitimation for authority, especially as there was no effective constitution during most of the period between 1946 and 1976. The king became a recognized presence in the world of northeastern villagers as a result of ritualized acknowledgement of his *barami* (Buddhist charisma) each morning in every school, in the photos that were distributed to every household, and in the news about the king and members of his family on the radio and in the occasional newspaper or magazine (TV would not become widely viewed in northeastern villages until the 1980s). While villagers felt increasingly frustrated or even alienated by the actions of local officials—especially in their extraction of fees for services and in their expectation of being entertained on visits to villages—they viewed the king as embodying benevolence, manifested in his highly publicized visits to rural areas.

Field Marshal Sarit encouraged these visits in order to counter the propaganda of the Communist Party of Thailand (CPT). The Sarit government expressed fear that the CPT would join with the Communist Party of Laos to woo Lao-speaking villagers in northeastern Thailand. His government also moved to promote "development" (*kan phatthana*) in the rural Northeast through programs that included a significant expansion of the road system and introduction of "community development." While the former did, in fact, help stimulate growth of the northeastern economy by making it easier for villagers to get produce to the market and to move to Bangkok or elsewhere for wage work, the latter served primarily to result in more visits to villages by patronizing government officials.

Although some northeastern villagers saw Sarit himself as a *khon Isan* because his mother was a native of the northeastern town of Mukdahan, they did not hold positive views of his successor, Field Marshal Thanom Kittikachorn, and the deputy prime minister/minister of interior, Field Marshal Praphas Charusathien. The period between the death of Sarit in 1963 and the early 1980s was one of intense political turmoil within the country, exacerbated by the conflicts in neighboring Laos, Cambodia, and Vietnam.

Despite this turmoil, or, more precisely, because of the large amounts of American aid that were given to Thailand because of the turmoil, the Thai economy continued to grow. Rural northeasterners increasingly oriented their economic activities toward the market both by expanding production of cash crops and by spending more time working in industries in and around Bangkok. While household income increased for rural northeasterners, they became increasingly aware of the degree to which they were disadvantaged relative to the growing urban middle class.

It was from the middle class, however, that the first significant political upheaval since 1932 occurred. Beginning in the late 1960s middle-class university students began to lead protests against military rule, and finally in 1973 succeeded in forcing, with the backing of the king, the military dictators to go into exile. The king then appointed an interim government and an assembly that was charged with writing a new constitution. A constitutionally based government with power vested in an elected parliament as had been originally envisaged in 1932 replaced the military-led government in 1974. This new democratic system had a very short life, being aborted by a coup in 1976. Rural northeasterners had had only a peripheral role in the shaping of this system, but after the 1976 coup they were once again deprived even of participation in any institution through which they could make their interests heard at a national level. By the late 1970s the Communist Party of Thailand was attracting increasing support from the rural populace throughout the country, and especially in the Northeast (chapter 6).

A communist-led revolution did not succeed, however. This was not only because a few leading members of the military who staged another coup decided on an amnesty program but at least as much because the CPT, with their adherence to a rigid form of Maoism, failed to understand the rural culture of Isan people. In short, most rural northeasterners found the revolutionary alternative advocated by the CPT to be unconvincing. The failure of the CPT did not, however, end the grievances northeasterners felt regarding the Thai state.

In the period between the early 1980s and 1997 the Thai economy became one of the fastest growing in the world. Although many rural northeasterners benefited from this expansion primarily through migration to urban centers or even abroad where they could find non-agricultural work, others found their access to local natural resources—notably, rivers and forests—severely curtailed because of government-sponsored projects to use these resources for the benefit primarily of the urban populace. Instead of turning to a revolutionary movement such as the CPT, many rural northeasterners, led by local people or by non-governmental organizations, were mobilized to join protest movements that sought to pressure the Thai government directly to give proper attention to their concerns (chapter 7). These movements had limited success, however, until a new constitution was adopted in 1997 in the wake of renewed middle-class-based protests against the reestablishment of military rule.

Northeasterners became significant beneficiaries of a new democratic order made possible by the 1997 constitution. Thaksin Shinawatra, a Sino-Thai from Chiang Mai in northern Thailand who had used his experience promoting new technology as a police officer to become a media magnate and had then entered politics, built the most successful populist party in Thai history. His Thai Rak Thai Party won large parliamentary majorities in both 2001 and 2005, in no small part because of the support of northeasterners as well as northerners. Thaksin had won this support because of his advocacy and then implementation of such policies as universal health care, loan programs for villagers, and devolution of power to local administrative organizations (see Pasuk and Baker 2009). At the same time, he alienated those close to the monarchy, many upper-level officers in the army, a large part of the urban middle class, as well as many in non-governmental organizations because he was seen as arrogant, corrupt, a violator of human rights, and a populist. In 2006 he was overthrown in yet another military coup.

The coup created a new crisis of legitimacy, one that was of a different order from the more localized one in the far southern provinces where since 2004 some Malay-speaking Muslims had been engaged in a bloody challenge to Thai rule. The coup—even justified in part as necessary to institute a new policy to resolve the crisis in the south[13]—raised the broader question as to who had the legitimate right to decide on who holds power in the Thai system. The new and increasingly intense crisis of legitimacy following the 2006 coup entailed different elements of Thai society struggling to reshape a consensus about the Thai nation. The elite conception of Thai-ness (*khwam pen Thai*), centered on a virtuous Buddhist king, that has its origins in the national integration policies of the late nineteenth and early twentieth centuries, has proved difficult to sustain in the early twenty-first century in the face of a politically conscious electorate, especially one that now includes those still thought of by the elite and much of the urban middle class as being unsophisticated peasants.

The large part of the Thai populace that lives in or has roots in rural northeastern Thailand has, through support of the populist Thai Rak Thai Party and its successors, and the Red Shirt movement, sought to ensure that access to power is determined by elections, thereby asserting its right to participate fully in the reshaping of the consensus about the nature of the national polity (chapter 8). By the late twentieth century rural northeasterners and their kinsmen who lived and worked outside the region have become increasingly sophisticated through more education, greater consumption of media, and travel not only within Thailand but also abroad for work. They have, nonetheless, continued to identify as *chao ban*, "villagers," but for many, perhaps most, the "village" now extends to the Isan region as a whole. Because these *chao ban* have an understanding of their place in a much larger world, they have become what I term "cosmopolitan villagers."

That the followers as well as the leaders of the Red Shirt movement should have embraced the term *phrai* as a label for themselves demonstrates their ability to engage the presumably more sophisticated cosmopolitan ruling elite of Thailand with irony and humor.[14] The term has, nonetheless, a deeper meaning. In this book I trace the evolution of *phrai* peasant villagers, with their particular relationship to the Thai nation-state, into the *phrai* who have become cosmopolitan villagers. I have sought, further, to trace how peasant villagers living in northeastern Thailand who have evolved into cosmopolitan villagers have become increasingly assertive in their claim for equal citizenship with both the old elite and the recently emergent middle class within the nation-state of Thailand.

2

THE FOUNDATIONS OF ISAN

A REGION APART

Northeastern Thailand, or the Khorat Plateau, as the region is also known in older literature, contrasts geographically, historically, and culturally with the central region, which has long been the core of the Siamese or Thai kingdom.[1] Whereas Thailand's central region is a low flood plain that receives fresh accretions of rich top soil from the north each year, the Northeast is a plateau with poor soils that tilts gently from the northwestern sector, where it is about 700 feet above sea level, to the southeast sector, which is only about 200 feet above sea level. The region is set off from the rest of Thailand by the Phetchabun range and by the smaller ranges of the Dong Phrayayen and San Kamphaeng, and from Cambodia by the Phanom Dong Rak escarpment. The Mekong and its tributaries, most notably the Mun and Chi Rivers, drain the whole plateau.

Except for a few hills in the northeastern corner, the region is primarily an area of gently undulating land, most of it varying in altitude from 300 to 600 feet. The porous and sometimes saline soils that are found in much of the region are "usually too infertile and insufficiently watered to be worth clearing for agricultural uses" (Pendleton 1943, 21). Even the areas that are suitable for cultivation often have too little rainwater during the rainy season or too much during the flood season to be as productive as the fertile flood plains of central Thailand.

Climatically the Northeast also differs from the central plains. The areas of the Northeast lying in the rain shadow of the mountain ranges dividing the Northeast from the rest of Thailand are the driest areas of all Thailand (Pendleton 1962, 118). Since these mountains stand as a barrier to the southwesterly monsoon, the Northeast as a whole is more dependent for its rainfall on the cyclonic storms that originate over the South China Sea. In general there is much more variation in rainfall from section to section and variability in specific localities in the Northeast than there is in the central region (Pendleton 1962, 117–8; Platenius 1963, 9).

The Northeast constitutes the largest region in Thailand, covering 170,226 square kilometers (about 66,250 square miles) or comprising nearly one-third of the total land area of the kingdom. Similarly, the population of the region accounts for about one-third of its inhabitants, the Northeast in 2010 having a population of 21.3 million, accounting for 31 percent of the total population of 68.9 million people.[2] This population ratio has held constant at least since the early part of the twentieth century when the first modern censuses were taken.

Because of different classifications used in all censuses, it is difficult to estimate the exact ethnic composition of the Northeast. Approximately 85 to 90 percent of the people living in the region are speakers of Tai languages,[3] most of whom speak domestic languages that are closely related to that of the lowland Lao living in the central Mekong region of Laos. In Nakhon Ratchasima (Khorat) and Chaiyaphum Provinces bordering on central Thailand there are several hundred thousand people whose domestic language is a Tai dialect known as Thai Khorat, a dialect that is closer to central Thai, but still retains features that are shared with neighboring Lao dialects. In Isan there are also some speakers of other Tai languages, the most significant being Phu Thai, spoken by peoples found in the northeastern part of the region.

At least 9 percent of the population of the region are speakers of Khmer or Khmer related languages.[4] Today, these people, like those who speak Lao and other Tai dialects, are also fluent in standard Thai, that is, the national language taught in schools. The towns of the region have long been centers of commerce, and the commerce of the region has been dominated since the nineteenth century by people of Chinese descent. Today, most of the *luk chin* or descendants of Chinese migrants in the region have developed a distinctive identity that entails speaking the dominant Thai-Lao dialect as well as standard Thai and sometimes a Chinese dialect.[5] It is difficult to get a precise estimate of the Sino-Isan population, but it would have to be at least 150,000. There are also upwards of 100,000 people of Vietnamese descent in northeastern Thailand, by far the majority being descendants of refugees who fled from Laos as well as Vietnam during the French Indochina war that ended in 1954 (see Poole 1970, Hardy 2008). The ethnic composition of the Northeast also includes a small but significant number of central Thai, most of whom hold positions in the Thai bureaucracy.

The large majority of the population of the region possess linguistic and cultural traits that differentiate them from the central Thai and relate them more closely to the Lao who live across the Mekong, beyond the boundaries of Thailand, and are the true *khon Isan*, Isan people.[6] The people of the Northeast sometimes refer to themselves as *khon phuenmuang* (natives) or as Lao. However, since the 1950s the term *Isan*, already used by people of other regions to indicate the people of the Northeast, has been taken up by a growing segment of the northeastern population to indicate their own ethnic identity. Northeasterners have begun to speak of themselves as being *khon Isan* or *phu Isan* (Isan people), as using *phasa Isan* (Isan language)[7] and as living in *phak Isan* (Isan region). The increasing usage of "Isan" by northeasterners bespeaks their growing sense of ethnoregional identity.

It should also be stressed that this sense of Isan identity is of very recent origin. Before we can attempt to assess what common interests the Isan people share and what common objectives they wish to pursue, we need first to understand how a distinctive region of northeastern Thailand evolved.

THE FORMATION OF ISAN

For several centuries prior to the end of the thirteenth century, the Khorat Plateau lay within the Angkor Empire and its population was probably predominately Khmer.[8] Exactly when Tai-speaking people first began to arrive in the area has yet to be discovered. The Thai and Lao chronicles, for example, bury the emergence of Tai-speaking people in the middle Mekong region in legend (Sila 1964, 13–16, 25–26). We do have evidence, however, that demonstrates that the appearance of Tai–speaking peoples in the areas which comprise present-day Thailand and Laos was not a sudden massive inundation stimulated by political events in the southern Chinese homeland of these people, as was once suggested. Rather, the process, as Coedès has so well described it, was probably one "of gradual infiltration of immigrants who began by holding positions of command over communities of sedentary agriculturalists, and ended by gaining control over the native peoples among whom they had settled and whose culture they had assimilated" (Coedès 1966, 102).

The first evidence of the presence of Tai-speaking peoples in territories dominated by the Khmer appears on one of the bas-reliefs of Angkor Wat in the twelfth century (Briggs 1951, 200–201), although they had already established themselves in principalities on the northwestern periphery of the Angkor Empire by the eleventh century. During the thirteenth century a Tai chieftain overthrew a Khmer provincial governor or commandant in an outpost of the Angkor Empire located at Sukhothai in north central Thailand and established the first important autonomous Tai state in an area formerly dominated by the Mon and Khmer. The second king of Sukhothai, Ramkhamhaeng (1270–1316), succeeded in extending the control of Sukhothai over most of north central and western Thailand, part of the peninsula, and the northern part of what is now northeastern Thailand. However, there is no evidence to suggest that there was any sizeable Tai-speaking population in the parts of northeastern Thailand controlled by Sukhothai at this time.

Shortly after its florescence, Sukhothai yielded to two other Tai kingdoms in the competition between the Tai-speaking people and the Khmer over the Khorat Plateau. At almost the same moment in time in the mid-fourteenth century, the Lao kingdom of Lan Xang (or Lan Chang[9]) and the Siamese (central Thai) kingdom of Ayutthaya were founded. Both remained important foci for political alignments in mainland Southeast Asia until the eighteenth century.

Although Ayutthaya lies in what is today the heart of central Thailand, until the fourteenth century it lay at the edge of Tai influence.[10] As the rulers of Ayutthaya sought to expand their domain, they were primarily interested in consolidating control over central and eastern Thailand and in reducing the power of the Khmer. Only secondarily, if at all, were they interested in extending their influence over what is today northeastern Thailand. Although theoretically successor to Sukhothai's control over the northern part of northeastern Thailand, Ayutthaya abandoned or ignored this claim at the outset in the face of a stronger claim exerted by the new Lao kingdom of Lan Xang.

Lan Xang originated in the small Lao principalities that had appeared sometime before the fourteenth century in northern Laos. Fa Ngum, the son of the ruler of one of these principalities based on the capital of Muang Swa (later to become Luang Prabang), was the first significant Lao political figure for whom we have historical record. Maha Sila Viravong, in his interpretation of the Lao annals, suggests that the Khmer gave their support to Fa Ngum because of their desire to see the expansion of the Siamese stopped: "The Khmers had gradually fallen down to the point where they were unable to defend themselves [against Siamese expansion]. The Khmer king had a strong desire to retaliate against the Thais [Siamese], or, at least, to check their advance. Hence the Khmer king's kindness to Prince Fah-Ngum so that he could use him to stop the Thai expansion" (Sila 1964, 27). The traditional date of the beginning of Fa Ngum's expedition to unify the Lao, AD 1349, is sufficiently close to the dates given for the founding of Ayutthaya and the initiation of the first Ayutthayan attacks against Angkor (Wolters 1966, 96–7) to lend credence to the hypothesis that the founding of the Lao kingdom was a consequence of the inability of the Khmer to prevent the emergence of powerful Tai kingdoms.

Fa Ngum started his expedition of conquest at the Khone Falls at the point which today divides Laos and Cambodia, moved up the Mekong, bringing the peoples and lands on both shores under his sway. From there he proceeded to the Plain of Jars, where he subjugated the principality of Xieng Khouang and continued on to Luang Prabang, where he was crowned king. He spent some time conquering the peoples of northern Laos upstream on the Mekong before moving downriver to take the area that lies around Vientiane. Until this time, only those areas of northeastern Thailand lying along the Mekong had been brought into the new kingdom of Lan Xang. However, once Fa Ngum reached Vientiane he decided to move on to take lands on the Khorat Plateau that belonged, in theory, to Ayutthaya as the successor to Sukhothai. An expedition in the 1350s was successful in deposing Ayutthayan officials at Roi Et and in convincing the Ayutthayan king that the Lao were powerful enough to meet any military challenge that Ayutthaya might mount in order to protect its interests in the Northeast. In consequence of his conquests, Fa Ngum was able to bring into the kingdom of Lan Xang all of the Khorat Plateau except the area around Nakhon Ratchasima, which remained in Khmer hands.[11]

In some remarks which Maha Sila Viravong has made in connection with Fa Ngum's conquest lie perhaps the first clue to the migration of a sizeable number of Lao into northeastern Thailand. Fa Ngum ordered the settlement of some twenty thousand Lao families around Vientiane and the northern part of the Khorat Plateau. "That was the reason," Maha Sila Viravong claims, "why a great number of Lao people established themselves in the Khmer territories" (Sila 1964, 34).

Lao, Siamese, and indigenous provincial histories make little mention of what took place in the Khorat plateau between the middle of the fourteenth century and the early part of the seventeenth century. However, what information exists provides some crucial clues that make possible certain conclusions about the relationship of the region to nearby kingdoms and about cultural developments within the region.

First, after the Lao capital was transferred from Luang Prabang to Vientiane in 1563, the interest of the Lao kingdom of Lan Xang in the Khorat Plateau contracted and by that time was restricted primarily to areas lying along the shores of the Mekong in what are today Loei, Nong Khai, and Nakhon Phanom Provinces. In these areas, which were integral parts of the Lan Xang kingdom, there was but one important religio-political center—namely, the Buddhist shrine at That Phanom that lies near the Mekong River between the present northeastern towns of Nakhon Phanom and Mukdahan (Pruess 1974, 1976a, 1976b). The chronicle of this shrine posits an ancient lineage going back to the Buddha himself, and there was probably a shrine of some type at That

Phanom in Khmer times. The more certain history is traceable to the restoration of the shrine by the Lao king of Vientiane in the sixteenth century (Pruess 1976a, 63). That Phanom lay in the narrow strip on the right bank of the Mekong that would most probably have been the extent of direct Lao control of part of the Khorat Plateau well into the seventeenth century.[12]

Prior to the seventeenth century, the Siamese kingdom of Ayutthaya had even less interest than Lan Xang in the Khorat Plateau as a territory that might be brought within its domain. The first Siamese foothold in the Northeast appears to have been established during the reign of King Narai (1656–88), when the two old Khmer towns of Muang Sema and Muang Khorakhabura were combined into a single fortified outpost of Ayutthaya with the name of Nakhon Ratchasima (cf. Manit 1962, 17).[13]

Lan Xang and Ayutthaya, however, shared a common interest in maintaining the Khorat Plateau as a wide border area between their two kingdoms. In wars between the Lao and Siamese kingdoms, first under Fa Ngum in the mid-1500s (Sila 1964, 50–51) and later at the end of the eighteenth and beginning of the nineteenth centuries, the Khorat Plateau, by virtue of its intermediate location, formed a major battleground. To prevent such confrontations between the Lao and Siamese kingdoms, both sides exerted some effort at various times to recognize the Khorat Plateau as a boundary region. For example, some time between the late fifteenth and late sixteenth centuries, Dan Sai, today in northern Loei Province, was officially named once and perhaps twice as the demarcation point between the two kingdoms.[14]

Although little of the Northeast was fully incorporated into either the Lao or the Siamese kingdoms prior to the beginning of the seventeenth century, culturally the region was becoming increasingly Lao as we define that ethnic tradition today. The migratory patterns of Lao into the region first mentioned in connection with the rule of Fa Ngum in the mid-fourteenth century continued during the subsequent period. In addition to what must have been a constant flow of a few Lao at a time into the region, the Khorat Plateau seems to have been a haven for the politically dispossessed of Laos. Maha Sila Viravong reports that in the last decades of the sixteenth century, large numbers of Lao around Vientiane migrated to areas extending from Roi Et to Champasak in order to escape the rule of a usurper who had come to the throne of Lan Xang (Sila 1964, 69–70). A history of Kalasin Province reports a steady migration of Lao people into the area between 1050 and 1750 and a large migration of political dissidents from Vientiane in the latter part of the eighteenth century (*Changwat Kalasin* 1957, 4–5). Champasak was settled in a similar fashion in the early eighteenth century while portions of the population of Roi Et came from Champasak shortly after the founding of that kingdom (*Changwat Roi Et* 1957, 4).

These migrations did not result merely in the supplanting of a pre-existing Khmer culture with a Lao culture. From the time of Fa Ngum on, the Lao had been borrowing many important elements of the Khmer "great tradition" as it existed during the period of contact. The migrants took with them some form of this syncretized Lao culture to the Khorat Plateau and once there they continued to borrow from Khmer culture. However, in a linguistic sense if no other, the Lao have shown a greater ability to absorb the Khmer with whom they have come into contact than have the Khmer the Lao. In consequence, the number of Khmer-speaking people remaining in the Northeast slowly diminished although they, along with the related Kui, still numbered about 1.8 million in 2010. Whereas Khmer and Kui also are competent in Standard Thai and many are competent in Lao as well, few Lao (or Thai) know Khmer or Kui.

Thus, at the beginning of the seventeenth century, only a few parts of the Northeast were fully incorporated within the Lao kingdom of Lan Xang and no part of the area lay within the kingdom of Ayutthaya. The definition by these two kingdoms of the rest of the region as a wide border zone made possible the autonomy of whatever sociopolitical units—villages and/or principalities—may have existed in the region. Culturally, the region was becoming increasingly Lao, but without a court center to look to, local variations developed perhaps to a greater extent than within Laos itself. Political autonomy and localism in the region were to become threatened only after the shift in the relative power of the Lao and Siamese kingdoms that began to take place early in the seventeeth century.

During the latter half of the sixteenth century both Lan Xang and Ayutthaya were drawn together in the attempt to protect themselves against attacks by the Burmese. By the time the Burmese were finally routed at the end of that century, both kingdoms had been weakened, although Ayutthaya had suffered more, according to the Thai annals. In 1610 Lan Xang attempted to take advantage of what it considered to be the greater weakness of Ayutthaya and staged an attack against the Siamese capital (Wood 1924, 61–62). However, the Siamese recovered faster than the Lao thought, and Siamese armies quickly rebuffed the Lao attacks and scattered the Lao forces. This event can be noted as the turning point in Lao-Siamese relations, for after this time the Siamese kingdom began to wax, albeit with temporary setbacks, while the Lao kingdom began to disintegrate.[15]

Although in 1670, when the stele at Dan Sai in Loei Province demarcating the boundaries between Ayutthaya and Lan Xang was erected, much was made of the "equality" of Lan Xang and Ayutthaya (Sila 1964, 76–77), the real indicator of the relative relations of these two kingdoms in regard to the Northeast was the establishment of a Siamese outpost at Nakhon Ratchasima during the reign of King Narai (1656–88). In fact, the king of Lan Xang ruling during the time of these two events, King Surayawongsa (1633–90 or 1633–95), was the last important king of a unified Lan Xang. On his death, the kingdom fell into a period of anarchy, ending with the split of Lan Xang into the three kingdoms of Luang Prabang, Vientiane, and Champasak early in the eighteenth century.[16]

The division of Lan Xang and the growing power of Ayutthaya brought the Khorat Plateau into focus much more than ever before. The weakened condition of the Lao states, although not the only factor, was undoubtedly one of the main reasons for the intensification of Siamese expansion towards the Northeast that was to continue, with only temporary abatements, until the end of the nineteenth century. In addition to Siamese interest in the area, the division of Lan Xang also stimulated Lao political interest in the interior of the Khorat Plateau. Although the evidence is scanty, it would appear that Vientiane inherited from Lan Xang territories lying on the right bank of the Mekong in present-day Loei, Nong Khai, and Nakhon Phanom Provinces. Champasak, itself located on the right bank, absorbed into its kingdom territories upstream on the Mun and Chi Rivers that lie today in Ubon and Roi Et Provinces (Archaimbault 1961, 562–63; *Changwat Roi Et* 1957, 4).

The stage was set for northeastern Thailand to become a meeting place for the interests of at least three states—Vientiane, Champasak, and Ayutthaya. However, before such a confrontation could occur, Burma, in 1767, again attacked and laid siege to Ayutthaya. In consequence the kingdom of Ayutthaya disintegrated into five parts, one of which emerged at Khorat or Nakhon Ratchasima (Wood 1924, 254).[17] This division was short-lived, for Taksin, a Thai of Chinese descent, was able to rally a sizeable military force and piece the kingdom back together with a new capital at Thonburi, across the river from Bangkok.

At the time of the Burmese attack, Vientiane was theoretically an ally of the Siamese, but following the fall of Ayutthaya, Vientiane was forced to support Burma or suffer attack itself. The kingdom chose to support Burma. Vientiane's offense to the Siamese was exacerbated by allowing the self-proclaimed ruler of Khorat to find asylum in Vientiane after Khorat fell to Taksin in 1768 (Wood 1924, 256). As punishment for disloyalty, Taksin ordered the invasion of Vientiane. During the punitive expedition, led by General Chakkri, who was later to found the Bangkok dynasty, Luang Prabang aligned itself with Bangkok, and as the Lao historian Maha Sila Viravong puts it, "was forced to accept the suzerainty of Siam" (Sila 1964, 103). Vientiane, after being sacked and almost completely destroyed, was placed under a Thai military commander.[18]

Champasak suffered the same fate. In 1777 Taksin ordered General Chakkri to attack Champasak for having attempted to expand its territories on the Khorat Plateau at the expense of the Siamese during the unsettled period following the fall of Ayutthaya. The expedition was successful and the ruler of Champasak was removed from his throne and sent to the Siamese capital. From this point on, although the king of Champasak was allowed to return home in 1780, Champasak became and remained a vassal of Bangkok[19] (cf. Archaimbault 1961, 560–64; Wyatt 1963, 19–20, 28–29).

As a consequence of the Siamese defeat of the Lao, the kingdoms of Vientiane and Champasak became vassals of Bangkok. More importantly for our consideration, the parts of the Khorat Plateau not included within the territories of these vassals were incorporated as "outer provinces" within the Siamese empire. This Siamese incorporation of "Lao" areas was a part of much larger expansion of the Siamese empire to the north, east, and south.

In 1804 a new king, Chao Anu, was placed on the throne of Vientiane by Bangkok. For the first part of his reign, which lasted until 1827, he proved to be a model vassal to Thailand and seemed to be personally close to King Rama II.[20] After the ascension to the throne of Rama III, however, Chao Anu decided that he would try to restore the independence of the kingdom of Vientiane. In 1827 he moved troops towards Bangkok, pretending to come to the aid of the Siamese court, reportedly threatened by British gunboats. He also obtained the support of Champasak in his expedition. Earlier, the Siamese king had been persuaded by Chao Anu to install one of his own sons on the throne of Champasak and this son came to the aid of his father when the latter launched his attack on Bangkok. Together, the forces of the combined vassals presented a formidable challenge to the Siamese. Chao Anu was able to lead his troops as far as Saraburi in the central plains of Thailand. The Siamese king was taken completely by surprise but quickly organized his troops and sent them against the Lao. During the year and a half it took the Siamese to rout the Lao armies, there was considerable fighting on the Khorat Plateau. The people of that region were involved in the war by being conscripted to serve in the forces of one or another of the armies or by having to supply the troops with foodstuffs.

For our purposes concerning northeastern Thailand, one of the most interesting parts of the story of the Chao Anu revolt concerns the role played by Thao Suranari or Thaoying Mo, the wife of the Siamese assistant-governor of Khorat. Thao Suranari was probably a Lao-speaking woman, but according to nationalist history she rallied the people of Khorat against the Lao (Manit 1962, 25–26). Thao Suranari is the only "northeasterner" who is accorded a prominent place in Thai (Siamese) history; even in a third grade primary school textbook she is acclaimed as a national heroine (Thailand, Ministry of Education 1961, 57–59).[21] Little is known about who the other rulers of northeastern principalities supported, although it is likely that some of them had to provide food and corvée labor for both the Lao and the Siamese.

When the Lao were finally defeated, Rama III ordered the complete destruction of the city of Vientiane, the deportation of its population mainly to the central plains, and the public ridiculing of Chao Anu and his family in Bangkok. The kingdom of Vientiane was eliminated and the territories under both Vientiane and Champasak were reduced to the same status as those of the Khorat Plateau—namely, that of being provinces responsible to Bangkok rather than vassal principalities. Among the Lao vassals, only Luang Prabang was able to retain a semblance of autonomy.[22]

In contrast to the demise of independent Lao political power, the Chakkri dynasty of Bangkok proved to be one of the most stable and effective in Thailand's history. The strength of the dynasty, although due in no small part to the personal abilities of several of the kings, was enhanced, ironically, by the arrival of European colonialists in mainland Southeast Asia. The British, while preventing Siamese expansion to the south and west, eliminated the Burmese kingdom that had for so long threatened Siam.

Even more significant was the Siamese ability to evolve a response to the West that made possible the preservation of independence when all Bangkok's neighbors fell under colonial rule. Still, Bangkok did not entirely escape the territorial ambitions of the colonial powers, and it was in the newly incorporated Lao territories that Siam suffered its greatest territorial losses.[23] French colonization in Southeast Asia had the effect of halting Siamese expansion eastward and northeastward and of establishing the present boundaries of the Thai Northeast. Such internationally recognized boundaries were an innovation in an area where control had been based on population rather than territory.

In 1862 France established itself in Cochin-China and continued its advance in Indochina until 1907. In 1867 Thailand ceded, under protest, its authority over Cambodia (excepting the provinces of Battambang, Siem Reap, Sisophon, and Melouprey). In 1888 Bangkok renounced any claim to the Sipsong Chao Thai area in northern Vietnam. However, the Franco-Siamese Treaty of 1893, signed by the Siamese under threat from a French military ultimatum, resulted in Thailand's first major territorial concessions to France. This treaty ceded all of the Lao areas on the left bank of the Mekong to France. Two areas on the right bank of the Mekong, Sayaboury Province opposite Luang Prabang and the province of Champasak (called Bassac by the French), passed to French control in consequence of the treaty of 1904.[24]

Many French officials agreed with the Siamese, albeit for different reasons, about the essential absurdity of the division of the Lao areas on ethnic grounds. Several of these officials argued strongly for French expansion into the Khorat Plateau since the people of this area were also Lao (cf. Lunet de Lajonquière 1907). But the period of French colonial expansion was over and, with the exception of a brief interlude in World War II, the boundaries dividing Laos and Thailand have remained unchanged since 1904.

Although the Thai Northeast did not acquire a distinct geo-political identity until the beginning of the twentieth century, a large portion of the population of the region shares a common historical heritage that has significance for the development of northeastern regionalism. In consequence of migrations and assimilation, the vast majority of the northeastern populace is today closely related culturally to the Lao on the opposite bank of the Mekong. Although there are slight cultural variations in the region due to a long period of local autonomy and the greater impact of Khmer culture upon the people of the Northeast as compared with the Lao of Laos,[25] in the main the people of the Northeast can be grouped ethnically with the Lao as differentiated from the Siamese or central Thai. Politically, however, the region has had a history of division. The areas lying along the Mekong were integral, but secondary, parts of the Lao kingdom for most of the period between the mid-fourteenth and early nineteenth centuries, while much of the interior of the Khorat Plateau was effectively politically autonomous. Inclusion of the region as a whole into one or another kingdom occurred only in the pre-fourteenth-century period under Angkor (when the populace was itself Khmer) and since 1827 under the Siamese. Still, these very factors of division and autonomy can be seen to bear some relation to the subsequent Isan search for a distinctive identity. One of the present-day manifestations of Isan regionalism is an attempt to foster a sense of ethnoregional identity in the face of Thai pressures without necessarily equating such a quest with the weak "national" destiny, both historically and currently, of the Lao. Such political objectives could emerge only after the people of the Northeast became aware of their common heritage and identity, however. This awareness developed in consequence of the intensified interactions between northeasterners and central Thai that had begun with the consolidation of Siamese control over the North.

CONSOLIDATION OF THAI CONTROL

The Ayutthayan period can be characterized politically by Siamese moves to consolidate and maintain control over the people living within the central plains of present-day Thailand. In the four centuries when Ayutthaya was the capital of Siam, there were continual threats to this political objective, mainly from the Burmese but also from the Khmer and from neighboring Tai kingdoms. However, the collapse of the Burmese empire at the beginning of the nineteenth century, the continued weakness of Cambodia, and the dissolution of the kingdom of Lan Xang, all occurring at a time when Siam had acquired a dynamic new dynasty, radically changed the traditional equation. Siamese policy towards the Tai-speaking peoples living to the northeast and to the north shifted from one of seeking vassals or alliances to one of attempting to incorporate these people into Siam proper. The Siamese defeat of the Lao in the war of 1827–28 marked the end of the vassal states of Vientiane and Champasak and led to increasing Siamese control of all the territories of the Khorat Plateau and the middle Mekong region. Towards the end of the nineteenth century, the old kingdom of Lanna or Chiang Mai was also brought within the Siamese domains. Only Luang Prabang out of all the Tai-speaking kingdoms bordering on the Siamese empire to the north and northeast remained independent, although only as a vassal.

The imposition of Siamese control over these areas was brought about gradually. At the beginning of the nineteenth century the Siamese instituted practices of indirect control that entailed incorporation of a large number of semi-autonomous principalities in a system whereby the Thai king confirmed local rulers in return for tribute, mainly in kind. For the populace of the northeastern region of Thailand, these methods of administration had the initial effect of perpetuating local autonomy. A nostalgia to return to this period of localism and autonomy can be noted in some of the political expressions of northeasterners at a later period. However, more crucial to the formation of Isan ethnoregionalism were the events at the end of the nineteenth century. Under the pressure and stimulus of Western colonialism, King Chulalongkorn introduced a number of reforms, partially based upon Western ideas and technology, that aimed at more direct Siamese control over these areas (Tej 1977). With these reforms and the demarcation of the boundary between Laos and Thailand established through the Franco-Siamese treaties of 1893 and 1904, the destiny of northeasterners was cast with Thailand. After these events, any search for common identity among northeasterners would be carried out within the context of the Thai state.

Beginning with the reign of King Taksin (1767–82), central Thai administration of the Lao areas, including present-day northeastern Thailand, was based on a semi-feudal principle whereby villagers were subject to indigenous elites and the elites in turn subject to Thonburi and, after 1782, Bangkok. Together, elites and peasantry were grouped in a large number of small principalities termed *hua muang*.[26] Although there is some evidence to suggest that the structure of the *hua muang* in Laos and northeastern Thailand was based on the Lao monarchical system (cf. Toem Singhatthit 1956, 2:489; Bunchuai 1962, 4) and although four *hua muang* had been established on the Khorat Plateau during the Ayutthayan period,[27] the creation of a *hua muang* system was a part of the Thai kingdom's system of control over its outer provinces during the Thonburi period and for the first four and a half reigns of the Chakkri dynasty. Between 1767 and 1882, 145 *hua muang* were created in the Lao areas of which about 95–100 were located on the Khorat Plateau.[28] These *hua muang* were divided into two basic types: major *hua muang* (*hua muang yai*) that were directly responsible to Bangkok, and minor *hua muang* (*hua muang noi* or *hua muang lek*) that were subordinate to the major *hua muang*. By the 1880s, when the system was changed, there were forty-two major *hua muang*, of which twenty-seven were located in the Northeast. At the head of each *hua muang* was a lord (*chao*) who together with the three other highest local officials formed a ruling group known as the *achayasi*. Below the *achayasi* was a group of officials charged with specific functions such as handling of the budget, management of the *chao muang*'s horses, and so on.[29]

Hua muang were lower in status and smaller in size than vassal states but were not of the same order as the "inner provinces" that surrounded the capital in the central plains of Thailand. They were similar to vassals in that their rulers belonged to local aristocracies and possessed considerable autonomy. They were like the "inner provinces," however, in that the rulers (the members of what was called the *achayasi*), had to be "appointed" (in practice, confirmed) by the Thai throne. Vella states that they were also "subject to the more important obligations of ordinary provinces: the payment of taxes in local products and the supplying of men (or a money substitute) for the corvée" (Vella 1957, 87). In an interview in 1963 with a descendant of the hereditary ruling family of the northeastern province of Maha Sarakham, I learned that prior to the reign of King Chulalongkorn (1868–1910) the *hua muang* comprising much of what is present-day Maha Sarakham Province sent a supply of wild cardamom as a tribute to Bangkok. Following the ascension to the throne of Chulalongkorn in 1868 Maha Sarakham shifted to tribute in silver. By 1883–84, according to a French official who made an extensive trip throughout the Northeast during these years (Aymonier 1895; 1897), most of the *hua muang* in the Khorat Plateau were sending tribute in silver, though a few such as Dan Sai, Sangkha, and Buri Ram were still sending such specialties as sticklac, beeswax, and cardamom. According to the same source, the tribute that varied according to the population size of the *hua muang* consisted of head taxes. These taxes apparently sufficed to satisfy the corvée requirement as well, since there is no record of corvée being raised in the Northeast after the Lao-Siamese war of 1827–28.

In addition to taxation, the Thai crown reserved the right of mediating disputes between rulers of the various *hua muang,* making decisions in cases involving capital punishment, and directing or initiating war within the area. Finally, Bangkok required each *chao muang* or his representative to come to Bangkok annually to drink an oath of allegiance to the king and to appear at court at the time of a king's coronation or funeral. Yet despite these formal restrictions, the absence of permanent representatives of the Thai government in the Lao areas and the difficulties in communication and transportation meant that the *chao mueang* and the *achayasi* could rule their *hua muang* without too much regard for Bangkok.

This situation in which local autonomy was circumscribed only minimally by Thai control continued until the Thai court began to fear that the expansion of British and French colonialism might endanger their hold over the *hua muang*. After successfully installing a Bangkok-appointed royal commissioner at Chiang Mai in northern Thailand in 1874, the Thai government instituted a system of royal commissioners for the Lao areas of northeastern Thailand and southern Laos as well (Vella 1955, 344). The authority of these commissioners was guaranteed by the Siamese troops that accompanied them. From the local point of view, the new system was, in effect, a military occupation. In 1882 a royal commissioner in charge of the Lao *hua muang* was stationed at Champasak (Toem Singhatthit 1956, 1:464) and in 1890 Lao *hua muang* were grouped into four divisions known as *monthon*, each with its own royal commissioner (Bunchuai Atthakon 1962, 69).

This four-fold grouping of *hua muang* was divided as follows: the northern or Lao Phuan division included sixteen major *hua muang* under a commissioner at Nong Khai. The eastern or Lao Kao division included eleven *hua muang* under a commissioner at Champasak. The northeastern or Lao Isan division included twelve major *hua muang* under a commissioner at Ubon, and the central or Lao Klang division included three major *hua muang* with a commissioner at Khorat. Each of the first three included territories that today lie in both present-day Laos and northeastern Thailand. These four were on a par, administratively, with three other groupings of *hua muang*: one in northern Thailand based on Chiang Mai, another in the south based on Phuket, and a third in territories today in Cambodia based on Sisophon (Toem Singhatthit 1956, 1:508–37; Bunchuai 1962, 69; Damrong 1960, 81–86).

The Franco-Siamese treaty of 1893, which resulted in the cession of territories on the left bank of the Mekong to the French, provided an important reason for the broadening of the administrative reforms which King Chulalongkorn had begun in the previous decade. In the first of a series of major governmental reform laws proclaimed in 1893, the administration of all *hua muang* that had formerly been under the jurisdiction of several quasi-ministries was centralized under the Ministry of Interior. The same proclamation created the new administrative unit of *monthon* or "circles" of which there were eighteen for the whole country. These were designed to bridge the gap between the central government and the *hua muang*. *Monthon* were administered by Ministry of Interior officials appointed by Bangkok. This administrative reform carried the Thai government a step closer to direct control over the "outer provinces," including those in northeastern Thailand.

The *monthon* established in the Lao areas reflected the loss of territories on the left bank of the Mekong. Whereas there had been four groupings of *hua muang* prior to 1893, there were only three *monthon*. Furthermore, because of a provision in the Franco-Siamese Treaty of 1893 forbidding the Siamese to have fortified or military establishments within twenty-five kilometers of the Mekong (Thailand, Department of Publicity 1941, 49), the headquarters of two of the northeastern *monthon* were transferred to new places. The three northeastern *monthon* were Khorat, centered on Nakhon Ratchasima; Isan, centered on Ubon (rather than Champasak); and Udon, centered on Udon (rather than Nong Khai).[30]

The extension of the authority of Bangkok over the Northeast, as well as over the northern provinces and those southern provinces whose population was predominately Malay-speaking, was challenged by the peoples of these regions who held to older precolonial ideas of political authority. Of these challenges, the most significant took place in northeastern Thailand.

3

BUDDHIST MILLENIALIST ROOTS OF ISAN POLITICAL CULTURE

BUDDHIST MILLENNIALISM

In the first years of the twentieth century, the rural populace in what is today northeastern Thailand and central and southern Laos rose in large numbers in opposition to new political regimes imposed by the Siamese on the right bank of the Mekong and by the French on the left.[1] The rising was led by men who styled themselves and were called by their followers *phu mi bun*—"men having merit." This concept derives from the Theravada Buddhist tradition adhered to by the Lao and is found in cognate forms among all followers of Theravada Buddhism.

Fundamental to Theravada Buddhism as it is practiced is the belief that every action has a moral consequence. Such is the law of *kamma*, to use the Pali term known in cognate forms by all followers of Theravada Buddhism.[2] According to popular Buddhist understanding every human being enters the world with a kammic legacy, that is, with conditionings that are the result of actions in previous lives. The actions performed in previous existences, if moral, have resulted in "merit" (Pali, *puñña*; Lao and Thai, *bun*), that is, positive *kamma*, or, if immoral or evil, in "demerit" (Pali, *papa*; Lao and Thai, *bap*). The accumulation of merit and demerit from previous lives determines one's kammic heritage. Some manifestations of this heritage—such as physical defects, gender, parentage, and place of birth (e.g., whether in a peasant hut or a princely palace)—are obvious at birth. Others, however, are indeterminate "because I do not know what my past sins and good actions have been" (Obeyesekere 1968, 21), and thus one cannot know when or how one's kammic heritage will be manifest. However, if one is suddenly struck down by a fatal illness, or has a serious accident, or has a miscarriage, or is punished by secular authorities for a crime, then such is understood as *pen kam*, that is, the consequence of demerit inherited from a previous existence. If one is enthroned as a king or is married or affianced to a prince or is able to be successful in whatever occupation one takes up or even if one lives a long life surrounded by family and friends, such is clearly the consequence of having merit from a previous life.

While everyone enters life with a legacy that comes from past *kamma*, certain persons—especially men—are seen by others to have inherited extraordinary positive *kamma* or merit (*bun*) or charisma (*barami*, from Pali *parami*). Such men can be recognized by the symbols of authority they are able to link themselves to and by the followers who are attracted to them. While those who wear the crown of kingship are—unless deposed—self-evident *phu mi bun barami*, others can be recognized as *phu mi bun* if they are able to perform acts that demonstrate their exceptional natures.

In Buddhist terms, the most significant of such acts are those that are deemed to reduce suffering (*dukkha*; Lao and Thai, *khwamthuk*) or increase prosperity (*sukkha*; *khwamsuk*). The concept of the "person who has merit" is obviously closely related to the Mahayana Buddhist idea of the bodhisattva, the being who, although having achieved enlightenment, has chosen to postpone his entrance into *nibbana* (nirvana) in order to alleviate the suffering and enhance the prosperity of other humans through "great compassion." While Theravada Buddhism formally recognizes only one bodhisattva—Mettaya or Ariya Maitreya, the future Buddha—many persons in Theravadin history have been acclaimed as possessing exceptional charisma and in the Lao tradition such men have been and are called *phu mi bun*, literally, men with merit.[3] Such men—and they have always been males—are assumed to have exceptional powers because they have inherited much merit from previous existences.[4]

Phu mi bun have arisen in the Thai and Lao worlds particularly in times of political crisis, that is, when the supreme authority of a political order has become problematic (see Chatthip 1984, C. Wilson 1997). Because *phu mi bun* do not have the charisma of office that a king or even a vassal prince has, they are dependent on performing or arranging for acts that are deemed miraculous (*saksit*) because the consequence of such acts are not the result of commonsensical cause and effect.[5] The *phu mi bun* who have offered their followers a restoration of an older political order or the establishment of a new moral order have become leaders of what comparative religionists term a millenarian or millennial movement.

Comparative religionists have taken the concept of millenarianism or millennialism from Christian history. Generalizing from the original Christian sense (a new order on earth to be established by Christ), the millennium is a new order on earth that will be established by a supernatural agency, i.e., by a force that is transcendental to man. Millennialism is distinguished from other eschatological belief systems

A diorama of the *phu mi bun* millenarian uprising, northeastern Thailand, 1901–2
(Art and Culture Center, Rajabhat University, Ubon, web page)

in that the millennium is believed to be imminent, and in that it will be located in this world rather than on some other plane of existence.[6]

The reforms instituted by King Chulalongkorn beginning in 1892 that aimed at creating a centralized state led to a radical devaluation in the current political order as it existed for large parts of the population of the country. In 1898 Prince Damrong Rajanubhab, half brother of King Chulalongkorn and minister of interior responsible for implementing the new administrative system, encountered in Phuket in southern Thailand an incident that foreshadowed more serious uprisings in northern and northeastern Thailand. In Phuket Prince Damrong discovered a monk who was honored by many people in the area, who ritually affixed gold leaf to his person in much the same manner as gold leaf was affixed to Buddha images.[7] Intrigued, Prince Damrong asked the monk why he was so honored by his followers. The monk told Prince Damrong that in 1876 there had been an uprising of Chinese miners in Phuket. The monk, then abbot of a village temple, was approached by several men who strongly encouraged him to flee to the hills as the other villagers had done. The monk refused to leave, saying that he had never known any home but the temple. Those who had come to persuade him to leave consulted among themselves and finally decided to stay with the monk. The monk then provided each of these men with a magical cloth *(pha prachiat)*—a white cloth on which he had written magical formula (Thai, *yantra*). Shortly afterwards, a band of Chinese attacked the village and, expecting no resistance, were unprepared when they were counterattacked by the monk's followers. The Chinese fled. When villagers heard of the successful resistance, they returned to the village; the monk provided each of the men with magical cloth to protect them against bullets. Again the Chinese (now a larger group) attacked; again they were repulsed, and the monk's reputation was made. After peace had returned (the Siamese government having suppressed the uprising), the monk's reputation continued to grow, as amulets he had distributed were reported to accomplish many different types of miraculous ends.[8] In this case, the monk had attracted a collective following because of the common threat the followers had experienced from the Chinese rebels. Significantly, the millennial possibilities of this movement were short-circuited by the Siamese government; by recognizing the monk in question as the senior abbot of the local sangha, the government was able to institutionalize the charisma of the monk.

There were more serious uprisings in northern Thailand in the late nineteenth century, both by rural peasants (Tanabe 1984) and by so-called Shan (Ngiao) who had migrated from Chiang Tung (Kengtung) in what is now Burma (Tej 1968).[9] Both the peasants and Shan were very much aware of the efforts by the Siamese court to replace local rulers and princes with Bangkok-appointed officials (Brailey 1973, 1974). Although the uprisings were successfully repressed, the memory of religio-political autonomy continued to hold great influence among the Khon Muang or Yuan of northern Thailand. Followers of the northern Thai charismatic monk Khruba Siwichai continued to resist Siamese efforts to subordinate the northern Thai sangha to a Bangkok-centered sangha hierarchy into the 1930s, and the memory of this monk continues to be the grounding for northern Thai (Yuan, Khon Muang) ethnoregionalism to the present (see Keyes 1971a, 1981; Cohen 2001).

By far the most significant millennial uprising in Thailand, however, to my knowledge, is one that began in the northeastern region of the country about 1899–1900, swept through much of the region, and reached a climax in 1902, when it was forcibly suppressed by the Thai government. It is this movement and its aftermath that foreshadows subsequent challenges by rural northeasterners to the authority of the Thai state.

THE *PHU MI BUN* UPRISING IN NORTHEASTERN THAILAND, 1900–1902[10]

In the last decades of the nineteenth century, the political order in northeastern Thailand and neighboring areas in Laos and Cambodia was radically disrupted. The change can be said to have begun in 1867, when the Siamese court was forced by France to relinquish its tributary authority over the kingdom of Cambodia. The threat of French expansion (together with the threat of British expansion from the west) led King Chulalongkorn, who ascended to the throne in 1868, to strengthen Siam's control over the peripheral areas of the realm. Beginning in the

1870s, the Siamese court began to evolve a new system of provincial administration. In 1882, Siamese high commissioners (*khaluang yai*) were sent to Champasak, Ubon, Nong Khai, and Khorat to begin instituting a new political system in northeastern Thailand and neighboring areas of Laos.[11] These high commissioners, whose authority was increased in 1890 and again in 1891, occupied a new position intermediate between the Siamese court and the local hereditary elite of the region. In 1892, the position of this elite was directly challenged by the appointment of Siamese officials as permanent administrative commissioners (*khaluang kamkap ratchakan*) with certain powers, especially with regard to taxation, that had previously been held by the local lords (*chao*) of the *muang* (Amorawong 1963, 136ff.; Paitoon 1972, 40–43).

While the Siamese court was carrying out these changes in provincial administration, the French were also subjecting it to increased pressure. After France had consolidated its authority over the whole of Vietnam in the late 1880s, it began to move into territory in present-day Laos that Siam claimed was under its control. In March 1893, in what is today southern Laos, war broke out between France and Siam. The military force Siam sent to the front was made up, in large part, of levies raised in northeastern Thailand (Bunchuai 1962, 72–73; Paitoon 1972, 53–55; Tej 1968, 138–40). In July 1893, the French sent gunboats up the Chao Phraya River; under threat of attack on Bangkok, the Siamese government agreed to sign a treaty dictated by the French. The Franco-Siamese Treaty of 1893 recognized French authority over all territory on the left bank of the Mekong River. Siamese officials and troops (including the levies from the northeastern provinces) were forced to withdraw across the Mekong. The treaty created a zone on the Thai side of the border twenty-five kilometers wide in which no Siamese officials, policemen, or soldiers could enter without specific permission from the French. As a consequence, political authority in this zone became very confused.

Following the war, the situation in northeastern Thailand grew increasingly tense. The French established consulates at Ubon and Khorat, and French merchants, missionaries, and others began to operate in northeastern Thailand. Disputes emerged regarding the status of the many refugees who fled from French Laos to resettle in Siamese territory. There is no question but that certain Frenchmen hoped to use the pretext of these disputes as a rationale for French advance into northeastern Thailand and, perhaps, into the whole of Siam. The Siamese court, for its part, accelerated its efforts to increase its control over the threatened northeastern region.

The importance the Siamese court attached to the northeastern border provinces was manifest in the appointment of the high-ranking and highly respected Prince Sanphasittiprasong as the royal commissioner plenipotentiary (*khaluang yai tang phra ong samret ratchakan*) for Monthon ("circle") Lao Kao (later Monthon Isan), the jurisdiction that included the northeastern provinces in the drainage of the central and lower Chi River (Toem Wiphakphachanakit 1970, 471; Paitoon 1972, 55, 57–58.). In 1894, the court began implementing in northeastern Thailand a plan of centralized provincial administration, the system later known under the name *thetsaphiban*. The units of this system were defined primarily in terms of territory rather than in terms of the subject population, as had been the case in the existing system. In 1894, a mapping expedition was sent out to determine the boundaries, and in 1897 a royal "Edict Concerning Local Administration" created a hierarchy of political units into which the populace was administratively organized (Tej 1968, 191, 195–206; Toem Wiphakphachanakit 1970, 2:463–65; Paitoon 1972, 67.). When this edict was implemented in the Northeast, only a few of the old "domains" (*muang*) were recognized as "provinces" (*changwat*); most were made into "districts" (*amphoe*) under the provinces, and a significant number were demoted to the status of *tambon* or "commune" and made subordinate to the districts. This political restructuring resulted in the downgrading of many of the local gentry, and those who remained as lords—now "governors" (*phuwa ratchakan*)—of provinces were left with little real power; the Siamese commissioners placed over them now held power in the name of the Siamese king.

The most important power preempted by the Siamese commissioners was that of taxation levied on the populace. Acting on orders from the court, the commissioners undertook to systematize all types of taxes. In 1899, Prince Sanphasit, the high commissioner at Ubon, issued a proclamation that fixed the head tax at 3.50 baht per eligible male (*chai chakan*)—a category excluding those under eighteen and over sixty years of age, the disabled, those serving in government service, local gentry and their families, Siamese officials, foreigners, ascetics and monks, artisans, and rich persons (Paitoon 1972, 75–76).[12] In 1901–2, the poll tax was raised to 4.00 baht per taxable person (94). Taxes on production were also made more efficient. The overall effect of the rationalization of taxation was to increase the tax burden on the peasantry (95–96). The Siamese commissioners also introduced other changes that directly affected the peasantry. In 1899, for example, Prince Sanphasit ordered that all sales of large animals be carried out in the presence of officials. Ostensibly this requirement was designed to reduce theft; in fact, it had the effect of giving local officials the opportunity to take part of the sale price of buffaloes, cattle, horses, and elephants (77–78). Prince Sanphasit also attempted to change those local customs (such as tattooing) that the Siamese regarded as uncivilized (75). In short, the peasantry in northeastern Thailand found their freedom of action increasingly restricted by Siamese officials.

The economic restrictions and the tax burden placed upon northeastern peasants fell heaviest on those who were finding it difficult to produce enough for their needs. The harvests in the Chi River basin in 1890 and 1891 had been extremely poor because of too little rain one year, and too much flooding in the following year (Bunchuai 1962, 69; Paitoon 1972, 43–44). Moreover, the population of the region had grown to such an extent that many peasants were cultivating marginal lands on which good harvests could not be expected unless conditions were optimal (see Keyes 1976). In 1902, Phra Ubali (then known as Phra Yanarakkhit),[13] the ranking monk in Monthon Isan, himself a northeasterner from Ubon, wrote the following about the combined effects of natural and political conditions on the life of the peasants in the area:

> The populace is impoverished because they lack economic progress. If they have good yields, there is no market. If they cannot (farm), they must starve. . . . The trade in beasts of burden is difficult in several respects. Buyers and sellers exist, but they lack the legal papers. When elephants and horses that have gone astray are caught and taken to administrative offices (*sala klang*), they are confiscated for the crown. . . . It is impossible for the populace to find work (for

wages) in their own land. The cost of labor is cheap to a degree.
. . . Since (the populace) lives far away from the commissioners
(*khaluang*), there are crooked people who collect head taxes before
the government is able to do so. Because (those who have been
cheated) have nothing left, they are ruined. (If they bring the crooks
to court), they have no evidence and are defeated.[14]

Given the conditions changing for the worse, some peasants turned
to banditry (Paitoon 1972, 47–49). By the end of the nineteenth century,
the attraction of banditry gave way as politico-religious leaders emerged
from among the people and these leaders offered ways to eliminate the
causes of suffering of the peasantry.

By 1899, Siamese officials began to receive reports about men claiming
to be "miracle men" (*phu wiset*), who were providing peasants with
sacralized water (*nam mon*), "medicine" (*ya*), and modes of worship
(Paitoon 1972, 107). At the same time, troubadour singers—apparently
from French Laos—were traveling about the region singing in a
popular form known as *kham phaya* about the coming of *phu mi bun*.[15]
Troubadour singing (*molam*) was probably the major way whereby
the *phu mi bun* message was spread from village to village. In addition,
handwritten manuscripts were also circulated, and at least four different
written versions of the message are known to exist.[16]

While different versions of the message are reported from several parts
of the region,[17] the content was very similar everywhere. All versions
begin with the prediction of an imminent dramatic catastrophe. For
example, in a version obtained in villages in the vicinity of Selaphum
(today in Roi Et Province), it was predicted that a terrible wind would
initiate a series of horrific events: "On Sunday, the day of the full moon in
the fourth month of the year of the Ox, third of the decade, Chulasakarat
[Era] 1263 [March 23, 1902], a windstorm so powerful that it can blow
people about will begin and it will be dark for seven days and seven
nights. One should burn the wood of the *mai linfa* (Lao; Thai, *mai pheka*:
Oroxylum indicum) for light and plant lemon grass at all stairways to
houses. During the windstorm, if one seizes a handful of lemon grass,
one will not be blown away."[18]

During this catastrophe, many normal things were to be radically transformed: pebbles would become gold and silver, while gold and silver would become pebbles, lead, or iron; gourds and pumpkins would become elephants and horses; pigs and buffaloes (especially albino or short-horned buffaloes) would become man-eating *yaksa*,[19] silkworms would become snakes or vicious dugongs; the fibers from the roots of trees from along the Mekong would become silk; flowers of the flame-of-the-forest tree (*Butea frondosa*; Lao, *mai can*; Thai, *mai thong kwao*) would become red dye for coloring silk.[20]

The message continues with the prediction that associated with the holocaust will be the coming of a savior, variously termed Thao or Chao or Phraya Thammikarat (Lord Righteous Ruler), the "meritful lord" (*chao ton bun*), or "meritful person" (*phu mi bun*). In one of the written versions, it said of Phraya Thammikarat that "in the past he ruled Muang Nong Sun [identified as Ayutthaya or old Siam] and then he ruled Muang Lang Chang [old Laos]. . . . In the year of the pig [1899/1900] the face of Chao Thammikarat was seen in our own time" (Paitoon 1972, 101, my translation). In another written version, Phraya Thammikarat is identified as a villager from Ban Nalao, Selaphum District, Roi Et Province, a man who had taken the title and name of Phra Ketsatthawiha Chao Fa (100–101). This man was by no means the only one who claimed to be a *phu mi bun*, as we shall see. Those who follow the savior(s) and undertake the actions prescribed by them or in the messages will not only escape disaster but will prosper:

Whoever wishes to remain free from these evil happenings should copy or retell this story and make it generally known. If one is pure and has not performed any evil or bad *kamma*[21] (or, if one wishes to become rich), one should collect pebbles so that Thao Thammikarat can transform them into gold and silver. If one has performed various evil deeds, then in order to become a pure person one should perform the ritual of *tat kam wang wen*[22] whereby one arranges to invite monks to come and sprinkle sacralized water.[23] If one is afraid of death, one should kill albino buffaloes and pigs before the middle of the sixth month to prevent them being transformed into *yaksa*. If one is still a maiden or a married woman who has not yet consummated her marriage, one should quickly take a husband. Otherwise the *yaksa* will catch you and eat you. (Toem Wiphakphachanakit 1970, 559, my translation)[24]

The millennialism of this message could not be more classic. First, there is a set date for the radical destruction of the existing social order. At that time, natural conditions will be inverted (gold and silver will become pebbles, pebbles will become gold and silver, and so on). A savior will come; he will be a returning king, a king of righteousness, and, in Buddhist terms, the legatee of great merit, which will enable him to alleviate the suffering of the just and punish the wicked. Those who have demonstrated themselves to be believers—by disposing of their gold and silver, killing off buffalo and swine, collecting pebbles, and performing ritual acts (like the *tat kam wang wen*)—will be saved and will prosper. Even a sexual element is added in that all maidens or women who have not yet consummated marriage should "take husbands" (the Thai phrase suggests having intercourse as well as entering into marriage). Those who do not follow these prescriptions and proscriptions will suffer a horrible death—being eaten by *yaksa*.

The message of the imminent holocaust and the establishment of a new order under a righteous and meritful ruler spread throughout much of northeastern Thailand,[25] as well as across the Mekong in French Laos. Siamese officials dismissed initial reports about the effects of the message, viewing it as mere superstition. However, by early 1902, the government could no longer ignore the fact that very disturbing events were taking place in northeastern Thailand. In February 1902, Phra Yanarakkhit, the ranking monk in Monthon Isan, reported that from Ubon to Sangkha in Surin Province, no one—from villager to official—could talk of anything but the *phu mi bun*. In some places, the monk reported, "rice in the fields remains unharvested and cattle and buffaloes are allowed to eat it; garden plots and sugar cane (fields) have often been discarded."[26] The first direct official Siamese action took place when three ranking monks in Yasothon Province were reprimanded for having performed the "cleansing" ceremony (Toem Wiphakphachanakit

1970, 2:560–61). Still, the movement continued to grow, and it became organized around several men claiming to be *phu mi bun*. Early in 1902, there were at least three major leaders of the movement in northeastern Thailand. A man from French Laos by the name of Man established himself in a village in Khemmarat District in what is today Ubon Province, claiming to be Chao (or Ong) Prasatthong (Lord Golden Serenity), "a divine being who had descended from heaven to be reborn as a favor to mankind" (Toem Wiphakphachanakit 1970, 2:564; also see Paitoon 1972, 106). A local official wrote of Man that he claims to be a *phu wiset* ["miracle man"] and has gone about [demonstrating his powers] by keeping the [eight] precepts, meditating in caves and in the hills, and preparing sacralized water. He deceives the populace that he is a *phu wiset* who can cure various illnesses with magic (*rut*), sacralized water, and enchanted medicine (*khunya*)" (Paitoon 1972, 108, my translation).[27] Man attracted an initial following of about two hundred and was responsible for several disaffected local gentry from the downgraded *muang* of Khong Chiam (in present-day Ubon Province) going to French Laos, where they claimed to be *phu mi bun* (Paitoon 1972, 93).

Another disaffected local noble, Thao Bunchan, was the leader of another sector of the *phu mi bun* movement located in the vicinity of Khukhan in what is today Si Sa Ket Province. When a new governor of Khukhan was appointed, Thao Bunchan, who felt that he should be governor but was not appointed, left the town together with two other disappointed local gentry and established themselves as *phu mi bun* in a village nearby (Paitoon 1972, 93, 106). Prince Sanphasit, the high commissioner at Ubon, estimated that by February 1902 Thao Bunchan had a following of six thousand.[28]

The third most important leader in northeastern Thailand was a villager by the name of Lek, who was apparently the same as the man mentioned in one of the written forms of the message as being from Ban Nalao, Selaphum District, in Roi Et Province. He and several other villagers, all with pretentious titles, established themselves in Phayakkhaphumphisai District (in today's Maha Sarakham Province). No estimates are available on the size of Lek's following, but it is known that they were from several provinces in the central Chi River valley (Paitoon 1972, 106).

It is not entirely clear how much prior coordination there was among the leaders of the movement in northeastern Thailand, and between them and those in French Laos. One minor leader, interviewed after the uprising had been put down, claimed that all the leaders shared the same objective: "to establish a kingdom that was not under either the Siamese or the French" (Paitoon 1972, 107). To obtain this objective, the movement was to destroy, by force, Siamese and French power in the area. Once this was accomplished, four of the *phu mi bun* would rule at Vientiane, Ubon, That Phanom, and Nong Son (Ayutthaya) (107). Whether or not such a grandiose plan existed, several of the *phu mi bun* leaders did undertake to wrest power from the Siamese by force of arms.

It appears that the hand of the *phu mi bun* was forced in late February and early March 1902 when several patrols, consisting of a few Siamese officers and soldiers and some local irregulars, were sent out to arrest those responsible for the growing unrest. One of these patrols succeeded in killing Thao Bunchan, the leader in Khukhan, and in dispersing his followers. However, the other patrols were less successful; in one case, the irregulars were persuaded to join the rebels. Meanwhile, Man and Lek had joined together and "led a force of about twenty-five hundred or more in an attack [on the Mekong River city] of Muang Khemmarat" (Paitoon 1972, 112; see also Toem Wiphakphachanakit 1970, 2:565). The rebels killed two of the chief nobles, captured the governor of the province, and burned and looted the town. The success of the rebels at Khemmarat attracted the support of many more people. It also spurred strong government response.

The rebels under Man and Lek started toward the city of Ubon, then the major city in the area. They established themselves at the village of Ban Sapho, fifty kilometers or so northwest of Ubon in the district of Trakanphuetphon. Here they were joined by some of Bunchan's followers from Khukhan. Before the rebel force could move towards Ubon, they were attacked at Ban Sapho by a Siamese force numbering perhaps as many as two thousand (Paitoon 1972, 114–15, 186–89).

On April 4th [1902] the Siamese force, armed with repeating rifles and cannons, attacked the rebel force. The rebels were ill armed, having knives, swords, spears, and old flintlock rifles. As the government troops approached, the rebels warned them: "Don't anybody shoot or do anything at all. Sit in meditation and our side will shoot but a single shot." The government troops did attack and a battle raged for four hours. Seeing their forces in defeat, the leaders of the rebels escaped before the battle was over. When it was over, more than 200 rebels had died, more than 500 had been injured, and another 120 had been captured. Not a single government soldier was even injured. (Paitoon 1972, 115–16, my translation)[29]

Following this decisive battle, government troops were sent to several other locations to eliminate any remaining rebel resistance. In this mopping-up operation, a number of rebels were killed—including six minor leaders in Khong Chiam District—and many more were captured. The total number of rebels captured in all encounters was estimated to be about four hundred (Paitoon 1972, 120). Lek was captured but Man escaped to French Laos, where he joined up with Ong Kaeo and was associated with him in an unsuccessful attack on Savannakhet on April 21, 1902 (120).[30]

Of the four hundred or so rebels whom the Siamese captured, all but nine major leaders and a few minor leaders were released. One of the nine major leaders was a monk; another, a local noble; the others, villagers (Toem Wiphakphachanakit 1970, 2:574–75). With the exception of the monk, the leaders were executed in their home communities as examples to the people of what happens to rebels. The monk, along with the three monks who had been involved prior to the rebellion, were ordered to remain in the monkhood for life; if they left the monkhood, they would be jailed instead. A number of the minor leaders were given prison sentences. As for the ordinary people who had become followers of the *phu mi bun*, they were ordered to participate in ceremonies at which they drank an oath of allegiance and pledged themselves to believe strongly in the king of Siam (Paitoon 1972, 67).

These events had not gone unnoticed by the French. In putting down the rebellion, Siamese forces entered the 25-kilometer zone along the border with French Laos, contravening the Treaty of 1893. The French vice-consul at Ubon, M. Paul Patte, warned that such infractions might lead to French forces crossing into Siamese territory. Through negotiations carried on between Siamese officials and representatives of the French Foreign Ministry in Paris, it was agreed that Siamese forces could enter the zone in pursuit of the rebels, but they could not stay there (Paitoon 1972, 118–19). M. Lorgeon, who had been French consul in Bangkok and was in 1902 legal advisor to the Siamese government, had gone to Ubon at the time of the execution of the rebel leaders. He had challenged Prince Sanphasit, the Siamese high commissioner, as to whether he had the authority to carry out the executions. On his return to Bangkok, M. Lorgeon asked the king about this and was reassured that Prince Sanphasit had been given the authority to act as he did (Toem Wiphakphachanakit 1970, 2:577). The potential for French intervention remained a threat to Siam for some years to come. Nonetheless, for reasons having to do with French foreign policy, the French did not exploit the *phu mi bun* uprising, nor the disaffection of many local gentry in the region, as pretexts for annexing northeastern Thailand to French Laos. French expansion to the west ended with the treaty of 1907, whereby Siam ceded to France the right-bank territories of Sayaboury (across the Mekong from Luang Prabang) and right-bank lands that had been under Champasak, as well as provinces in what is today northern Cambodia.

THE LEGACY OF THE *PHU MI BUN* UPRISING

Insofar as the thousands of northeasterners who had been followers or sympathizers of the *phu mi bun* were concerned, the Siamese government—through the use of superior military force and the subsequent punishment meted out to the captured *phu mi bun* leaders— proved itself to be the dominant political element in the region. Yet Prince Damrong, Prince Sanphasit, and other high-ranking Siamese officials recognized that force alone would not ensure that the local gentry as well as peasants in the northeastern region would accept the authority of the Bangkok government. Following the uprising, the Siamese government undertook investigations into its causes. Phra Yanarakkhit, the ranking monk in Monthon Isan, who was called upon for his opinion regarding the causes, argued that the poverty of the region served to stimulate unrest among the populace (Tej 1968, 273).

In saying this, he was sounding a theme that would be repeated by nearly every analyst of the causes of unrest in northeastern Thailand from then on to the present. The Northeast relative to the rest of the country was then and remained throughout the twentieth century and into the twenty-first century the locus of the poorest sector of the population of the country. But economic deprivation was far from the only, or even primary, reason why northeasterners rallied around the *phu mi bun*.[31]

As Paitoon and Tej (Paitoon 1972, 93, 95, 122; Tej 1968, 272–73) have both observed in their analyses of the *phu mi bun* uprising, the rapid introduction of politico-administrative reforms served to create a whole class of potential dissident leaders out of displaced local gentry and a large body of followers among the peasantry who were subjected to new tax demands and legal restrictions. The increasing intrusion of the Thai state into northeastern society, namely village society, would remain a significant source of northeastern dissent even into the twenty-first century.

The causes of the rebellion were to be found not only in the new political conditions and in the underlying poverty; in addition there was an ideological cause. In the various communiqués circulated among Siamese officials—particularly between Prince Damrong (minister of interior) and Prince Sanphasit (the high commissioner of Monthon Isan)—there was constant reference to the "stupidity" and "ignorance" (*ngo*) of the northeastern populace.[32] Paitoon, in his analysis of these documents, wisely observes that what was behind these statements was the fact that the northeastern populace had not yet come to appreciate the meaning of the new ways for ordering behavior which the Siamese officials were attempting to introduce (Paitoon 1972, 96–97); in other words, the Siamese officials and northeasterners understood power in quite different cultural terms. Perceiving this cultural gap, King Chulalongkorn, Prince Damrong, and others of the king's advisors, promoted policies, such as the integration of the Buddhist sangha and the institution of compulsory primary education, that would bring the Siamese cultural view to the populace at large, including the northeastern peasantry. Nonetheless, the characterization of northeasterners as stupid did not disappear and, indeed, has been so reinforced in Thai popular culture through such media as TV soap operas and films that it has become the conventional understanding of northeasterners held by many in Thailand's expanding urban middle class as well as by the elite.

In the wake of the *phu mi bun* uprising, the central Thai government set out systematically to transform the Lao of northeastern Thailand (as well as northern Thailand) into Thai citizens (*chat Thai*) as Prince Damrong had envisioned. This effort entailed the institution of a system of compulsory primary education based around a set of texts emphasizing the connections between Thai Buddhism, the Thai nation, and the Thai monarchy. In the early decades of the twentieth century, government resources were also used to disseminate the idea that the Thai king was the only "person with merit" who has the power to share the benefits of this merit with others.

In northeastern Thailand, the reason these efforts were successful to some degree was because a number of respected senior northeastern Thai monks were affiliated with the Thammayut *nikai*, the reformed sangha established by King Mongkut. Until 1902, when monks throughout the country were placed under the authority of the Thai sangha, monks were divided by the ordination lineages to which they belonged. There were many distinct ordination lineages, but roughly they could be grouped as (1) Thai, which included Thai-speaking monks in central and upper southern Thailand; (2) Yuan, which included monks in northern Thailand; (3) Khmer, which included monks in the southern part of northeastern Thailand; and (4) Lao, which included monks in northeastern Thailand. In addition, in central Thailand there were some monks who identified with the tradition of the Mon, a people found primarily in lower Burma but also with significant representation in Thailand.[33] All Theravadin monks recognized a fundamental differentiation in clerical practice between those who studied and explained the dhamma, the teachings of the Buddha (Pali, *pariyattidhura*) through sermons, and those who devoted themselves to strict practice of these teachings (*patipattidhura*). While it appears to have been the case that historically many monks throughout what became Thailand observed the strict practice early in their careers or on occasional retreats, almost all were primarily students and expounders of the dhamma. The exception was the Mon tradition that placed much greater emphasis on meditation and asceticism, practices associated with *patipattidhura*.

A major change began in the nineteenth century when a princely monk who would later become King Mongkut (born 1804; ordained 1827–51; reigned 1851–68) decided that the Mon tradition was closer to true Buddhism. He attracted a number of other monks who shared his commitment to adhere strictly to following the path leading to *nibbana*. Although most of these monks who became the core of what would constitute a reformed order within the sangha were from members of the Siamese elite, at least a few came from more humble roots. Several came from northeastern Thailand (Taylor 1993, 46).[34] These monks strongly disapproved of magical (*saksit*) practices and, thus, were willing to denounce the *phu mi bun*.

The rise of a distinctive and widely respected forest meditation tradition in northeastern Thailand centered on Achan Man Phurithatta (Bhuridatto Thera), who lived from 1871 to 1949 and who had been ordained by Phra Ubali. Achan Man was probably a more significant factor in the decline of the type of magical Buddhism associated with the *phu mi bun* than was the coercive force deployed by the Thai state.[35] Achan Man was revered not because he was seen as a "man of merit," that is, the embodiment of great *barami*, but because he succeeded in emulating the Buddha in withdrawing from the world and devoting himself to meditation. As I have written elsewhere (Keyes 1981), Achan Man was acclaimed as an *arhat*, a saint, rather than a bodhisattva, a "Buddha-to-be."

The older idea that powerful men known by their religious charisma could emerge from among the people did not, however, completely disappear in the Northeast in the wake of the influence of Achan Man and his "forest monk" disciples. The lack until quite recently of adequate health care for villagers in northeastern Thailand (as for villagers elsewhere in the kingdom) has served to keep the idea of *saksit* power very much alive. To this day there are curing cults in the region focused on those who claim to have extraordinary powers. Thus, when political crises have occurred in Thailand, there has continued to exist the potential for the emergence of a person having *saksit* power who claims to be able to alleviate suffering caused by political action.

A number of cases from northeastern Thailand demonstrate the continuing viability of the idea that local persons with merit can

A widely circulated photograph of Achan Man Phurithatta (Bhuridatto Thera)

effect radical political changes in the lives of their followers.[36] In 1924, for example, there was a man in Loei Province, located in the far northwestern corner of the Khorat Plateau, who claimed "himself to be a representative of heaven who had received the task of coming to protect men from the calamity of man-eating *yaksa*" (Toem Wiphakphachanakit 1970, 2:551, my translation). He acquired a following, which he led in a quixotic attack on the local district office. A government force quickly put down this small uprising and the leader wound up in jail (579–87). This affair can probably be seen as a final reaction, in an isolated district, to the implementation of King Chulalongkorn's provincial administrative reforms.

In 1933, a troubadour (*molam*) singer in Maha Sarakham Province claimed to have extraordinary powers he would put to use in overthrowing Siamese power and establishing a new, independent Lao kingdom. Again, this man gained a small following, but before anything could happen he was arrested and given a jail sentence (Bunchuai 1962, 94, 96–98). I believe that it is not coincidence that this man emerged at a time when the structure of political authority had been radically changed by the 1932 revolution, when a group of civil servants and military officers forced the king to proclaim a constitution under which the king would remain the symbolic head of state while real power was to be vested in "representatives of the people."

In 1959, "a minor incident in the *phu mi bun* style took place in Khorat which cost several lives including that of a Thai district officer. Even more extraordinary, its leader laid claim to being a reincarnation of the revered and much more recent monarch, Chulalongkorn" (Ishii 1975, 126).[37] In 1974, a cult around a man prophesying that Ariya Maitreya was about to appear imminently attracted followers in Udon and Loei Provinces.[38] Such incidents notwithstanding, millennialist movements never again achieved the significance they had at the beginning of the twentieth century. Northeasterners have, nonetheless, continued to find in their distinctive Buddhist traditions moral critiques of the exercise of power by the Thai state even as they have turned to more secular forms for asserting them.

4

ISAN BECOMING THAI

INTEGRATION OF THE NORTHEAST INTO THE THAI NATION-STATE

The extension of Thai political control over outlying regions, including the Northeast, was inexorably connected with the creation of modern communication and transportation networks that were begun in the last decades of the nineteenth century. Without more rapid means of communication and transportation between Bangkok and outlying regions, the political reforms of King Chulalongkorn could never have been so effective in breaking down the autonomy and isolation of the northeastern *hua muang*. Traditionally, messages between the government and provincial outposts had been carried by relay runners on horseback or by fast boat. During the reign of King Chulalongkorn the Ministry of Interior maintained a schedule whereby messages between Bangkok and Nong Khai took 12 days, between Bangkok and Ubon, 12 days, and between Bangkok and Luang Prabang, 17 days going and 13 days in returning (Damrong 1960, 58). The normal movement of people and goods was far slower. According to one report in 1895 it took about three weeks to travel by ox cart from Nong Khai to Khorat and another eight or nine days to travel from Khorat to Bangkok (Smyth 1895, 83, 93). Travel by water, which was important in connecting the north with the central plains, served in the Northeast only to connect internal points on the Mun, Chi, or Mekong, or to connect northeastern communities with other communities on the left bank of the Mekong.

Trading patterns between the central plains, in particular, Bangkok, and the Northeast were altered radically with the completion of the first rail line to Khorat in 1900. Whereas the shipment of goods had formerly taken at least eight or nine days to go from Khorat to Bangkok, it could now be accomplished in a day. The traditional routes within the northeastern region were, of course, unmodified by the rail connection between Bangkok and Khorat, but the speed with which goods could reach Khorat from Bangkok facilitated the introduction into the region of items previously too expensive or too perishable to transport. By 1928 one section of the northeastern rail line had been extended to Ubon and by 1933 the other section had reached Khon Kaen (Thailand, Ministry of Communication 1947, 11–13).[1] Automobile transport made its first appearance in the Northeast sometime in the 1920s but did not expand rapidly until after World War II.

Modern communication connections between the Northeast and Bangkok were inaugurated at about the same time as the beginning of railway construction. The Post and Telegraph Office was first established in 1883. According to a French official, there were two major northeastern telegraph lines in 1907, each branching out from Khorat, the terminus of the Bangkok–Khorat line. The first went north to Nong Khai and the second went east to Ubon, with a section going from Buri Ram to Champasak (Lunet de Lajonquière 1907, 283). Subsequently telegraph services were extended to every district in the Northeast. Telephone service would, however, come much later and did not begin to become significant until the 1960s.[2]

Both the extension of Thai political control and the expansion of communication and transportation networks helped to bring northeasterners into more intimate contact with the central Thai and to make them aware of Bangkok as an economic and political focus. Neither set of innovations was, however, as important as the educational reforms, also begun by King Chulalongkorn, for making northeasterners aware of their inclusion within a Thai nation-state and for transforming them into Thai citizens.

Traditionally, village education throughout Thailand had been in the hands of Buddhist monks attached to local temples. Education was, thus, locally circumscribed and dependent upon the training and knowledge of the monk teachers.[3] King Chulalongkorn felt that to modernize Thailand and to inculcate in the populace of the kingdom an awareness of their national heritage, the educational system, like the administration, must be centralized and standardized.[4] In 1871 he established the palace system in which princes were given Western-type education. After his success in this endeavor, he decided, in 1885, that the government should extend "modern" education modeled on a Western curriculum to the whole country. In 1889 a Ministry of Education was founded with the extremely able Prince Damrong as its first head. In November 1898 King Chulalongkorn promulgated the Decree on the Organization of Provincial Education.

The hybrid school—part religious, part state-sponsored—created by the 1898 decree proved to be only a transitional type. By the reign of King Vajiravudh, who came to the throne in 1910, the government became dissatisfied with schools being staffed by monks who were ill trained and not committed to education as a vocation. While King Vajiravudh retained Chulalongkorn's ideal that modern education should be tempered by instruction in Buddhist morality, he and his advisors envisioned a system of popular education in which teachers would be trained by and responsible solely to the state. This system was outlined in the Primary Education Act of 1921, an act that made state-sponsored education compulsory for all citizens. Although the actual establishment of government schools in most villages did not take place until the 1930s, traditional Buddhist education offered by monks, including in the Northeast (Tambiah 1968), was sometimes modified to include some of the government-prescribed curriculum.

One of the most important social implications of the 1921 Act was that it made school attendance mandatory for girls as well as boys. The requirement was not an empty one; between 1921 and 1925 the percentage of female students throughout the country jumped from seven to thirty-eight (Vella 1978, 159). The government also instituted measures designed to centralize and standardize education (cf. Vella 1978, 165); the success of these measures depended on replacing monks with trained persons who had taken up teaching as a vocation. The government established teaching-training institutions throughout the country, and, by the late 1920s, secular teachers were graduating in increasing numbers.

Progress in implementing the 1921 Act was slow, primarily because the governments of King Vajiravudh (1910–24) and King Prajadhipok (1924–35) allocated rather modest amounts of money for education. The situation changed significantly after the revolution of 1932 that led to the establishment of a constitutional monarchy and a shift of power from royalty to a bureaucratic and military elite.

INTRODUCING DEMOCRACY

The most crucial date in modern Thai political history is undoubtedly 1932, for in that year a group of civil servants and disaffected military elements in Bangkok led a successful coup d'état against the Thai throne and established a constitutional monarchy. The most important consequence of the change in government insofar as the development of political identity in the Northeast was concerned was the creation of a parliament. For the first time provincial representatives were given an opportunity to express themselves in a national forum on issues affecting the future of both their home areas and the nation as a whole. Within this context representatives from the Northeast were to assume particularly significant roles. Even before the experiment in parliamentary democracy was begun, however, the coup against the throne ushered in a brief period of uncertainty about the political future of Thailand that affected northeasterners as well as the other peoples of the kingdom. Certain events in the Northeast during this period suggest, although not very strongly, the first stirrings of dissent based on a regional identity.

In 1933 a royalist military leader, Prince Bovaradej (Boworadet), led troops under his command from the Khorat garrison into rebellion against the government of the coup leaders. Although the rebellion was mainly backed by elite royalists, "it was generally recognized . . . that the aims of Bovaradej were shared by the more conservative elements throughout the country; and many provincial officials and officers had openly sympathized with the rebels" (Thompson 1941, 81). David Wilson confirms that a few indigenous leaders in the Northeast supported this rebellion (D. Wilson 1962, 223). New research is needed in order to determine how much support for the rebellion came from the peasantry in northeastern Thailand. Whatever the extent of this support may have been, the government of the "Promoters," as the members of the coup group were called, was concerned about the "rebelliousness" of the people of the region.

An incident that occurred in the province of Maha Sarakham soon after the 1932 coup suggests that it may have stimulated some sentiments that echoed those of the *phu mi bun* uprising three decades earlier. Attempting to take advantage of the confusion following the coup, a traveling folk opera singer, known as Molam Noi (Noi the troubadour) tried to stir up the populace against the government and advocated such policies as non-payment of taxes, non-conformance with regulations requiring children to go to school, and cessation of paying obeisance to the monks because "the sangha of today is not composed of real priests" (Bunchuai 1962, 95). Molam Noi planned to resurrect the kingdom of Vientiane, of which he would become king. The Lao, including northeasterners, would be divided between this kingdom and another in Khorat under a Mom Ratchawong Sanit (who was not further identified) also as a king. Both kingdoms, Molam Noi declared, would be independent of Bangkok. Molam Noi attracted a following through his claims to be a *phu wiset* (a magically-endowed one) who could fly through the air and exercise other supernatural powers. His efforts came to an abrupt halt in 1933 when he was captured and was unable to escape by flying out of jail as his followers expected (Bunchuai 1962, 96–7).

In 1934 in the aftermath of the Bovaradej Rebellion the government erected in Khorat the first monument of the post-1932 period. The monument memorialized Thao Suranari (Thaoying Mo), who had led resistance to forces sent by Chao Anu, the Lao king, in an invasion of Siam in the early nineteenth century. Although Thaoying Mo had long been revered locally as a powerful spirit, the monument re-positioned her as a heroine of the Thai nation. The building of this monument so soon after the Bovaradej rebellion has been interpreted as an act to ensure the loyalty of northeastern people (Saipin 1995; also see Keyes 2002a).[5]

Statue of Thaoying Suranari in Khorat memorializing the only northeasterner
accorded a prominent place in Thai and Siamese history

In the aftermath of the coup and the unsuccessful Bovaradej rebellion,
the new government in Bangkok made a large number of arrests of people
suspected of being involved in anti-government activities. Some of those
arrested in the Northeast were accused, somewhat paradoxically, of being
"communists." One individual so charged, Yuang Iamsila, later to be an
MP from Udon, maintained that he did not even know at the time what
communism was (D. Wilson 1962, 222–23). Whatever the reason for the
"communist" charges, they marked the first occurrence of suppression
of northeastern political leaders by the central government for alleged
left-wing activities.[6]

One source has advanced the not very plausible hypothesis that
governmental fears of communist activity among northeasterners at

this time had arisen because of the involvement of some northeasterners in the embryonic revolutionary activities of Vietnamese (referred to as Annamese or Tonkinese) refugees in northeastern Thailand. This linkage was made by Thompson and Adloff in their book, *The Left-Wing in Southeast Asia.*

By early May 1934 leaflet distribution on the part of a group calling its members the "Committee of Young Siam" began to be concentrated in the northeast provinces. It was there that political refugees from Indochina were grouped, and the cells formed in Sakol Nakon [Sakon Nakhon] and Bichitr [Phichit] were supposed to be closely allied to similar Cantonese and Tonkinese groups. Fear of this potential linkage undoubtedly accounted for the severity of the prison sentences imposed at this time by the Thai courts on a number of Annamite revolutionaries. (Thompson and Adloff 1950, 56)

That Vietnamese refugees in the Northeast at this time were being wooed to an anti-colonial revolutionary cause is certainly true. Political cadres had followed the Vietnamese refugees into the Northeast and had joined them in their centers at Udon, Sakon Nakhon, Nakhon Phanom, Nong Khai, Mukdahan, and That Phanom (cf. Le Manh Trinh 1962, 118). Ho Chi Minh himself, under the alias of Thau Chin,[7] had spent from 1928 to 1930 working among these people, particularly in Udon and Sakon Nakhon, where he established cells and Vietnamese schools (Le Manh Trinh 1962). Ho is reported to have told Vietnamese in Udon: "Viet Nam is a colony, Thailand is a semi-colony. Viet Nam is oppressed by the French. Thailand has been bullied by the French into signing several unequal treaties. We detest the French, the Thai do not like them either. Moreover, Thailand and Viet Nam are neighboring countries. It's certain that the Thais have sympathy for the anti-French movement of the Vietnamese" (Le Manh Trinh 1962, 121–22). Yet, despite such words of encouragement, it is doubtful that the Vietnamese proselytized very much among their northeastern neighbors. For the most part the Vietnamese community in the Northeast retained the characteristics of a ghetto or caste group and Vietnamese restricted their interactions with northeasterners to the market.[8]

The few sporadic manifestations of real or apparent political dissent that appeared in the Northeast following the coup of 1932 probably reflected more the instability in the country as a whole than they did an emerging regionalism. This instability was short-lived as the government in Bangkok quickly restored order throughout the kingdom and moved on to define the new directions that the state would take under its aegis.

The government of the Promoters continued the trend towards bureaucratic and administrative centralization that had begun under King Chulalongkorn. In 1932 the eighteen *monthon* of the country were reduced to ten and in 1933 the *monthon* system was abolished (Landon 1939, 45). The latter move signified that the government now considered the provinces and districts of the country to be sufficiently integrated within a national administrative system to obviate the need for an intermediary level of government between nation and province.

The most important innovation of the new government was the creation of a national parliament with elected representatives from every province. This institution provided the first mechanism in modern Thai history whereby local and regional interests of the country could be represented at the political center of the kingdom. The Thai parliament has had somewhat of a checkered history since being founded in 1933. It has been disbanded and reorganized, used and abused by successive prime ministers. However, when extant it has assumed a special significance for representatives from the Northeast.

For the rural people of the country, including the Northeast, democracy would hold no meaning unless they understood it. As a consequence, governments in the 1930s accelerated the expansion of compulsory primary education. The Promoters who staged the revolution saw popular education as "the best preparation for full democracy" (Landon 1939, 98) in the country. Governments in the 1930s allocated much higher percentages of their budgets for education than had the preceding royal governments. Between 1933 and 1936, appropriations for education were raised from 3.7 million baht to almost 12 million baht (ibid.).[9]

During the 1930s, the process of replacing monks with government-trained lay teachers was also accelerated. Moreover, the government established new schools in many communities where *wat* schools had not previously existed. By the outbreak of World War II, as Thompson and Adloff (1948, 37) observe, "centralization of educational facilities by the government [was] far more complete in Siam than in neighboring countries." Nowhere else in Southeast Asia, except in the American-administered Philippines, had a state-created school system become so well established in rural communities as it had in the villages of Siam by the late 1930s.[10]

Although the tasks of training secular teachers to replace the traditional monk-teachers, of establishing schools that would be within walking distance of every child, and of enforcing the teaching of all parts of the government-determined curriculum were not fully completed until after World War II, by 1934 compulsory primary education had become a reality for most villagers in the country. For the rural northeasterners the required participation in four years of government education resulted in every northeasterner learning about Thai geography, Thai history, and Thai language. Interspersed throughout their educational experience, these same children were taught to respect and honor the nation and religion.

There is no evidence to suggest that anywhere in Thailand did villagers (or townspeople, for that matter) actively resist the establishment of state primary schools. Nor did they resist the supplanting of religious schools by secular schools as some villagers in southern Thailand, Malaya, and Indonesia have done, and continue to do, with regard to Islamic schools. The Buddhist sangha would seem to have had reason to encourage such resistance. While monastic schools continued to exist, they were subordinated to secular schools. Boys had less incentive to enter monastic schools since they now acquired literacy in a secular school. Moreover, a regulation instituted under Prince Vajirañana, patriarch of the sangha and brother of King Chulalongkorn, and enforced after 1932, that required a boy to complete primary education before entering the novitiate, had a dampening effect on the interest of boys in becoming novices (cf. Holmes 1974, 91–92). In turn, fewer monks emerged from the ranks of novices.

Most monks, far from leading villagers in an effort to retain or restore the monastic schools in opposition to secular schools, actively participated in promoting the new school system. Owing to the efforts of Prince Vajirañana, the leadership of the sangha in the early part of the twentieth century was co-opted into assisting in the creation of a new system of mass education. When, from the 1920s on, government policy sought to replace monk teachers with lay teachers, the sangha leadership remained supportive because the government included moral instruction as part of the curriculum. Monks continued to be called upon to provide this instruction, albeit for a very small number of hours out of the total teaching week. Even after monks ceased to teach all subjects except morals in the new type of schools, the fact that most village schools continued to be lodged in buildings belonging to *wat* perpetuated the link between these schools and premodern monastic schools. Despite the fact that the local school had a fundamentally different mission, village monks and laypeople alike often viewed it as an extension of the *wat*. Indicative of this is the fact that local monks have often provided a religious rationale for the raising of money to be used toward constructing a new school on grounds separate from that of the *wat*. Hanks reports that in the central Thai village of Bang Chan in about 1950 the local abbot attempted to encourage villagers to make available the resources to build a new school building to replace one that had blown down. The abbot told villagers "that making merit by building schools equals the merit of building temples" (Hanks 1960, 23). In 1963 the monks in the northeastern Thai village of Ban Nong Tuen, where I carried out research, joined in the sponsoring of a temple fair whose purpose was to raise money for a new school; again donations to the school fund at the fair were designated by the monks as merit-yielding, thereby giving them a religious significance. These cases, which are far from atypical, reflect the extent to which the sangha has gone in participating in the transfer of legitimation from monastic schools to state-sponsored secular schools.[11]

While villagers were neither incited by monks nor motivated themselves to defend traditional monastic schools against secular schools, they did not accord a positive reception to the new schools. Rather, to paraphrase Hanks (1960), the new secular schools were received by villagers with "indifference," that is, they were viewed as contributing only marginally to the enhancement of life within rural society. Yet, as alien as the school might have seemed (cf. also Aree Sanhachawee 1970, 107; Holmes 1974, 46, 97), and as unenthusiastic as villagers might have been about it, the fact remains that from the 1930s on most villagers everywhere in Thailand have spent the requisite four years (and recently six years) attending a government-sponsored school. An anthropologist who in 1959–60 worked in a then remote Thai-Lue village in the northwest of Thailand observed that government-mandated schools brought traditionally isolated people into a Thai frame of reference: "It is our strong impression that in areas like Chiengkham where officials are estranged, the draft widely scattered, official radio broadcasts largely irrelevant to village life, and government services almost nonexistent, the local elementary school is overwhelmingly the main source of national consciousness and loyalty. Lessons in the national language, in Thai history, religion, and geography—however superficial and imperfectly remembered—have a profound effect on village life" (Moerman 1961, 80). As I have argued elsewhere (Keyes 1991a; also see Keyes 1966a, 140–91), the government school literally created the Thai nation-state as a meaningful framework for villagers.

The educational reforms, like the administrative reforms and the expansion of communication and transportation networks, served to bring northeasterners into much closer contact with central Thai culture and society and to make them aware that their future would be affected by decisions in Bangkok. At the same time, these innovations also began to make northeasterners realize that their local culture and patterns of living were considered inferior to those of central Thai. Such was apparent in the attitudes of the new government officials and in the content of the educational curriculum. As the impact of direct Thai control increased, northeasterners began to develop ambivalent attitudes towards central Thai culture. Such ambivalences towards their own local culture and elite culture are characteristic of most peasant societies. What was to make northeastern Thailand different was that northeasterners came to recognize that their "local" culture and values were shared by a large proportion of the Isan populace. This recognition did not follow immediately upon the consolidation of Thai control in the area. Rather, the first hints of the merging of local interests in larger ethnoregional interests appeared in consequence of the activities of northeastern elected representatives during the period of the parliamentary experiment from 1932 to 1947.

THE SHAPING OF AN ISAN POLITICAL IDENTITY[12]

The first general election in Thailand took place in November–December 1933, and successive elections were held in the prewar years in 1937 and 1938. Political parties were illegal throughout all these elections and only half of the members were elected, while the other half were appointed. Consequently, the Promoters were in little danger of a threat by parliamentary opposition to their hold on the reins of government. However, the period between 1932 and the war was marked by competition among the leaders of the 1932 coup, and the political allegiances of all elected representatives tended to coalesce around one or the other of these leaders. Although Phraya Phahon became prime minister in 1933 and remained so until 1937, Pridi Banomyong (Luang Pradit Manutham) and Luang Phibun Songkram (Plaek Kittisangkha) became the most important figures around whom the majority of MPs grouped themselves.

Pridi, a son of a Sino-Thai farming family in Ayutthaya, was the main intellectual force among the Promoters. In his legal training in France he apparently found the source of his ideas about the construction of a new Thailand. Although some of his ideas appeared in the permanent constitution of 1932, they were most apparent in an Economic Plan proposed in 1933 that envisaged the nationalizing of both industry and farms thereby making all farmers employees of the state.[13] The plan was subsequently branded as communist and Pridi was forced to leave the country for a short time. Although he was later exonerated and returned to a position of power within the government, Pridi's plan was thoroughly discredited and was never proposed formally again. Nonetheless, some of his ideas that sought to introduce a radical method for economic development were later to reappear in the solutions proposed by postwar Isan representatives as solutions to the economic difficulties of the region.

Although Pridi's political ambitions suffered a setback with the rejection of his economic plan, by 1934 he had not only returned from abroad but had also assumed the important post of minister of interior. His strength was among the "liberal" group in the Promoters, a faction made up, in large part, of young civilians who had studied abroad as

Pridi himself had done. His influence spread not only among a large number of elected representatives in the National Assembly[14] but also to others of the emerging elite who had attended Thammasat University (University of Moral and Political Sciences), of which he was the founder and first rector.

Pridi's major adversary in the competition for political power was the then young military officer, Phibun Songkram. Phibun, also of Sino-Thai farming background, had studied military science in France. His strength lay in his popularity among military officers who had been impressed by his leadership of the forces that suppressed the Bovaradej Rebellion. His military orientation and his own political ambitions were the main basis for the approach he adopted towards the type of government he felt Thailand should have. People rallied around him not because of his ideological position but because of the belief that he would be a powerful ruler of the country. He can been seen as the first in a series of military men—Sarit Thanarat and Prem Tinsulanond being the most well known—who have been similarly viewed and have so viewed themselves.

The political struggle between Pridi and Phibun was projected against the backdrop of the National Assembly. Many of the appointed assemblymen were military officers who sided with Phibun. But it is the elected representatives in whom we are most interested since among them were the few northeasterners who had become involved in national politics. One type of Isan MP included the descendants of old *chao muang* families who sought election as a means of perpetuating their influence in their home areas and for gaining access to power which had been denied them after the administrative reforms were implemented. How many Isan representatives of this type there were is difficult to determine. I have been able to identify two definitely—Thongmuan Atthakon from Maha Sarakham and Thongdi na Kalasin (Kwang Thongthawi) from Kalasin—and the names-cum-titles of at least three others suggest that they too may have been of this type. Associated with these MPs were a few local provincial and district officials who left their positions in the civil service to seek national office. Phraya Sarakham Khanaphiban (Anong Phayakham), an ex-governor of the province of Maha Sarakham who was elected to the National Assembly in 1933 (Bunchuai 1962, 90–2,

96) exemplifies this type of representative.[15] These deputies attached themselves to another representative of similar background who was later to become one of the most important figures in national policies— Khuang Aphaiwong. Nai Khuang himself was a descendant of the traditional ruling family of Battambang, which had been ceded to the French by the treaty of 1907 and is today a part of Cambodia. These representatives, and others of like mind, tended to be conservative since their own way of life was rooted in the traditional past.

The most vocal type of Isan MP was the northeasterner who, through education, had risen from a relatively humble background and whose ties were still strong in the countryside of his constituency. Among the most prominent parliamentary supporters of Pridi were men such as Thawin Udon (Roi Et), Thong-In Phuriphat (Ubon), Tiang Sirikhan (Sakon Nakhon), and Chamlong Daorueang (Maha Sarakham). I suggest that one of the reasons why such men committed themselves to the liberal faction was because these men had less of an investment in the traditional Thai social system than did MPs from the central plains or representatives who belonged to the old provincial or national aristocracies. On the contrary, they had much to gain by the greater democratization of the system. Their political strength did not lie with whom they knew in Bangkok, at least not initially, but with the rural people who had elected them. To enhance their positions they needed to espouse, dramatically if possible, programs and policies that would both increase their popularity in the countryside and bring them to the attention of the national leadership.

During the 1933–38 period, Thong-In Phuriphat (Ubon) established himself as the most persistent critic of the government. In 1935 he and two other members filed a vote of no confidence in the State Council over a combination of issues including increased military involvement in civil government, an opium scandal, and the alleged inefficiency of the Ministry of Economic Affairs (Thompson 1941, 90; *Bangkok Times*, October 16, 1935). In 1937 he led a parliamentary protest over the inadequacy of funds allocated for education and public works as compared with the defense budget (Thompson 1941, 93). In the same year he also demanded an explanation from the government of a speech by a young military officer who had demeaned the elected MPs (Landon

1939, 50). Shortly thereafter he requested permission to found a political party that would have branches throughout the country (ibid.). However, the Council of Ministers rejected the request on the basis that the time was not yet suitable for such (ibid.; *Siam Chronicle*, May 20, 1941).

In 1938 Phibun became prime minister after the retirement of Phraya Phahon. Although Pridi and some of the other liberal Promoters were included in Phibun's first government, they soon became dismayed at his tendency towards military dictatorship and ultra-nationalism. In keeping with these themes, in 1941 Phibun led the country into a brief war with the French in Indochina for the purpose of regaining some of the territories that had been lost earlier by Siam to France. The war ended inconclusively due to intervention by the Japanese, who foisted mediation on the two belligerents. Indochina, which was in the hands of the Vichy French and nominally an ally of the Axis powers, had no alternative but to accept Japanese efforts. As a result of the negotiations, the lands on the right bank of the Mekong (Sayaboury Province and the area around Champasak), as well as certain portions of Cambodia ceded to the French in the treaties of 1904 and 1907, were restored to Thailand.[16]

The war, and the irredentist atmosphere in which it was fought, had an impact on the people of the Northeast. The theme was struck by officials in Bangkok that "racially" the peoples in the territories claimed by Thailand belonged within the Thai kingdom.[17] Northeasterners who heard such proclamations were thus made aware that Bangkok considered that Isan and Lao were ethnically inseparable. Since the battles took place along the Lao–Northeast Thailand border, the Thai troops who fought the war were stationed in large numbers in the Northeast. Moreover, large numbers of central Thai officials went to the Northeast, some perhaps for the first time, to inspect the war preparations and defenses. Through these actions rural people along the Mekong were made aware of the artificiality of the border drawn between them and the people of Laos. The Thai prosecution of the war underscored the fact that decisions about the future of the Northeast lay with the Bangkok government.

Shortly after the conclusion of this war the Japanese began their military advance into Southeast Asia. After offering token resistance the Phibun government agreed to become an ally of the Japanese. This decision led Pridi to resign from the government and to take up the post as regent for the young King Ananda who was studying in Switzerland. With Pridi's departure the military under Phibun assumed almost total control of the government, although the Parliament was permitted to continue, perhaps as a symbolic legacy of the 1932 revolution. Opposition to the government, although small at the outset, was now unified since Pridi had broken with Phibun. In Parliament followers of both Pridi and the more conservative Khuang under the leadership of several northeastern MPs joined in opposition to the military.

As the war progressed Pridi became the leader within Thailand of a secret Free Thai Movement that opposed both the alliance with Japan and Phibun's military government. This movement included many prominent Isan MPs.[18] One important facet of the Free Thai activities was its connection with the anti-Japanese underground in Indochina. Although it is difficult to document, the events that transpired after the war suggest that certain of these Isan members of the Free Thai Movement must have established close ties with the followers of Ho Chi Minh and the Lao prince Suphanouvong during the war.[19]

In July 1944 Phibun's government fell on the issue of transferring the capital from Bangkok to the hinterland province of Phetchabun. Early in 1944 Phibun had begun to conscript labor to build a road to Phetchabun with disastrous results.[20] Coast provides a good summary of the situation and the consequent parliamentary defeat of Phibun's government:

> After a couple of months there was serious trouble with the labor force. Men were dying fast of malaria, which was of a vicious variety in this unwholesome area. By July, it became necessary to take strong measures and Phibun drafted a bill for the compulsory conscription of workers on this national project. He presented the bill personally to the Assembly, only to find that the overwhelming majority of the members were against him. This reverse came about largely because he had filled the Assembly with military members [as appointed members of Parliament] who had always supported him, and at this time of national emergency most of them were outside Bangkok. Led mainly by Nai Thong-Indr Buripat [Thong-In Phuriphat, MP from Ubon] and Nai Tieng Sirikhand [Tiang Sirikhan, MP from

Sakon Nakhon], two staunch Pridi men, the Opposition blocked the Premier's scheme. (Coast 1953, 26)

In August, Khuang Aphaiwong, who was later to become the main leader of the Democrat Party independent of both Phibun's and Pridi's factions, became premier and immediately appointed a committee to investigate Phibun's Phetchabun scheme. The chairman of this committee, Fong Sitthitham (Ubon), was joined by several other northeasterners including Chamlong Daorueang (Maha Sarakham), Liang Chaiyakan (Ubon), and Tiang Sirikhan (Sakon Nakhon).[21]

In the period between July 1944 and the coup d'état of November 8, 1947, although various people were in name prime minister,[22] Pridi held the real power. Opposition to Pridi began to appear among some of his former associates in the Free Thai Movement, however. After the 1946 elections many of the former Free Thai men who remained loyal to Pridi, including such prominent northeastern MPs as Chamlong Daorueang, Thawin Udon, Thong-In Phuriphat, and Tiang Sirikhan, helped organize the Sahachip (Cooperative) Party.[23] Those who broke with Pridi, including Fong Sitthitham, Liang Chaiyakan, and Kwang Thongthawi among the northeastern representatives, joined with Khuang Aphaiwong, Seni Pramoj, and his brother Kukrit in forming the Democrat Party. Although it is misleading to suggest for these two factions ideological labels that have currency in the West, there was definitely a difference in political philosophy between them. Pridi and his followers were anxious to have Thailand associate with, and perhaps even lead, the nationalist forces which were beginning to appear in Indonesia, Burma, and Indochina. They were also willing to consider introducing new, perhaps even radical, ideas, particularly in the economic sphere, to the unfinished task of modernizing the kingdom. The Democrats, on the other hand, tended to be more concerned with preserving the cultural continuity and many traditional institutions of the kingdom. In consequence, the Democrats were less concerned with relationships with neighboring peoples and more cautious regarding plans for modernization. These two positions, in their various subsequent guises, both held attractions for the populace of the Northeast as well as for the rest of the country. Both factions, at least publicly, remained committed to parliamentary rule.

For the brief three-year period just preceding and following the end of World War II, members of the anti-military groups ruled the country. During this period, a number of northeastern representatives in the National Assembly rose to positions of major importance in the government. Chamlong Daorueang (Maha Sarakham) was made a cabinet member, acting for the minister of commerce and industry in the first Aphaiwong cabinet (1944–51) and a minister without portfolio and later assistant minister of commerce in the Thamrong cabinet (1946–47). Liang Chaiyakan (Ubon) was a minister without portfolio in the second Aphaiwong cabinet (January–March 1946). Thong-In Phuriphat (Ubon) was first a minister without portfolio and then deputy minister of the interior in the first Aphaiwong cabinet and a minister of industry and minister of communication under Thamrong. Tiang Sirikhan (Sakon Nakhon) was in the cabinet of Seni Pramoj (September 1945–January 1946) and a minister without portfolio and later assistant minister of the interior in the Thamrong government. Thawin Udon (Roi Et) was made a senator and in April 1947 was appointed manager of the government-owned Thai Industrial Development Corporation.

The theme that dominated the first years of the postwar period was the attempt by the Thai government, under Pridi's guiding hand, to regain international acceptability in contrast to the low esteem in which Thailand was held by the Allied powers for its alliance with Japan during the war. In addition Pridi was also interested in seeing Thailand play a crucial role in the drama of resurgent nationalism that spread across Southeast Asia in the immediate postwar period.

> Pridi had very definite ideas about the role that Thailand should play in Southeast Asian affairs. While maintaining good official relations with the victorious Allies, particularly with the United States, Pridi also was ambitious for Thailand to become the leader of independent nations in this strategic area of Asia. He foresaw that nationalist forces in Burma, Indonesia, and Indochina would one day force the weakened colonial powers to recognize the futility of trying to rule these areas in the prewar manner, and that it was only a matter of

time until the powers were forced to grant them independence. Pridi believed that Thailand's long history of independence and political stability and its success in dealing with European powers made it a natural leader among these emergent nations. It was an ambitious vision, but Pridi was an extraordinary person who seemed to have unlimited faith in his ability to lead Thailand and Southeast Asia in the new postwar era. (Nuechterlein 1965, 94)

To advance this objective Pridi allowed Bangkok to become a place in which representatives of the Indochinese independence movements could contact armament supplies and present their cases to the outside world.[24] In May 1947 he also tried, with little success, to mediate the dispute between the French and the Viet Minh. While in Paris on this mission, he hit upon the idea of a Southeast Asian Union that would include Thailand, Laos, Cambodia, and Vietnam (cf. Coast 1953, 38; Nuechterlein 1965, 94–95). Although the French were unsympathetic to such an idea, Pridi persisted, and in September 1947 an organization designed to promote this end, the Southeast Asia League, was founded. The list of officers of the league is extremely interesting in that it reveals the connections between several of the important northeastern politicians and leaders of the independence movements in Indochina. The president (Tiang Sirikhan, MP from Sakon Nakhon) and the public relations officer (Sen. Thawin Udon, a former MP from Roi Et) were both well-known Isan political leaders, while the vice president (Tran Van Giao) and treasurer (Le Hi) were important figures in the Viet Minh, and the general secretary (Prince Suphanouvong) was to become the leader of the Pathet Lao.[25]

What the Southeast Asia League might have accomplished is purely speculative, however, for it survived only two months. While Pridi was pursuing his desires to make Thailand a significant force outside its borders, events within the kingdom greatly undermined his position. In June 1946 the young King Ananda died of a gunshot wound under mysterious circumstances. Rumors abounded that the king had been assassinated and that Pridi was in some way responsible.[26] The inability of an investigating group to come up with definite conclusions as to the cause of death coupled with widespread corruption in the Thamrong government helped to discredit Pridi and to make possible the military coup of November 1947. Pridi, Thamrong, and some of their supporters (although apparently no northeasterners) fled the country and many of those who remained were arrested or went into hiding. Although the coup had been managed by the military with Phibun as at least its nominal sponsor, Khuang Aphaiwong was allowed to become prime minister once again. However, his actions were subject to strict surveillance by the military authorities.

For the time being, thus, the semblance of parliamentary democracy was preserved. On January 29, 1948, new elections were held. However, few of Pridi's supporters stood for election since they had been dispersed or arrested after the coup. The election gave a resounding victory to the Democrats. This same pattern also appeared in the Northeast; among the twenty-nine out of thirty-four representatives from the Northeast whose party identification I have been able to discover, fifteen were Democrats. Of the remaining fourteen, four were members of the pro-Pridi Sahathai Party, seven were members of Liang Chaiyakan's nominally pro-Pridi Prachachon Party,[27] two were independents, and only one was a member of the pro-Phibun Thammaphiphat Party. These results indicated that the Northeast, despite the reemergence of military power within the central government, remained heavily committed to political leaders who supported parliamentary rule.

Although the Democrats had won a decisive majority, Khuang Aphaiwong was not allowed to consolidate his parliamentary gains. In April 1948, the military staged a *coup de main* against Khuang, and Phibun was again returned to power.

REPRESSION OF ISAN POLITICIANS

The Democrat interlude had merely temporarily postponed the consolidation of power by Phibun. Even before he actually assumed power, however, the military and police under his control began to move against the major northeastern MPs and ex-cabinet officials who had supported Pridi. The charges and the ultimate actions taken against these men were extremely critical in shaping subsequent political attitudes in the Northeast. Initially, Pridi and all of his followers, including those from the Northeast, were charged with having conspired to subordinate Thai national identity within a larger communist-dominated Southeast Asian union.

In order to justify the coup, the military produced stories of communist and republican plots, or the intended murder of the king, and of an armed rebellion that had been planned for November 30 [1947]. The purveyor of the more fantastic stories was Luang Kach, who claimed that Pridi had been about to establish a Siamese Republic as a cornerstone for a South East Asia Union; that radio orders had been intercepted and documents found bearing out these contentions; that agents were on their way to Switzerland to murder King Bhumipon; and that an arms cache, including many Russian weapons, had been discovered at the house of Thong-Indr [Thong-In Phuriphat, MP from Ubon], one of Tamrong's Ministers—arms indubitably intended for the communist revolution. (Coast 1953, 42)

As the possibility of arresting Pridi was thwarted by his exile abroad, the charges began to be focused more specifically on the northeasterners. The main northeastern supporters of Pridi had been in hiding in Thailand, but they reappeared in middle and late 1948 and were almost immediately arrested. Tiang Sirikhan (Sakon Nakhon), Chamlong Daorueang (Maha Sarakham), Thong-In Phuriphat and his brother Thim (Ubon), and Thawin Udon (Roi Et), along with another Pridi minister from the central plains, Thongplaeo Chonlaphum (Nakhon Nayok), were charged with plotting a separatist movement in which the Northeast would be joined to Indochina in a communist-dominated Southeast Asian Union.[28] Tiang Sirikhan, "himself a Laotian and a person of great prestige in the Northeast, denied the pro-communist charge while quite openly admitting his sympathy with the aim of forming some sort of South-East Asian Union, though not one that would infringe upon Siam's sovereignty. Many Laotians, while not wishing to cut themselves loose from Siam, felt that the administration of the northeast was too feebly controlled from Bangkok, and that greater local autonomy was essential for proper administration" (Coast 1953, 50).

Phibun's government was spurred to action by an attempted counter-coup by Pridi-led forces in February 1949. In the aftermath to this attempt a number of Free Thai leaders were found dead of gunshot wounds in their homes. In March 1949 Thong-In, Chamlong, and Thawin, along with Thongplaeo, were re-arrested although they had just been released a short time before. Shortly after their arrest they were shot to death by the police "while attempting to escape." "The official story was that the four men were being transferred by bus to another prison, when suddenly a rescuing party of their friends fired on the bus, killing the prisoners and missing the escorting policemen" (Coast 1953, 53). This incident, known as the "Kilo 11" incident because the four were shot at the road marker eleven kilometers north of Bangkok, received widespread publicity at that time.[29] In March through May, two other northeastern leaders, Thim Phuriphat and Tiang Sirikhan, were brought to trial on charges of separatism.[30] However, the outcome of the trial was inconclusive, perhaps in consequence of the public outrage over the Kilo 11 incident, and both men were released. For Tiang Sirikhan, the respite was temporary. He stood in a by-election in Sakon Nakhon in April 1949, although he was under indictment at the time, won his seat back, and was again reelected in 1952. In December 1952, however, Bangkok newspapers reported that he had escaped to Burma to evade arrest in conjunction with a new plot by communist conspirators (*Bangkok Post*, December 16 and 17, 1952; January 13, 1953). He never again appeared, and the popular belief, later corroborated in a court trial, was that he too had been assassinated under the direction of Phibun's lieutenant, Police-General Phao Sriyanond.

The elimination of these men had lasting repercussions in the Isan region. Northeasterners had taken pride in the accomplishments of local men who had risen to cabinet level. This pride was severely injured when these men were killed. Moreover they were killed not only because they had been followers of Pridi, but, more damaging, because they had been northeasterners. The main charge against Chamlong, Thong-In, Thawin, and Tiang was that they were involved in a plot to separate the Northeast from the rest of the kingdom. The Northeast was thus accorded a political identity that heretofore it had not had.

In the subsequent period these four men became symbols of the growing sentiments shared by a large part of the northeastern populace that they were discriminated against as a whole by the central Thai and the central government. The death of these prominent northeastern leaders was a major catalyst in the development of Isan regional political identity and purpose, for it demonstrated most dramatically the attitudes of the central government towards those who were identified with Isan political aspirations. In addition, northeasterners began to feel that central Thai political discrimination was but a symptom of more basic economic and cultural discrimination.

INCREASING ECONOMIC DISPARITY

Although the Kilo 11 incident captured the attention of the northeastern public in the period just following the reappearance of military rule, the impact of the postwar expansion of the Thai economy, although less dramatic, was beginning to stimulate the development of northeastern ethnoregionalism in other ways. While Bangkok became a boomtown and the central plains in general shifted ever further to a commercial economy, the Northeast remained tied to a subsistence economy. Difficulties restricting the enlargement of the cash sector of the rural economy motivated an increasing number of northeasterners to seek temporary work in Bangkok and elsewhere outside the Isan region. Out of the interrelated phenomena of economic underdevelopment in the Northeast and temporary migration of northeasterners to Bangkok grew a more widely held sense of Isan regional identity.

The inability of the northeastern region to respond as well as the central region to the new economic forces that appeared after the war stemmed primarily from the poor natural endowment of the region. Soil fertility, rainfall patterns, flooding, and population pressures on cultivatable land in the Northeast all compare unfavorably with the same features in the central region. For example, production figures for paddy show that in 1950–51, whereas the average yield in the central plains was 227 kilograms per *rai*, the comparable figure for the Northeast was 145 kilograms per *rai* (Thailand, Ministry of Agriculture 1961, 39).[31] However, such a comparison signified little to the average northeastern villager so long as the country as a whole was geared primarily to subsistence agriculture and so long as he produced sufficient quantities of rice for the needs of his family.

In the immediate postwar period commercial rice production in the central plains expanded rapidly in order to meet the demands of neighboring countries whose economies had been severely damaged by the war and by subsequent revolutions. In contrast, little surplus rice could be produced in the Northeast and what was produced was not easily saleable since it was of the glutinous or "sticky" variety, the staple of the region, rather than white rice. Poor resources and inadequate transportation connections inhibited the entrance of many northeastern farmers into other forms of commercial farm production.[32] By the early 1950s a marked discrepancy in cash income between the Northeast and the central plains was apparent not only to the outside observer but also to the northeasterners themselves. In 1953, for example, average annual cash income per farm family in the Northeast was only 954 baht (US$51.93) as compared with 2,888 baht (US$157.21) in the central plains.[33] Moreover, the cash income of the northeastern farm family was less than that of farm families in any other part of Thailand (Thailand, Ministry of Agriculture 1955, 26).

While the Northeast remained relatively untouched by the new economic expansion, Bangkok was developing rapidly. In previous periods of expansion in Bangkok immigrant Chinese had comprised most of the unskilled labor force. As one group of immigrants rose in status, a new group arrived to take positions at the lowest socioeconomic rung of the urban ladder. However, after 1949, mass immigration of Chinese into Thailand ended following the imposition of quotas of two hundred immigrants from any one country per year (Skinner 1957, 117–18). The demands of a rapidly expanding Bangkok at a time when a major source of labor was shut off created a vacuum in the urban labor force. This vacuum was filled by the migration of people indigenous to Thailand into Bangkok at a minimum rate of 37,800 persons annually between 1947 and 1954.[34]

Among those who poured into Bangkok were large numbers of rural northeasterners in quest of wage-labor in order to supplement the subsistence endeavors of their families (cf. Textor 1961, 15–16). Although northeasterners were by no means the only immigrants to Bangkok, the place of Isan villagers in the Thai capital was unique. Since World War II northeasterners have constituted by far the largest percentage of rural people who have migrated to Bangkok. Initially, and through the 1970s most of the Isan rural migrants to Bangkok were "temporary." That is, migrants came to Bangkok only seasonally, between harvest and planting times, or, at most, spent only a few years in Bangkok before returning to settle permanently in their home villages (Textor 1961, 11; Keyes 1966a, 312 passim). Most rural migrants were young, unattached, (or temporarily separated) males between the ages of twenty and twenty-nine.[35] Finally, most of the northeastern rural migrants again through the 1970s entered the unskilled labor force as pedicab drivers (and after a ban on pedicabs was promulgated in 1960, as taxi drivers), construction workers, or workers in various Chinese-operated mills and factories.

How many northeastern villagers participated in this practice of temporary migration to Bangkok in the period from the late 1940s through the 1970s is unknown. However, enough evidence exists to suggest that a sizeable percentage of the men from all parts of the region who came of age in the postwar period were involved. In a survey I carried out in 1963 in the village of Ban Nong Tuen in Muang District, Maha Sarakham, for example, I found that 49 percent of the men twenty years of age and over or 67 percent of the men between thirty and thirty-nine had worked in Bangkok. (Only one woman had ever worked in the Thai capital). Other studies suggest such temporary migration by village young men was typical of Isan villages in the period.[36]

In Bangkok northeastern migrants found themselves considered inferior by urban Thai. Not only were they employed in lowly occupations, but they also discovered that Bangkok Thai thought of them as unsophisticated and uncultured provincials (cf. Textor 1961, 17, 24–5). Faced with such attitudes northeasterners tended to congregate together in Bangkok, "drawn . . . by a common sub-culture, dialect, taste for food and music, etc." (Textor 1961, 22). In Bangkok the northeastern sector of the labor force emerged as a relatively distinctive lower class whose organization and shared interests were utilized to advantage by Isan MPs.

There is, in fact, considerable evidence that a Thai lower class is emerging [in Bangkok] with common interests and some class consciousness. Low in possession of most values important in Bangkok society, the class is primarily concerned with basic well-being, i.e., the health and safety of the organism. Some elements within the class, pedicab drivers, for instance, are formally organized for the attainment of group interests, while others—domestic servants and market gardeners for example—are informally organized. The class has been wooed by some Thai politicians in hopes of support at the polls. The fact that a large proportion of this class consists of recent immigrants from up-country, especially Northeast Siam, provides a natural basis for some working arrangement with assemblymen representing the [provinces] in question. (Skinner 1957, 309)

Textor suggested that the northeastern pedicab drivers, one of the most important groups among the Isan migrants in Bangkok, were more politically aware than laborers from elsewhere: "The great majority of [northeastern] drivers have cast ballots for members of Parliament in their native province; perhaps well over half of the drivers can accurately supply the name of one or more of their home province's representatives in Parliament. The degree of interest in parliamentary politics is probably greater than that found among other working people, in Bangkok or elsewhere in Thailand" (Textor 1961, 44).

From his experiences in Bangkok the returned migrant carried home with him feelings of class and ethnic discrimination directed towards him as a rural northeasterner by the central Thai inhabitants of Bangkok and an enhanced awareness of the common culture and problems which all northeasterners shared. In brief, the pattern of the increasing temporary migration of northeastern villagers to Bangkok beginning in the postwar period greatly spurred the development of "we-they" attitudes among northeasterners. Moreover, the "we" (*ban hao*, lit., "we villagers") was beginning to assume a more ethnoregional character.[37]

PARLIAMENT AND ISAN ETHNOREGIONALISM

During Phibun's second period in power between 1947 and 1957, many representatives from the Isan area played upon a growing sense of ethnoregionalism to put pressure on the central government to direct more attention towards the Northeast. The objective which these MPs promoted on behalf of their regional constituency was the reduction or elimination of alleged discrimination by the national government towards the Northeast. These representatives claimed that there was ample evidence that the central government ignored, and even suppressed Isan political leadership (for example, the Kilo 11 incident and the disappearance of Tiang Sirikhan) and overemphasized bureaucratic centralization to the detriment of the northeastern region. They also claimed that the government was not doing enough to stimulate development in the Northeast so that the region could attain the same economic level as the rest of the country. Finally, they maintained that the central government, and the central Thai in general, treated northeasterners as cultural or class inferiors. If ever Isan MPs in Bangkok needed to "prove" their points, they would call public meetings of the northeasterners working in the city who were very responsive to "exposing" the discrimination of the central government towards the Isan people.[38]

In parliamentary debates in the first years after Phibun's return to power a number of northeastern MPs continually raised the charge of economic discrimination of the government against the Northeast. In July 1949, for example, Bunpheng Phrommankhun, a Prachachon Party deputy from Si Sa Ket, attacked the government for its economic neglect of the Northeast. In the same month several Isan MPs raised an issue that had found its way into earlier debates—namely, government discrimination against northeastern rice millers in the international marketing of rice.[39] In December 1950 Liang Chaiyakan (Ubon) organized a rally of northeasterners in Bangkok at which he planned to announce government appropriations for irrigation works in northeastern provinces. However, several other northeastern representatives, including Lieutenant Charubut Rueangsuwan (independent, Khon Kaen), and Bunkhum Chamsisuriyawong (independent, Udon), took the opportunity of the rally to protest publicly how little the government really was doing for the Northeast.

Although the theme of economic discrimination began to be important at this time, feelings of political discrimination also continued to run high. In the parliamentary debate on a new constitution in January 1949 several northeastern MPs spoke out strongly against the constitution, and one group led by Chuen Rawiwan (Sahathai, Nong Khai) attacked the "indivisibility of the kingdom" clause on the grounds that it was potentially injurious to the rights of northeasterners. In December 1949 six MPs (including four from the Northeast) rather quixotically at the time (or perhaps foresightedly) proposed that Thailand be divided into six autonomous regions.[40] Opposition of northeastern MPs to the military government appeared again in November 1950 when a large number of northeastern MPs (including all of the Democrats and several followers of Pridi) supported a Democrat-sponsored petition for a general parliamentary debate on government policy. In December 1950 at the rally of northeasterners in Bangkok, Nat Ngoenthap (Independent, Maha Sarakham) delivered a speech in which he stated that although the three northeastern MPs who had been killed in the Kilo 11 incident were gone, he and others would continue to fight for the cause of the Northeast as they had done (Thompson and Adloff 1945–50).

The public positions of the Isan MPs together with the majority of opposition Democrats in the Parliament were an embarrassment to Phibun. It is somewhat surprising that he did not eliminate Parliament altogether, particularly after attempted coups in 1949 and 1951 proved that opposition to him was not without its strength. However, his control of the country through the military must have appeared sufficiently sure to convince him that he could permit the window dressing of parliamentary rule.

He did, however, call new elections in February 1952 with the expressed hope that they would provide him with a popular mandate. Nationally, the results were favorable for Phibun, for the pro-government Farm Labor (Kasikammakon) Party led by the minister of foreign affairs won approximately 50 of the 123 seats. To these were added the 27 seats of the Prachachon Party, taken into the Phibun camp by its leader, Liang Chaiyakan (*Bangkok Post,* May 6, 1952).

Comparison of the 1952 election results with past and subsequent elections suggests that those elected from northeastern constituencies in 1952 might be grouped as follows:

TABLE 4.1 Party Affiliations of MPs from Northeastern Thailand, 1952 Election

Party affiliation	Number of MPs
Pro-Phibun	11
Pro-Pridi or leftist	11
Democrat	3
Independent	7
Unknown	10

Source: *The Siam Directory* 1955, 4–6

It would appear that the Northeast electorate was still reluctant to give a military-led government a majority even at a time when the military was firmly ensconced in power and had won (or coerced) a parliamentary majority in the rest of the kingdom. Moreover, the leadership of the non-Democrat opposition of the new parliament seemed to have come from the northeastern MPs. Most influential, until his "disappearance" later in 1952, was Tiang Sirikhan from Sakon Nakhon. In addition, Thep Chotinuchit from Si Sa Ket, who was to become a major figure in the "new left" revival of 1955–58, emerged as an important opposition leader.[41] The strength of the Isan-led opposition was apparent in the 35 votes, out of 241 cast by MPs of both appointed and elected categories, which Thep received in the election for the president of the Assembly (*Bangkok Post*, March 21, 1952).[42]

Although political parties were banned shortly after the opening of the Assembly, an opposition continued to flourish under the leadership of Thep and another northeastern deputy, Klaew Norapati (Klaeo Noraphat) of Khon Kaen (Darling 1965, 124–26).[43] In addition to the regional objectives that the northeastern component of this opposition advocated during the next three years, it also pressed continually for a loosening of the military's grip on the government. Further, it began to advocate a neutralist foreign policy in contrast to the pro-American policy of the Phibun government. Mainly in reaction to the neutralist position of the opposition, the government accused its leadership of subverting national interests (*Bangkok Post*, January 23, 1954; Darling 1965, 124–26). General Phao, Phibun's head of the police, was more specific. He accused Thep and his followers of being connected with the Viet Minh (*Bangkok Post*, January 23, 1954). Such accusations attest to the fact that the belief was yet alive among some members of the ruling elite that the opposition leaders from the Isan region were allied with the Viet Minh, Pathet Lao, and Red Chinese leadership in a communist conspiracy.

Haunted, perhaps, by the ghosts of the earlier northeastern leaders who had been eliminated because of similar fears, Phibun held in check those members of his government who would have liked to remove the more vocal of the present opposition leadership from the Isan region. Moreover, in 1955 Phibun decided to lead the country once again on the road to the development of "democracy." He legalized the establishment of political parties and decreed that an election would be held shortly for a new parliament. Three recognizable political groupings then began to emerge: the pro-government Seri Manangkhasila and associated parties led by Phibun himself, the old Democrat Party led by Khuang Aphaiwong, and a group of small parties which represented various shadings of what Wilson has called Thailand's "new left" (D. Wilson 1959). The two most important of these "leftist" parties, the Economist (Setthakon) and the Free Democrat (Seri Prachathipatai), were founded by MPs from the Northeast.

The leader of the pro-government Seri Manangkhasila Party in the Northeast was Liang Chaiyakan (Ubon) who had spent more time in the Assembly than any other northeasterner and had moved through all political groupings (Democrat, pro-Pridi, and pro-Phibun) at various points in his career. Almost as long-tenured, but politically more consistent, was the northeastern head of the Democrat Party, Nai Fong Sitthitham, also from Ubon. The leaders of the Economist Party, Thep Chotinuchit (Si Sa Ket) and Thim Phuriphat (Ubon), had stirred considerable interest and received much publicity for making a trip to communist China in 1956 without government sanction. On their return they had been arrested, but were released shortly thereafter. However, although this act had made them well known in Bangkok circles, both Thep and Thim gave more emphasis to internal economic problems than to foreign policy in their attempt to win support for the Economist Party. The Free Democrat Party, the other major leftist party, was founded by Sa-ing Marangkun from Buri Ram. A somewhat more colorful (and more doctrinaire) leftist party which was more restricted in appeal, was the Hyde Park Movement led by Thawisak Triphli from Khon Kaen.

There were minor leftist parties and some limited support for the northeastern-led leftist groups outside the Isan region, but for the most part the whole leftist movement was predominantly a northeastern product.[44] For example, the Free Democrat Party put up forty-five candidates in the February 1957 elections, of whom twenty-nine were from the Northeast (*Bangkok Post*, January 7, 1957). However, of the eleven seats this party captured, all were from the Northeast. As can be seen from the following table, this pattern was repeated for other leftist parties.

TABLE 4.2 Results of the February 1957 Election for Thailand
and for the Northeastern Region

Party Affiliation	Party Name		Number of Seats	
			Nationwide	Northeast
Pro-Phibun	Seri Manangkhasila		85	15
	Thammathiphat		10	2
		Total	95	17
Democrat	Democrat		28	10
Leftist	Economist (Setthakon)		8	8
	Free Democrat (Seri Prachathipatai)		11	11
	Hyde Park Movement		2	1
		Total	21	20
Other	Nationalist		3	0
Independent			13	6
TOTAL			160	53

Sources: *The Siam Directory* (1957, 1–6) and Darling (1965, 157)

Following the February election the government was accused of rigging election results, leading students to demonstrate against Phibun. General Sarit Thanarat, the head of the army, disassociated himself from the government, and the position of Phibun and his lieutenant, Police-General Phao, deteriorated. In September Sarit led a military coup d'état that forced Phibun and Phao into exile. Sarit himself did not, however, assume control of the government because ill health forced him to leave the country for medical treatment. From September 1957 until October 1958, two of Sarit's associates, Phot Sarasin (September 1957–January 1958) and Thanom Kittikachorn (January–October 1958), served as prime ministers. During this period considerable political freedom existed in the country.

TABLE 4.3 Results of the December 1957 Election for Thailand and for the Northeastern Region

Party Affiliation	Party Name	Number of Seats	
		Nationwide	Northeast
Pro-Phibun	Seri Manangkhasila	4	0
Pro-Sarit	Sahaphum	45	20
Democrat	Democrat	39	3
Leftist	Economist (Setthakon)	6	5
	Free Democrat (Seri Prachathipatai)	5	5
	Hyde Park Movement	1	1
	Total	12	11
Other	Nationalist	1	0
	Issara	1	1
	Total	2	1
Independent		58	18
TOTAL		160	53

Sources: *Bangkok Post*, December 17, 18, 19, 1957 and Thailand, Institute of Public Administration, Thammasat University (1958, 45–51)

In December 1957 the kingdom was given the opportunity to express itself once again at the polls as the caretaker government claimed it was necessary to provide "clean" elections to offset alleged misconduct by Phibun and his cohorts. The December elections indicated, on the surface at least, not only a marked decline in electoral support for followers of Phibun (as might be expected), but also a reduction in the number of leftist MPs (see preceding table).

However, contrary to the interpretations of some observers (D. Wilson 1959, 98; Darling 1965, 183) that the December elections represented a major drop in the popular appeal of the leftists in the Northeast where such sentiments were to be found, the new election really did not reveal, in fact, such a shift. For one thing, three candidates elected as leftists in February, including Thim Phuriphat (Ubon), were elected in December on the pro-Sarit Sahaphum ticket. In addition, at least four other Sahaphum deputies elected from the Northeast (Kiat Nakkhaphong [Maha Sarakham], Prathip Sirikhan [Sakon Nakhon], Khrong Chandawong [Sakon Nakhon], and Ora-in Phuriphat [Ubon]) also espoused political objectives similar to those of the leftists. This affiliation of leftist-leaning representatives with the Sahaphum or pro-Sarit party reflected the belief held in some circles at the time of the election that the Sahaphum Party had socialist inclinations. To these "disguised leftists" must be added at least three independent MPs (Chuen Rawiwan [Nong Khai], Plueang Wansi [Surin], and Suthi Phuwaphan [Surin]) who ran on much the same platform as the leftists.[45] In short, northeastern support for candidates designated loosely as leftist remained relatively strong in the December elections. Furthermore, in both of the 1957 elections, leftist appeal was almost exclusively restricted to the Isan region and in that region at least one-third of the elected representatives could be said to espouse the rather diffuse ideals of the "new left."

What explained the popularity of the leftist candidates in the Northeast as contrasted with the rest of the country? The day before the February 1957 election the *Bangkok Post* published the following evaluation:

Political circles noted that it is a peculiarity of the northeast to prefer any opposition candidate to a government one, and opposition candidates have stressed in publicity posters that they are in opposition.

The observers also noted that the Seri Manangkhasila Party candidates in the northeast are further handicapped through noncooperation and through actual dissension . . .

The Sethakorn (Economist) Party is reportedly leading in many of the northeastern provinces. The party leader, Nai Thep Jotincuchit [Thep Chotinuchit], is considered at present, the most popular candidate in [Si Sa Ket] while the deputy leader, Nai Tim Buripat [Thim Phuriphat], is one of the most popular in [Ubon]. Both went to communist China last year and were arrested on their return, and both had stirred up some interest regarding trade with communist China.

However, according to [Si Sa Ket] Governor Kitthi Yothakari and [Ubon] Governor Prasong Issarabhakdi, the people of these provinces are not much interested in international politics, being more concerned with their own living conditions and their own means of livelihood.

Nai Prasong reported that "Poujadists" have appeared on the scene in [Ubon]. He said that some opposition candidates are promising the people that if they are elected to the government, they would abolish taxes. (*Bangkok Post*, February 25, 1957)[46]

The governors were undoubtedly correct in their assessment that the international concerns of the leftist politicians probably had very little appeal for the relatively unsophisticated northeastern rural people. But pointing to the villagers' preoccupation with their own means of livelihood does not lead us much further in understanding why leftist candidates emerged and succeeded primarily in the Northeast. I would suggest that leftist candidates were generally more successful than many other Isan candidates in exploiting the ethnoregional sentiments that had reached a peak in the Northeast in 1957.

In some ways the leftist parties could be equated with regional parties. Whereas the leftist candidates traced their ideological heritage to the "martyred" northeastern leaders and were associated with a leadership that was almost exclusively from the northeastern region, the non-leftists were much more tied to political leaders who were central Thai. David Wilson questioned whether the leftist identification of some northeastern candidates was not secondary to a more basic regional oppositionism:

> Political figures from the Northeast seem to stand or fall on the vigor [with] which they oppose the government. Such opposition has often taken the form of more or less radical "leftist" ideology, although it has as often been pure oppositionism. The consistent ingredient has always been opposition, and it may be assumed that such an attitude is necessary for success in politics in the Northeast. This situation has earned the region a reputation for breeding radical politicians. Whether or not such a reputation is deserved is difficult to say. (D. Wilson 1959, 81)

Wilson's analysis notwithstanding, it does appear that the radical solutions to the economic problems of the Northeast proposed by many of the leftist candidates also fell on sympathetic ears among the northeastern, predominantly rural, electorate. Returned migrants who had seen the contrast between the standard of living in Bangkok and in their home villages and who had developed new expectations would have been especially receptive to promises of candidates to work for the raising of economic standards in the Isan countryside. However, the ability to play upon an emerging ethnoregionalism was not associated exclusively with the leftists. Many non-leftist candidates who had already attained some status in Bangkok were preferred by the northeastern electorate over leftist candidates who, however appealing their campaign promises might have been, were relatively unknown. Even so, an important apologist for the Phibun government, Liang Chaiyakan (Ubon), was reelected by a large majority in both the February and December 1957 elections.[47] It should be noted that although he was a member of Phibun's party (and at one time a member of Phibun's government), Liang had been a major advocate of government action for economic improvement of the Northeast.

The northeastern populace returned representatives whom they believed would best represent their interests in the national forum. Often the elected MPs were leftists who promised to further the regional interests of Isan. But just as often the chosen deputy was seen by the electorate as a man who had some influence in ruling circles in Bangkok and could, thus, act as an advocate for his northeastern constituency. It is significant that 66 percent of the northeastern representatives elected in December 1957 had been elected in either the 1952 or February 1957 elections.[48]

During 1958, although the northeastern MPs of the various parties differed in their views on such non-regional matters as attitudes towards Pridi, the Anti-communist Act, neutralist versus pro-Western foreign policy, or relations with communist China, there seemed to be consensus among all in seeking "cooperation to bring about improvements of conditions in the Northeast" (*Bangkok Post*, February 27 1958). In April 1958 all of the northeastern MPs who were in the pro-government party presented an "ultimatum" to the government. The deputies presented a set of four demands that they asked to be acted upon within fifteen days or else they would leave the party and form a separate Northeast party, presumably together with leftist Isan representatives who had been making overtures to all northeastern MPs about the possibility of forming an Isan party. The demands were as follows:

1. An urgent short-term project for improving conditions in the Northeast should be started in order to relieve suffering and hunger there as soon as possible.
2. The Government should also draw up a longer term project "like the Yanhee Hydro Electric Project, through foreign loans as in the central and southern projects."
3. The Government should establish heavy industries in the Northeast "which has plenty of raw materials."
4. The Government should increase educational facilities in the Northeast. (*Bangkok Post*, April 11, 1958)

The report did not mention how the northeastern deputies thought that these proposals could be met within fifteen days, and subsequent reports indicated that no representative resigned from the party.

However, the idea of forming a northeastern party that would advocate immediate and radical solutions to the economic problems of the Isan region remained. In May twenty-one northeastern MPs from twelve of the fifteen Isan provinces and representing leftist, pro-government, and independent parties, held a meeting in which it was "approved in principle . . . that "only through socialism can conditions in the Northeast be improved"" *(Bangkok Post,* May 2, 1958).[49]

The growing regional loyalties of a majority of the representatives from the Isan region caused concern among the leadership of the Thai government. But far more worrisome to the government were the attitudes adopted by the leftist MPs from the Northeast on international issues. The leftist parties were opposed to Thailand's membership in the Southeast Asia Treaty Organization and the Asian People's Anti-communist League, to the receiving of American aid that they alleged had strings attached, and to a pro-Western foreign policy. Officials in the government close to General Sarit viewed the pressures, exerted primarily by northeastern representatives, for "socialistic" programs to improve the economic position of the Northeast, for greater toleration of leftist political action within the country, and for a neutral foreign policy with grave apprehension. They were beginning to feel that if given free reign the activities of the northeastern MPs could seriously threaten the security of Thailand. There was a growing awareness among these government leaders of the need to deal with what they considered a "northeastern problem" *(panha Isan).* After Sarit inaugurated a new period of military rule in late 1958 this problem and its solutions were to become major preoccupations of the Thai government.

5

MONARCHY, SECURITY,
AND DEVELOPMENT

THE SARIT ERA

The political relationship between the Northeast and the Thai polity was transformed in a markedly negative way during the period between 1957 and 1973, a period in which the Thai government was presided over by military dictators. In September 1957, Field Marshal Sarit Thanarat led a coup against the government headed by Phibun Songkhram. This coup did not simply entail the replacement of one military ruler by another. Sarit's coup was to lead to the most significant reconfiguration of the Thai political order since 1932. The results were not immediate, however, because after the coup Sarit had to go to the United States for medical treatment. He then returned to Thailand to stage a second coup in 1958, replacing Field Marshal Thanom Kittikachorn, who as Sarit's chosen deputy had served as an interim prime minister. Although Sarit would be prime minister for only five years, dying in 1963, he would, in the words of Thak Chaloemtiarana, who wrote the definitive biography of Sarit, "more than any other person in the modern period set the pattern for present day politics in Thailand" (Thak 1979, 152). Sarit himself, as Thak observes, did not have "a clear 'vision' of how to reorganize the Thai political system," but "he did have certain ideas about politics and these came to have a decisive effect on Thai politics" (152–53). This effect significantly shaped subsequent relations between rural northeasterners and the Thai government.

The most basic change Sarit made to the Thai polity was the renewal of the monarchy. Phibun, as one of the original Promoters of the 1932 coup, had always viewed the monarchy as marginal to Thai politics. He had felt compelled, however, to publicly support the young King Bhumibol Adulyadej's ascension to the throne and, in 1950, his return to Thailand from Switzerland where he had been studying.[1] Once back in Thailand the king began to assume a more public role. Sarit, on the other hand, could not claim the legitimacy of having been one of the Promoters and, thus, of constitutionalism. He turned, instead, to the monarchy to legitimize his coup and to secure the political leadership of the military (Thak 1979, 311). Beginning with Sarit's time, political legitimacy in Thailand would come to depend more on the approval of the monarch than on popular sovereignty as embodied in the constitution.

In turn the military made protection of the monarchy its basic role. At the time Sarit assumed power, he and the military considered—in no small part because of American influence—the primary threat to the nation to be communism, both externally as represented by the People's Republic of China and the Democratic Republic of Vietnam, and by the communist movements in neighboring Laos and Cambodia supported by Vietnam and China, and internally as manifest in the Communist Party of Thailand, the presumed ally of neighboring communist-led states. Sarit made "security" (*khwam mankhong*) the primary basis of Thai government policy and welcomed the very significant military assistance of the United States in the form of materiel, joint military exercises, and the establishment of American bases on Thai soil.

The "Northeast problem" (*panha Isan*) became a particular focus of the security policy of the governments under Sarit and his successors. In part this was based on the assumption that the kinship and cultural connections of the dominant population of the Northeast with Laos made the region susceptible to communist infiltration from across the Mekong. It also stemmed from a continuing concern about the history of leftist politics in the region. At the same time, however, the proximity of the Northeast to Laos and Vietnam made it the ideal location for

American bases in Thailand. Four of the seven military airbases used by the United States in the period between 1961 and 1976 were located in the Northeast and it was from the one at Udon that most of the sorties over northern Vietnam were flown.[2]

Sarit is memorialized in a monument in Khon Kaen, a major city of the Northeast, not for his role in safeguarding the security of the country but for his promotion of "development" (*kan phatthana*).[3] Sarit did not simply continue the laissez-faire capitalism of Phibun, but oversaw, with the assistance of a cadre of technocrats, the deployment of government resources as well as much American aid in the infrastructure and other projects designed to facilitate overall national economic growth. As discussed below, in conjunction with the first National Development Plan of 1962, a subplan was also devised that focused solely on the Northeast. While the development policies it entailed led to a significant change in the economy of the region as northeastern villagers began to shift from subsistence-based production to production for the market and to seeking jobs in the non-agricultural sphere, these changes also served to exacerbate the economic disparities between the Northeast, especially the rural Northeast, and Bangkok and central Thailand.

Sarit himself identified with the Northeast because his mother was from the region and he had spent part of his childhood there, although he was sent to Bangkok at about the age of ten or eleven by his central Thai

Memorial to Field Marshal Sarit Thanarat in Khon Kaen depicting him helping the people (Charles Keyes, 2002)

father (himself an army officer) to the Royal Military Academy. His early experience, as well as the fact that his mother lived in the northeastern town of Mukdahan, contributed to his focus on the region when he became prime minister. His legacy for the region, as symbolized by the neglected monument in Khon Kaen,[4] included a continuing government concern for the "development" of the region, but few in the region would be able to point to anything other than the road network as a positive outcome of this concern. His more significant legacy has been the dominant role the military has played in Thai politics since his time, a role legitimated not by a popular mandate but by the monarchy.

RETURN OF KING BHUMIBOL AND THE RURAL ISAN VIEW OF THE THAI MONARCHY

In 1963–64, while Jane, my wife, and I were engaged in fieldwork in the northeastern Thai village of Ban Nong Tuen in Maha Sarakham Province in northeastern Thailand, we witnessed what was still the initial stage of the growing significance of the Thai monarchy for Isan villagers. Between the early 1930s and early 1950s the Thai monarchy had been all but invisible to the citizens of Thailand. King Prajadhipok (r. 1924–35) had gone into exile and abdicated after the coup of 1932 that established a constitutional monarchy. From 1935 to 1946, Ananda, his young nephew, had been recognized as king, but lived in Switzerland until after World War II. In 1946 he had returned to Thailand to be crowned, but had died shortly after his coronation from a still not fully explained gunshot wound. Although his brother, Bhumibol Adulyadej, became king in his place, the young monarch returned to Switzerland shortly after the royal funeral in order to complete his studies.

Phibun Songkhram, as one of the promoters of the 1932 coup, had resisted allowing the monarchy to have any significant role, but he was in no position to stop or control King Ananda's return having himself been removed from the premiership in a coup by a pro-Allied group led by his arch nemesis Pridi Banomyong. When in 1946 Pridi and his associates failed to provide a satisfactory explanation of King Ananda's death to the Thai public, Phibun and his supporters were able to stage another coup and return to power. Phibun then used an inquiry into the death of King Ananda to destroy Pridi, with Pridi being accused (wrongly) of the king's death. Having put himself forward in this guise as a defender of the monarchy, he was in no position to prevent King Bhumibol from returning to the country to be officially crowned in 1950.

King Bhumibol brought with him his young wife, Sirikit, whom he had married the previous year. The birth in quick succession of four children, three daughters and a son, expanded the presence of the monarchy beyond the king and queen, the king's mother, and his sister. King Bhumibol and Queen (as she became after his coronation) Sirikit soon began to take an active role in reintroducing the monarchy to the people of Thailand by traveling to different parts of the kingdom as well as giving radio broadcasts. In 1956 the king was ordained as monk for a period of fifteen days to make merit for his grandmother, Savang Vadhana, Queen Consort of King Chulalongkorn. Photos of him in yellow robes (and wearing sun glasses because of his blindness in one eye) were widely circulated and many *wat*, including most in northeastern Thailand, prominently displayed this photo.

By the time Sarit assumed power in 1958, the Thai government had ensured that a photo of the king would be displayed next to the altar of the Buddha and the national flag in all primary schools. Every weekday morning, as we witnessed in Ban Nong Tuen, school children would start the day by showing respect to the three "pillars" (*lak*) of the Thai nation—the Buddha, the king, and the nation. All three symbols were linked with a "sacred thread" (*saisin*), a cotton string that had been blessed by monks. By the time village children had completed four years of compulsory schooling, these symbols were deeply imprinted in their minds.

The government with support from the United States Information Service (USIS)[5] reproduced photos of the king, or the king and queen, or the king and the whole royal family and distributed these to many, perhaps most, households in the kingdom. One widely distributed photo showing the king touching a woman who is presenting him flowers was particularly significant because it conveyed the message that the royal touch was magically (*saksit*) efficacious.[6] In June 1963 when Jane and I were engaged in fieldwork in Ban Nong Tuen, we observed that many villagers traveled to a neighboring district because the king was there to visit a military institution. Although there were only a few radios in the village, when the king spoke many gathered around to listen to him.[7] Even more villagers were aware of the king as an impressive royal person because of the photos of him at the school and in many homes.

In my dissertation (Keyes 1966a, 330) I noted, based on my research in Ban Nong Tuen, that the splendor in which the king lived could be imagined with "reference to the images of all kings created upon the stage of the folk opera." The Lao folk opera, *molam mu*, shares with central Thai *like* the dramatic performance to musical accompaniment of a story drawn from the *jataka*, or birth stories of the Buddha, or from legend. The actors in both forms of folk opera don costumes that are based on what are thought to be royal garments. *Molam mu* differs from *like* in that the musical accompaniment is provided primarily by the *khaen*, a polyphonic reed mouth organ that has become the iconic symbol of northeasterners.[8]

In one all-night *molam mu* performance we witnessed in Ban Nong Tuen in 1964, the suitor for the hand of a princess was at first deemed to be unsuitable because he appeared at first to her relatives to be a crazy old man. After they eloped, however, his true nature as the god Indra became apparent. Gods (*thewada*), like royalty, belonged to a category of beings that in Lao and Thai are subsumed under the classifier *ong*, a classifier that contrasts with *khon*, the classifier used for ordinary human beings. The elements of the narrative of the life of the young King Bhumibol—the tragic death of his brother, his wooing of Queen Sirikit, the birth of his children, and especially his visits to ordinary subjects where his charisma was clearly evident—were very much in keeping with the elements of folk opera stories. In short, by the early 1960s villagers throughout the Northeast recognized in King Bhumibol a man of extraordinary charisma (*phu mi bun barami*), one who far surpassed in charisma the local *phu mi bun* of a half-century earlier.[9]

The villagers of Ban Nong Tuen had no problem in distinguishing the king from the prime ministers and bureaucrats who exercised actual political power. As I wrote in my fieldnotes, in villagers' "conception of the social universe of the state, the king is more necessary in villagers' eyes than is the P.M. [prime minister]. P.M.s come and go, but the king

Portrait of King Bhumibol at a village school in Maha Sarakham Province
(Jane Keyes, 2005)

as a symbol remains."[10] Although prime ministers and other officials are
"royal servants" (*kharatchakan*), many such "royal servants" have proved
by their actions that they did not always act in accord with the king's
concern for the general welfare of his subjects.[11]

A villager in Ban Nong Tuen spoke for many others when he told me
that he considered General Phao Sriyanond, the head of the police in
Phibun's post-1947 government and a rival of Sarit, to have been "evil"
(*phu rai*). General Phao had been responsible for the Kilo 11 incident
and had also arranged for the detention and execution of many others
he considered opponents. Something of the view of Phao also extended,
in villagers' eyes, to the police more generally. As I concluded in my
dissertation:

The villagers' only contacts with the police are on those occasions when the police are enforcing rules and laws to the detriment of villagers. Police come to the village to look for illegally made liquor, to uncover local lotteries which are popular all over village Thailand and extremely unpopular with the government, or to expose village gambling games. The police are never viewed, as they are supposed to be in the West, as the preservers of law and order on the people's behalf. In instances of theft, and even murder, in the villages, villagers attempt to conceal the facts from the police and prefer to adjudicate or rectify the problems themselves. "To call the police is only to create trouble," commented one old man in Ban Nong Tuen. Hence, communication initiated by villagers with the police is almost non-existent. (Keyes 1966a, 92–93)

In other words, the police were considered not as appropriate "servants of the king," but as the wielders of amoral or immoral power.

Villagers held similar negative attitudes towards the district officer (*nai amphoe*), the primary representative of the government in their lives. Again, to quote my dissertation:

For Ban Nong Tuen villagers the Nai Amphoe [for Muang District, Maha Sarakham] is an immediate and powerful embodiment of the government. He could drive up in his jeep and demand that villagers repair a road or build a bridge. He could and did demand that villagers give him such items of local produce as watermelons, honey, and fish or that they provide his party with a meal.

The relationship between villagers and the district officer is further strained by the fact that the Nai Amphoe is a central Thai who holds the local villagers in low esteem. He boasts that he has lived fourteen years in the Northeast and cannot speak in Isan dialect. His power is only rarely kept in check by supervision from his superiors. The social distance created by his superior status, his ethnic difference, and his local power make it nearly impossible for villagers to approach him with complaints or demands. For Ban Nong Tuen villagers, the district officer is a person to be both feared and avoided. (Keyes 1966a, 92)

In short, by the early 1960s Isan villagers had come to distinguish between the king, whose manifest moral authority was derived from his Buddhist charisma, and most of the servants of the king, who were seen as exercising power without moral constraint. However, the king was more a mythical than a palpable presence in their lives. Attitudes toward the Thai military in rural Isan in the early 1960s were mainly neutral. While a few village men had been conscripted, they had seen their service more as an adventure than an imposition.[12] While we were engaged in our research in Ban Nong Tuen, the Thai military carried out a joint exercise, called "Exercise Thanarat," with US forces encamped a few kilometers away from the village. This was the first time, at least since World War II, that most villagers had had any firsthand contact with Thai military personnel.[13] They were curious about the exercise, but none of their experiences made them view the Thai military in either positive or negative ways. The recognition of Sarit as a fellow northeasterner and as one attentive to the king contributed to some positive impressions of the Thai military. That perception was to change after the middle of the decade as Thai military forces engaged in actual combat with presumed communist insurgents in the region.

THE "NORTHEASTERN PROBLEM"

Whereas northeasterners viewed government officials as servants of the state legitimated by the monarchy and not as servants of the people, they saw those they elected to Parliament from the region as representing them. Although Phibun's government had moved to control MPs through cooptation, intimidation, or even murder, it had still allowed a parliament to exist. While Phibun was overthrown by a military coup rather than an election, the coup was welcomed by many of the politicians who had been opposed to Phibun and Phao. During the interim government of Thanom Kittikachon between September 1957 and October 1958 while Sarit was abroad for medical treatment, there seemed to be an opening for a reemergence of politicians who promoted the interests of the Northeast but who had been previously marginalized (or worse) because of their presumed leftist orientation. Although Thanom and his deputy, Praphas Charusathien, had no sympathy with those who desired to see Thailand move towards the left, Sarit's absence abroad made them cautious about moving against what appeared to be a growing popular movement. To some extent the first Thanom government even attempted to accommodate the interests of the Thai left. Thim Phuriphat, MP from Ubon, for example, who had been a major leftist leader before the December 1957 election, was included in the cabinet. In June 1958 Thanom even publicly stated that the government was working for "mild socialism" (*Bangkok Post*, June 18, 1958). Such accommodation did not extend, however, to allowing the Thai Communist Party to have legal status; in June MPs led by those of the pro-government party that had taken the rather strange name of National Socialist voted 40 to 11 to keep the Anti-communist Act (*Bangkok Post*, June 4, 1958).[14]

By mid-1958 the Thanom government's position was becoming shaky as it ran into serious economic troubles. The opposition, including both Democrats and leftists, began to call for a "General Debate." In addition, the government party was faced with insubordination by some of its own members who made or planned trips, along with opposition MPs, to Russia and communist China. Isan members of the pro-government party were particularly conspicuous for their participation in these trips. For example, in August 1958 two pro-government MPs (Banchoet Saichya [Roi Et] and Burana Campaphan [Si Sa Ket]), together with three opposition MPs (To Kaeosena [Free Democrat, Buri Ram], Sa-ing Marangkun [Free Democrat, Buri Ram], and Thawisak Triphli [Hyde Park Movement, Khon Kaen]), all from the Northeast, went to communist China on an unauthorized trip.

Such was the state of affairs when Sarit suddenly reappeared on the scene. He only stayed in Bangkok for a short time, but his sentiments soon became known and felt. The two major Isan representatives in the cabinet, Thim Phuriphat (Ubon) and Ari Tanwetchakun (Khorat), were forced to resign because of their occasional outspoken opposition to some government policies. Sarit openly voiced his disapproval of National Socialist members who had gone on visits to Russia or China and asked that the name of the party no longer be translated in English as "National Socialist" because it was not socialistic. Then he left for more medical treatment in England. In October 1958 he suddenly appeared again, and on the twenty-first of that month the "Revolutionary Group," under his direction, took over the government and declared martial law, leading to the suspension of the constitution and the abolition of Parliament.[15] It would not be until the early 1970s that a parliament once again provided Isan representatives a venue in which to have a legitimate voice in Thai politics.

During Sarit's premiership, terminated by his death from sclerosis of the liver in December 1963, and continuing under Thanom and Praphas, the Thai government predicated its policies regarding the Northeast on what was designated the "northeastern problem" (*panha Isan*).[16] Whereas previous governments had sought to address some of the complaints of northeastern politicians, Sarit and his successors now viewed such complaints as potentially dangerous to the continued existence of the government and of Thailand itself. This shift in the understanding of dissent in the Northeast was closely related to growing official fears—very much fueled by Thailand's alliance with the United States—concerning the renewed civil wars in Vietnam and Laos.

The Thai government feared that if communist-led movements in South Vietnam and Laos were to succeed, then the Northeast could prove to be the Achilles heel in Thailand's attempt to maintain its own security. The Thai leadership saw the northeastern problem stemming not only from the connection between the peoples of northeastern Thailand and those of Laos but also from the economic underdevelopment in the northeastern region. These conditions, the government feared, might make the region fertile ground in which the seeds of insurrection could grow. Isan ethnoregionalism might, it was thought, develop into a Lao separatist movement that would look to North Vietnam, communist China, and the Pathet Lao for support. Finally, the government felt there was sufficient evidence to suggest that some northeastern political leaders were already involved in a communist conspiracy to overthrow the pro-Western government of Thailand (Keyes 1964).

The United States found in Sarit and his successors men who were fully committed to fighting communism.[17] By the early 1960s the United States was providing significant aid for the Thai military in the form of weaponry, training, and direct grants of money. The United States also gave Thailand large amounts of aid for economic development, with much of this aid being earmarked for use in the Northeast, the region deemed by the United States as well as the Thai government to be the primary locus of communist-led insurgency.[18]

During the 1960s United States military assistance to Thailand included, as mentioned above, the building of airbases for support of the war in Vietnam and Laos, the most significant of which was one in Udon in northeastern Thailand. While these bases generated jobs for many northeasterners, primarily in construction (men) and prostitution (women), they also became the source of increasing criticism, especially by an emerging student movement, leveled against the Thai government for the distortions they created in the social fabric of rural society in the Northeast.

Throughout the 1960s the Thai government's solution to the northeastern problem centered primarily on implementing policies to ensure the security of the region through counterinsurgency programs. The solution was also tied to government interventions designed to promote economic development.

THE NORTHEAST DEVELOPMENT INITIATIVE

After assuming power, Sarit had turned increasingly to technocrats or trained experts (*nak wichakan*) for help in formulating government policies, giving their advice more weight than that of officials enmeshed in the long-standing patronage networks of the bureaucracy (Thak 1979, 276ff). In 1957 and 1958 the International Bank for Reconstruction and Development, later known as the World Bank, sent a mission to Thailand at the request of the Thai government. The World Bank mission report (World Bank 1959) laid the foundation for a profound transformation of the Thai economy, forming the basis for the first five-year national development plan in Thailand, promulgated in 1962 by Sarit's government. A major focus of this plan was the problem of underdevelopment in the Northeast.

In about 1960, the Thai government under Sarit created a Committee on Development of the Northeast (*Khana kammakan phatthana phak tawanok chiang nuea*) under the National Economic Development

Cover of the publication, *The Northeast Development Plan*, 1962–1966

Board in the Office of the Prime Minister. The committee included many ranking members of the government and was chaired by Sarit himself. In 1961, this committee completed its major task and submitted *The Northeast Development Plan, 1962–1966* to the Sarit government for approval. The goal of the plan was stated as follows:

> The aim of the Northeast Development Plan is to raise the standard of living of the Northeastern people to levels comparable with that of other regions, bringing about greater welfare and happiness to the inhabitants of this region, and to lay down economic and social infrastructures for future economic stability and progress. The Committee holds above all the fact that the Northeastern part is an integral and inseparable part of the Kingdom of Thailand and that the Thai nationals living in the Northeastern region are Thai citizens

(*phak tawanok chiang nuea pen phak nueng khong ratchanacak Thai lae prachachon thi mi phumilamnao nai phak ni pen phonlamuang Thai*). (Thailand, Committee on Development of the Northeast [Khana kammakan phatthana tawanok chiang nuea] 1961, 1)

This plan, although by no means the first effort of the government of Thailand to deal with the economic problems of the Northeast, was the first government-sponsored plan designed specifically for the improvement of the region not subsumed in some larger national scheme. When the plan was first made public, the government announced that it would be spending about US$3 billion on its implementation over the following five years (1962–66). The money to finance such a large undertaking was to come, in great part, from aid grants from the United States (*New York Times,* April 14, 1962).

There were six specific objectives in the plan:

1. To improve water control and supply.
2. To improve means of transport and communication.
3. To assist villages in increasing production and marketing.
4. To provide power for regional industrial development and (later) rural electrification.
5. To encourage private industrial and commercial development in the region.
6. To promote community development, educational facilities, and public health programs at the local level. (Thailand, Committee on Development of the Northeast 1961, 1–2).

After the plan was first published in 1961 a Northeastern Committee in the National Economic Development Board, Prime Minister's Office, was charged with supervising, coordinating, or carrying out research in the Isan region in order to bring the original proposals more in line with the existing realities.[19] The implementation of the plan, however, was divided between a large number of agencies, departments, and ministries with overall coordination supplied theoretically by the Ministry of National Development (subsequently the National Economic and Social Development Board) and the Prime Minister's Office. The United States Operations Mission to Thailand (part of the United States Agency for International Development) devoted a large share of its resources to assist those Thai governmental bodies working on northeastern development plans.

Among the more striking consequences of aid to the Northeast was the improvement of the region's economic infrastructure. Completion of the Friendship Highway, which was built at a cost of US$20 million (almost all from American sources), connecting Bangkok with Khorat and then Nong Khai and other less spectacular highway and communication connections, followed quite logically from the desire, expressed first in King Chulalongkorn's reign, to reduce the isolation of the region from the central plains. While the road network was created primarily for security reasons, it had a marked effect on the economy and society of the region (see Louis Berger International, Inc., 1979; Moore et al. 1980; and Thung 1972). As the network expanded, more and more businesses and small entrepreneurs purchased trucks and small buses to carry goods and people between the Northeast and Bangkok (see *Bangkok World*, January 21, 1964).[20]

The rapid increase in bus transportation in the region was particularly noticeable by the early 1960s even before the highway from Khorat was completely paved.[21] By the 1970s, after the Friendship Highway was entirely paved, the preferred mode of transport between northeastern villages (except those close to a railhead) and Bangkok were long-distance buses. Although the government also began in the 1960s to invest in expanding air services to several cities in the region, roads, supplemented by trains, remain to this day by far the major link between rural northeastern Thailand and the Greater Bangkok Metropolitan Area.

In the 1960s the Thai government, again using American aid funds, began the construction of irrigation and multi-purpose dams as part of a large international scheme for the eventual harnessing of the power of the Mekong and its tributaries. The two most important dams being constructed in the period were the multi-purpose Nam Pong project (later known as the Ubol Ratana Dam) in Khon Kaen, which was expected to provide both water control and electrical power for the central provinces of the region, and the Lam Pao project in Kalasin, which, together with the Nam Pong Dam, was projected to provide irrigation for the Chi River basin.[22] While these dams did significantly increase the hydroelectric power of the country, and while there was some expansion of irrigated land near the dams, the significant displacement of villagers living in the areas that were flooded, most of whom received inadequate or no compensation, made the dams a source of discontent among a significant segment of the rural people directly impacted by them (see Ingersoll 1969; Jerachone Sriswasdilek 1979).[23] The negative consequences of dam building would in later years, especially following the decision to build the Pak Mun Dam in Ubon (see chapter 7), contribute significantly to tensions between rural northeasterners and the central government.

In addition to infrastructure, the Northeast Development Plan called for the introduction of a community development program (*khrongkan kan phatthana chumchon*). The Community Development (CD) program had its antecedents in the Thailand-UNESCO Fundamental Education Centre program of the 1950s (see Nairn 1966); under Sarit this program was moved from the aegis of the Ministry of Education and placed under the Ministry of Interior. From that time on, the Ministry of Interior became the primary locus of programs directed toward the rural areas of the country.[24]

While the CD program was first established in those northeastern districts that were deemed to be the least developed, and, thus, in government eyes, most likely to be susceptible to insurrectionary appeals, the program was eventually expanded so that by the 1970s nearly every *tambon* had its own CD organizer (*phatthanakon*) operating under a district CD supervisor. For the most part, CD workers were young men and sometimes young women whose status was somewhere between that of district clerks and that of assistant district officers. They typically operated with very small budgets and were not permitted to use large sums of government money for any of the village-based projects they initiated. Rather they were charged with organizing villagers into various types of groups to undertake community projects usually predetermined (by central authorities) and implemented with local labor. While some CD workers had excellent rapport with villagers and had some success in stimulating actual changes that villagers deemed beneficial to themselves (I describe one such exceptional CD worker in my dissertation—see Keyes 1966a, 97–103), most assumed a role of being a sometime liaison between district officials and villagers and a sometime compiler of local statistics. While some CD officers who were recruited from the local northeastern populace genuinely empathized with villagers and sought to be their advisors rather than spokesmen for often authoritarian district officers, most workers, including many native northeasterners, were openly contemptuous of village ways. Community development workers could be good patrons, they could be petty nuisances, or they could be yet other power figures who must be placated by villagers. Whatever roles they played, they could never be held accountable by the people they were supposed to serve; they always remained government officials constrained by the ethos of the bureaucracy. The CD program thus suffered from the fact that it was not really a local-level institution but rather an extension of the administrative apparatus of the central government. In other words, many, perhaps most, northeastern villagers perceived the CD program as another government intrusion into their world.

With an increase in reported insurrectionist activity in the 1960s, the Thai government, and its advisers in the United States Operations Mission, began to fear that the community development program and other development schemes for the rural Isan region might not stimulate development rapidly enough to offset the possible blandishments of cadres from the Thai Patriotic Front which had been established under Chinese auspices in 1965 (*Taiwan Today*, February 14, 1965). Without question, the Sarit government and subsequently the Thanom government spent far more on military and paramilitary actions in northeastern Thailand than they did on development programs. The linkage between "development" and "security" was most evident in the Mobile Development Unit (MDU) program set up by the Sarit government under the National Security Command in 1962. According to Scoville and Dalton, the purpose of the MDU program "was to promote intensive and rapid development in a few model villages of . . . [a district], to win the friendship of the people and to gain information on subversion. Each MDU program was intended after a year or so to be phased out and to be replaced by strengthened regular civilian government services" (Scoville and Dalton 1974, 55; also see Huff 1967). The first MDU was situated in Kalasin Province and the program subsequently operated primarily in areas of the Northeast and North that were designated as especially "security-sensitive." As special-purpose projects operated by military personnel, the MDUs had only a limited impact on the economy and society of rural northeastern Thailand. Of far greater significance has been the experience that a number of members of the military elite gained through participation in the MDU program.[25] These men, among them being General Kriangsak Chomanan, prime minister from 1977 to 1979, and General Prem Tinsulanonda, prime minister from 1980 to 1988, gained some insight into conditions of northeastern rural people that was not shared by other members of the elite, many of whom rarely left Bangkok.

The Mobile Development Unit program most clearly illustrated the government's belief that economic development could not be implemented effectively without the securing of village loyalty. In fact, all of the government's rural development schemes included as an essential component the dissemination of information designed to increase villagers' sense of attachment to Thailand and to the Thai government. With similar ends in view the government increased its radio service to the Northeast with stations located in Khon Kaen, Ubon, Udon, Sakon Nakhon, and Khorat. All of these methods for making the Isan populace more conscious of its sense of belonging to Thailand added to the traditional methods of education and local administration that in the past had aimed at inculcating in villagers a sense of belonging to the Thai state. However, as Morrell and Chai-anan (1981, 91) concluded after reviewing US support for Thailand's counter-insurgency programs, including MDUs, "in general, US assistance programs worsened rather than improved" the "negative behavior and corruption" of officials that "increasingly alienated the villagers from the government and its political system."

MIGRATION AND THE RESHAPING OF NORTHEASTERN THAI RURAL SOCIETY

An increasing number of northeastern villagers became very much aware of the marked difference between their lives and those of the elite and growing middle class mainly in Bangkok not only as a consequence of what government officials did or did not do in their rural communities but also because by the 1960s many had had extended firsthand experience with these disparities while working in very low-paying jobs in Bangkok. While new non-agricultural jobs in relatively significant numbers were generated in Thailand during the first half of the century, those who filled these tended overwhelmingly to be Chinese migrants (see Skinner 1957, 117–18). Chinese immigration was sharply curtailed by World War II, and after the war was over the Thai government instituted a policy that effectively put an end to large-scale immigration from China. At the same time, the economy of Thailand began to grow again, and with this growth came an increasing demand for unskilled (and some skilled) non-agricultural labor in Bangkok and (to a considerably lesser extent) in other centers.

This demand was met by people from rural Thailand who left their homes in large numbers to take up non-farm jobs. Those villagers who went to Bangkok, where most new non-farm jobs were created, tended at first to be from provinces in the central region, but northeastern villagers also responded to the demand in significant numbers. In the 1960 census it was found that while 67 percent of all migrants to Bangkok for the period from 1955 to 1960 came from central Thailand, a still significant 22 percent came from the Northeast (Thailand, Central Statistical Office 1961, table 6).[26] The relative proportion of northeasterners among migrants to Bangkok increased substantially after the 1955–60 period. A study carried out in 1977 under the auspices of the Thai National Statistical Office found that 43 percent of all male migrants and 51 percent of all female migrants who had arrived in the capital after November 1975 and who were still present in October 1977 had come from the Northeast (reported in Lightfoot 1980, 9).

In the 1960s, while a few northeasterners who found employment in Bangkok and elsewhere ended by making a permanent shift of residence, most spent only a temporary period of time away from their homes, returning eventually to settle down to an agricultural way of life. The typical pattern of rural to urban migration in the 1960s involved a migrant leaving his or her home community for a period of months or even years, and then returning home (cf. Keyes 1966a, 312–15 and Lightfoot

1980, 8; also see Lightfoot, Fuller, and Peerasit Kamnuansilpa 1983; and Lightfoot and Fuller 1984).

In a survey I carried out in Ban Nong Tuen in Maha Sarakham Province in 1963, I found that 44 percent of males over the age of sixteen had worked for at least some time in Bangkok. The growing pattern of temporary migration had led to a differentiation within the rural populace between those (mainly women) who oriented themselves entirely within family and village and those (mainly men) who developed social relations with people outside of their natal communities. While some of these relationships were with the foremen and labor recruiters who were from Bangkok, the much more significant ones were with other northeastern men. On the basis of my interviews and more informal conversations in 1962–64 with many villagers who had spent time working in Bangkok, I concluded that the "temporary migrant has been only too acutely aware of the extent to which central Thai, and particularly urbanized Bangkok Thai, look down on the northeasterner as a provincial hick. The migrant returns home with a heightened sense of ethnic identity with all Isan which he has obtained through realizing his common background and common interests with other northeasterners from other parts of the region" (Keyes 1966a, 324). The stories the 1960s migrants told of their experiences, combined with the negative experiences many villagers had with representatives of the government, shaped the sense that *chao ban* (villagers) and especially *chao ban Isan* (northeastern villagers) were discriminated against by other members of Thai society.

AMBIVALENCE TOWARD THE THAI NATION-STATE

By the end of the 1960s northeasterners, especially those living in rural communities, had a somewhat schizophrenic relationship to the Thai nation-state. On the one hand, they had come to see themselves as Thai citizens, even if they were culturally Lao. As I quoted a villager in an early paper on "Ethnic Identity and Loyalty of Villagers in Northeastern Thailand" (Keyes 1966b), "we are Lao people, but Thai citizens (*pen phu Lao tae sat Thai*)."[27] This identification had come about because of the effectiveness of government-sponsored compulsory education and because of their recognition that King Bhumibol Adulyadej was their legitimate ruler. No local leader or any leader in neighboring Laos was seen as having anything approaching the Buddhist charisma (*bun barami*) of King Bhumibol. In addition, the greatly expanded road system was making it possible for northeasterners to become much more integrated than before into the national economy. This made it much easier for villagers to find work in Bangkok or its vicinity and to transport village products to market. Villagers appreciated having the additional cash income that this integration had made possible.

On the other hand, the actual interactions northeasterners had with government officials, which increased significantly in the 1960s, were often very far from positive. When officials came to villages, even if the ostensible reason was to promote "development," they often acted as *chaonai*, lit., "royal-aristocratic persons," but used by northeastern villagers to mean arrogant superiors. The demands placed by ranking officials such as district officers and educational supervisors on villagers for lavish entertaining, including commercial whiskey, is well described in Khammaan Khonkhai's novel about school teachers in a northeastern Thai village, *Khru Ban Nok* (Rural Teacher), set in the late 1960s or early 1970s (Khammaan 1979, 1982). Villagers sometimes had to go to the district office to request permits for such enterprises as a small rice mill. Not only were such requests often turned down, but also those that were approved typically entailed a bribe.

No other representative of the government has had a greater negative impact on villagers than the police. The police entered villages primarily to enforce laws against illegal cutting of timber that villagers sought to use for house building or charcoal-making and especially to stop villagers making their own rice wine or whiskey. In May 1963 I myself witnessed a raid in Ban Nong Tuen. The tenth day of the waxing of the moon of the sixth lunar month (which in 1963 fell on May 2) was deemed especially auspicious among rural northeastern Thai for the holding of weddings. In Ban Nong Tuen a few village men had prepared rice whiskey through a traditional distillation process instead of, as the law required, purchasing alcohol prepared under government license. Police were clearly aware of the fact that many weddings would be held on this day. In Ban Nong Tuen the police arrived shortly after four o'clock in the morning when the wedding festivities began. They came to the village with guns and arrested a number of men who were subsequently sentenced to several months in prison. When released from jail, these villagers strongly expressed their view that they had been punished unjustly for following village practice.

In 1967 on a return visit to Ban Nong Tuen, I learned that the friend with whom Jane and I had lived in 1963–64 had been robbed and nearly killed by a group of bandits, who, although identified, were not brought to justice because they had protectors in the provincial police and court system. Our friend's efforts to get justice led to his paying nearly as much in bribes as he had lost in the robbery. In an article I wrote about him and published anonymously in Thai in 1968, I ended by noting that "people in similar predicaments elsewhere in the region have been offered help by those who say that they can rid Thailand of both bandits and corrupt officials. Could we blame them for listening?"[28] Such incidents were very common and led to a significant increase in disaffection with government institutions.

In another village in the province of Nakhon Phanom, a similar incident occurred. A study carried out in 1968 by a US defense contractor, the Philco-Ford Corporation for Advanced Projects Research Agency, United States Department of Defense, reported that in one village "the common attitude is that "the police interfere with prerogatives which should not be the government's right to grant or withdraw." The report continues:

> One man who was arrested, jailed for three days, and charged a four hundred baht fine for making illegal whiskey, tore up his receipt in front of the policemen and told them that "You only arrest ordinary people and don't do anything useful." Another man, arrested for cutting wood even though he had a permit, put it like this: "I do not like the actions of the officials about these little things, because we don't do them to make money. We just want the wood to build houses, and making whiskey is our custom. We only do it from time to time. But when they arrest us they get money from the whiskey factory, and from the lumberman. That is the reason why the

policemen like to do these jobs instead of catching thieves." (Philco-
Ford Corporation, 1968, 151–52)

Although the relations between northeastern villagers and police
were the most fraught, even officials who went to villages to promote
development such as community development organizers were often the
sources of friction. Those villagers who had been resettled because of the
hydroelectric dam schemes were particularly upset with the government.

The grievances northeastern villagers had with the Thai government,
especially as they lacked any legitimate institutional means, such as
through elected MPs, to express those grievances, became reasons for
some to listen to other voices. By the mid-1960s the Communist Party
of Thailand was finding increasing support from among the rural people
of Isan.

6

THE FAILURE OF COMMUNIST REVOLUTION AND THE RISE OF NON-GOVERNMENTAL ORGANIZATIONS

ROOTS OF THE COMMUNIST INSURRECTION IN NORTHEASTERN THAILAND

Although there had been a few supporters of communism in Thailand in the 1930s, especially among some of the overseas Chinese in Bangkok and among Vietnamese refugees who had settled in northeastern Thailand after the French crushed the Nghe-Tinh soviets in 1931, the Communist Party of Thailand (CPT) itself dates its founding to December 1, 1942 (de Beer 1978, 144–45).[1] The party had briefly been legalized after World War II, but when Phibun Songkhram returned as prime minister in 1947 his government moved to repress all leftist movements. As discussed in the preceding chapter, during this period a number of left-wing Lao-speaking northeastern leaders who had emerged from the anti-Japanese Free Thai Movement during the war were assassinated.

Despite or perhaps because of this repression, the party continued to attract new followers. In 1961 the party at its third congress, according to the CPT's official history, "gained a firmer and more profound understanding of the revolutionary path of using the countryside to encircle the towns and of the role of the peasantry in national-democratic revolution" (Communist Party of Thailand 1978, 164). The rural areas that became the base for the party were located primarily in northeastern Thailand.[2]

In 1961 the government twice made raids that resulted in numerous arrests of alleged communist agents and supporters in several northeastern towns. The biggest of these raids occurred in December 1961 when over a hundred suspects were arrested in Sakon Nakhon and Udon. The government claimed that those arrested were "recruiters of villagers to the cause of communist separationists who want to effect secession of the Northeast from the rest of the Kingdom" (*Bangkok Post*, December 15, 1961). The government also claimed that these arrests were a follow-up to the arrest of a former pro-government MP from Sakon Nakhon, Khrong Chanthawong, who had earlier been executed as a communist ringleader. During the December 1961 raid the police also engaged in the first recognized "battle" between government forces and indigenous communists in Nakhon Phanom Province. Although stressing that those captured were northeasterners, not Lao nationals, the government alleged that the suspects had been trained by and were under orders from the Pathet Lao. Fears of a tie-in between a suspected northeastern "liberation" movement and the Pathet Lao were suggested by the formation of a Thai Exiles Group comprising some former MPs from the Northeast in Xieng Khouang, Laos. This group was plotting, so one reporter claimed, "to carve the Northeast out of Thailand and join it to Laos" (Theh Chongkhadikij, *Bangkok Post*, March 5, 1962).[3]

The Thai government under Thanom Kittikachorn, who became prime minister after Sarit's death in December 1963, continued the policy of suppressing Isan political dissent. Although Thanom promised a new constitution and a new act that would permit the existence of political parties once again, the country remained under military rule. The government felt that the increasing number of incidents in the Northeast, the creation of an organization called alternatively the Thailand Independence Movement or the Thailand Patriotic Front (cf. Close 1965) and formed with the support of Peking and Hanoi, and the continued gravity of the war in Vietnam precluded any liberalization of the political system. Instead, the governments of both Sarit and Thanom offered as solutions to the "northeastern problem" military or police responses to the appearance of organized political opposition in the region, accelerated programs in economic development, and intensified Thai-ification of the Isan populace.

The Thailand Independence Movement or the Thailand Patriotic Front in the early 1960s, like the CPT, was led by Sino-Thai from central or southern Thailand rather than men from the Northeast (Battye 1966–67, 9–12). Although the Thanom government believed that former MPs from the Northeast such as as Thim Phuriphat, Sa-ing Marangkun (Free Democrat, Buri Ram), and Amphon Suwannabon (Free Democrat, Roi Et) were leaders of the Thailand Independence Movement/Thai Patriotic Front, the names of these men did not appear in the broadcasts from Radio Hanoi, Radio Peking, or "The Voice of the Thai People" (Battye 1966–67, 13–14, 38). Yot Tisawot, the only "guerrilla leader" identified as a northeasterner, was not known for any role in northeastern political activities prior to this time (ibid., 430). Many of the insurrectionists in the Northeast were not Thai citizens but were Chinese or Vietnamese Tai or Lao who had been sent as *agents provocateurs* into the region (37–38, 41–43, 45).

By the mid-1960s the situation began to change. The CPT began to achieve increasing success in recruiting northeasterners to their cause since efforts by villagers to seek redress for their grievances through legitimate means had proved either futile or, in some cases, fatal. Most villagers still found their political reality to be predicated on their relationship to civil servants, whose demeaning attitudes toward them had only become more evident as the government implemented new policies. Those officials that villagers dealt with were accountable only to their bureaucratic superiors and not to the citizenry or to their elected representatives. The party now sent some of its recruits, including some northeasterners, for training at a school in North Vietnam (Hoa Binh) that they reached through a network of Pathet Lao and Vietnamese agents (*Bangkok Post*, December 2, 1966). They then returned to become cadres in an insurgency movement.

In 1965 the CPT formally initiated armed struggle against the government in northeastern Thailand. During the late 1960s the party recruited a small but steady number of villagers primarily in the provinces near the Mekong River to become active combatants in the insurgency. They also gained the tacit or active support of many more villagers who provided food, other supplies, and safe havens. "The 'forest fighters'[4] as the guerillas call themselves, are not ideologically committed, but they have been persuaded by the few who are—the communist cadres who have been working among the villagers for years—that under the present conditions they face only hardship and suffering. They hear that the government is corrupt, oppresses the people, and is interested only in Bangkok" (Girling 1981, 259).

The communist parties of Laos and Vietnam, especially following the building of American bases in northeastern Thailand, provided significant support for the CPT in the form of training of cadres as well as facilitating the supply of weaponry. In May 1966 Peter Braestrup reported in the *New York Times*, "clashes between Communist guerrillas and Thai security forces in border areas along the Mekong River have become more frequent and bloodier. The change, United States sources believe, is attributed both to more aggressive countermeasures and to Communist efforts to spread terrorism. North Vietnam and Communist China, it is believed, have ordered the 18-month old Thailand United Patriotic Front to launch a major effort now—for tactical reasons tied to the Vietnamese war" (*New York Times*, June 26, 1966).

In 1967 Louis Lomax, an African-American journalist, made a brief visit to northeastern Thailand, where he met with some in the communist-led movement. Later he claimed in his book, *The War That Is, the War That Will Be*, that the insurgency in northeastern Thailand would soon be comparable to that in Vietnam. The attack in 1968 on the American airbase in Udon notwithstanding, the number of violent incidents attributable to insurgents in the late 1960s remained quite low and were restricted to only a few places. Peter Bell, a political economist with research experience in the Northeast, wrote that "Lomax's book is a journalistic exercise, not based on thorough investigation, but it does point indirectly to the deficiencies and dangers posed by the mechanistic military response to the northeast problem" (Bell 1969, 51). Those "deficiencies and dangers" would become much more evident in the 1970s.

FROM OCTOBER 14, 1973, TO OCTOBER 6, 1976

By the end of the 1960s, the Thai military dictatorship began to face a more direct challenge to its authority. Middle-class students at universities, especially in Bangkok, had organized protests that sought the replacement of military rule by parliamentary government authorized by a constitution. These protests reached a climax in 1973. On October 14, 1973 (in Thai, *Sipsi tula*, a date that became one of the most significant in Thai political history), the military rulers ordered army and police to attack tens of thousands of protestors—many others besides students—who had gathered at the Democracy Monument in the heart of the government section of Bangkok. When General Kris Sivara, then commander-in-chief of the army, chose not to follow the order of the government headed by Thanom Kittikachorn and Praphas Charusathien, the king intervened and sent Thanom and Praphas into exile. The 1973 events did not, however, usher in a new order, especially for rural people in Thailand.

In the year after *Sipsi tula* the political situation appeared very hopeful. A caretaker government appointed by the king and headed by Sanya Thammasak, a respected judge and former rector of Thammasat University, called into existence a national convention that, in turn, was charged with electing a national assembly that would draft a new constitution. This convention included 658 village and commune headmen, constituting the largest bloc (27 percent) among the 2,436 members of the convention (Morrell and Chai-anan 1981, 102–3). Officials, particularly those associated with the Ministry of Interior, were able, however, to impose their will on many of these rural representatives when it came to the choosing of members of the National Assembly. As Morrell and Chai-anan observe, there "was a sharp decline in participation in the national legislature by local leaders and farmers" while "representation of the old guard elements increased from 48 to 69 percent" (103). Even so, this legislature produced the most liberal constitution Thailand would know for twenty-five years.

The constitution laid the foundation for a system of government to be controlled once again by an elected parliament rather than by the military. In January 1975 a democratic election of members of Parliament took place but the government, formed by a coalition led by the Democrat Party, was almost immediately undermined by conditions outside parliamentary control. Most significantly, many in the security forces (police, military, and border patrol police) were not willing to see their own powers curtailed by Parliament. Some members of these forces fostered the creation of right-wing movements and, even more frightening, death squads that targeted left-wing politicians, labor leaders, and leaders of rural protest groups. These counterrevolutionary elements capitalized on the negative reaction many in the Thai middle class had to the communist victories in Vietnam, Laos, and Cambodia. The Khmer Rouge evacuation of Phnom Penh in April 1975 was particularly disturbing to many urban Thai who feared that the CPT might one day succeed in imposing a similar action in Bangkok.

Even before *Sipsi tula* some members of the Bangkok-based student organizations undertook to establish links with rural people by going to the countryside to "teach democracy." The most successful student organizers were those who joined the Graduate Volunteer Centre at Thammasat University, later becoming the Thailand Rural Reconstruction Movement founded by Dr. Puey Ungphakorn, the highly respected economist and later rector of the university. Some at Chiang Mai University allied themselves with a Farmers' Federation of Thailand movement in North Thailand, but this alliance did not prevent the movement from being suppressed. The Farmers' Federation of Thailand (*Sahaphan chao rai chao na haeng prathet Thai*) was founded in November 1974, becoming the first formal organization in Thailand whose purpose was to promote the interests of rural people (Turton 1978, 122; Haberkorn 2011). In 1975 several leaders of the Farmers' Federation of Thailand were assassinated by death squads backed by the military or police. "The police were said to have put about forged letters purporting to show that the killings were the result of internal dissension. No arrests of suspects were made except in [one] case" (Turton 1978, 123). The repression of the Farmers' Federation of Thailand, led by rural leaders from northern Thailand in 1975–76 even when a democratically elected government was in office, reinforced the view held by many villagers in the Northeast as well as the North that rural people would never be allowed a legitimate voice in the Thai political system (Haberkorn 2011).

The majority of students who went to the countryside to "spread democracy" had no real understanding of how to frame their message in terms meaningful to villagers. One group who went in 1972 to Ban Nong Tuen, the village in Maha Sarakham where I have carried out long-term research, was probably far from atypical. They camped out at the *wat*, the village temple-monastery, and made work cleaning up the *wat* grounds. Villagers said the students spent most of their times singing protest songs comparable to those sung by anti-Vietnam War protestors in the United States. Even though these "songs for life" (*phleng phuea chiwit*) often spoke of the plight of the poor, they did not appeal to villagers who considered them the music of the urban young rather than music with roots in the popular culture of rural people.[5]

The vision that many Thai shared of a more open democratic society following *Sipsi tula* was shattered in October 1976 when elements in the police and military backed by right-wing groups overthrew the democratically elected government and brutally suppressed student activists in Bangkok. The new government instituted a broadly defined law that allowed almost anyone critical of the government to be accused of "endangering society" (*phai sangkhom*) and imprisoned without due process. This law was frequently used against rural people. In response to these developments, the CPT began attracting to its ranks new recruits from among villagers as well as from among Bangkok students. Two to three thousand students, including most of the leaders of the *Sipsi tula* movement who were not killed or arrested in the crackdown at Thammasat University, fled to the jungle to join the insurgency (Morell and Chai-anan 1981, 293). There they joined thousands of villagers who had joined the insurrection.

By 1977, according to one source (Stuart-Fox 1979, 346), the number of armed fighters for the CPT had reached 6,000–8,000, while another source estimated that by the late 1970s "communist military strength in Thailand . . . stands at something like 12,000 to 14,000 armed guerillas in all regions" (Girling 1981, 257).[6] What was probably more significant was that these fighters were given food and shelter in many villages especially in the Northeast. A map first published in the *Far Eastern Economic Review* in September 1977 showed that the insurgency was present in all but two provinces in the Northeast, all but two provinces in the South, half of the provinces in the North, and nearly half of the provinces in central Thailand (the map is reproduced in Girling 1981, 261).

While the CPT had had little success, as the map indicates, in the central part of the Northeast, in the areas of the region located near the Lao and Cambodian borders as well as in the hill country of the Phuphan mountains, communist cadres, who were often "friends, relatives, or neighbors of the people they aim to contact" (Girling 1981, 263, citing Somchai Rakwijit 1976, 47) were successful in persuading many villagers that the CPT was more understanding of their difficulties than were representatives of the government. These cadres capitalized on many incidents of very negative interactions between villagers and government officials. The following story from Buri Ram, a province bordering on Cambodia, was not atypical.[7]

On June 5, 1976, a group of somewhat agitated people (the number unspecified) gathered at the office of the district officer of Amphoe Prakhonchai in Buri Ram Province. They sought official approval to allow small privately owned truck-buses to operate in the district on routes that the owner of a 1arge bus company claimed to have the exclusive right to serve. The small truck-buses had succeeded in competition with the larger bus company and in retaliation the larger bus company had used strong-arm tactics as well as reported police harassment to scare off the small truck-bus owners. The conflict reached a climax when a village woman in the process of childbirth hired a truck-bus to take her to the provincial hospital. As the vehicle on which she was traveling reached the main road, the intersection was blocked and a driver of one of the larger buses forced the truck-bus to turn back to the village. The woman died during the delay that ensued. Her death greatly intensified the anger of villagers and the village-based owner-drivers of the small truck-buses.

The district officer and then the governor initially expressed sympathy with the villagers, but neither, in fact, moved to do anything to meet their concerns. Following renewed demonstrations on June 8 and 9, representatives of the governor told the protesters to seek action through formal bureaucratic means. As often is the case, such a response was simply a way of denying a request. Villagers perceived then as they still do that they are at a severe disadvantage in lodging formal bureaucratic complaints. Not only did the protestors view this action as a rebuff on the part of the governor, but they were also upset by the news that a man was taking down all the license numbers of the truck-buses parked outside the building where the protest took place. The protest ended inconclusively, with villagers finding no redress for their complaints.

On June 10 a large contingent of policemen from Buri Ram and neighboring provinces sought out and arrested nine persons who had been at the demonstration. Of the nine demonstrators, only three had been bailed out by June 1977, a year after the original demonstration. Moreover, another man involved in the protest activities was murdered and the eyewitness to this murder was also murdered. Those arrested were victims, in part, of a radical change to the right that occurred following the October 1976 coup and the installation of a new right-wing government under Prime Minister Tanin Kraivichien, a judge and the personal choice of the king for the role. Since one of the charges against the demonstrators was "treason," lodged because of suspicion of communist involvement in the demonstration, the legal proceedings against the demonstrators became much more drawn out. The demonstrators were also charged with hindering traffic, using an amplifier without a license, and libeling government officials. Such incidents as this lent significant credence to the CPT's message that the Thai government was the enemy of villagers.

Even in Maha Sarakham Province where I had carried out my own fieldwork, located in the part of the Northeast where CPT cadres had the least success, villagers were still very much aware that there were reasons to support the insurgency. On a return visit to Ban Nong Tuen in 1980 one very articulate man talked at some length of the grievances toward the government, which led certain villagers to turn to the communist-led insurrection. He said, "Villagers have no faith in the government (*mai waichai ratthaban*) because of the continual experiences of corrupt practices that they have when dealing with government officials." However, he immediately added that villagers (very much including himself) were not attracted to the communists because they "do not see anything good in the communist systems found in neighboring countries."[8] To my knowledge only one person from Ban Nong Tuen—a young man from one of the poorest families in the village, who had spent several years working in Bangkok—had joined the insurgency in the mid-1970s. I later learned he had been killed in a fight with government forces in another province. His death was said by one Ban Nong Tuen villager to demonstrate the futility of resisting the government. Such sentiments notwithstanding, the negative attitudes among northeastern villagers toward the government continued to fester and elsewhere in the region led many to join the communist-led insurrection. By the end of the 1970s, many observers were convinced that the 1976 coup combined with the growing grievances of rural people were conducing to civil war between forces of the Royal Thai Government and those led by the Communist Party of Thailand. Despite such predictions, however, by the early 1980s the communist-led insurrection had collapsed.

END OF THE COMMUNIST-LED INSURRECTION

One major reason for this collapse was, somewhat paradoxically, a consequence of the success of communist revolutions in China, Cambodia, Vietnam, and Laos. By the late 1970s, the communist parties in those countries had fallen out over ideological differences and nationalist interests. The Communist Party of Thailand, strongly linked to the Communist Party of China, found itself without nearby allies. Unquestionably of greater significance for rural northeasterners was the large number of refugees from Laos and Cambodia who fled to Thailand bringing with them disturbing stories about life under communist rule in those countries.

The communist takeovers of governments in Laos and Cambodia as well as Vietnam in 1975 were especially disturbing to the military and monarchy in Thailand. The reaction of these institutions contributed significantly to the success of rightist elements in seizing control of the Thai government in 1976. What is less well known is that these changes also had the unintended consequence of making many rural people skeptical of a communist political system. As the villager in Ban Nong Tuen quoted above said, he and other villagers were not convinced that the CPT offered a real alternative. In part, he and the many other villagers who shared this view were influenced by what they learned from the radio and from stories that circulated widely by word of mouth about what had happened following the success of communist-led revolutions in Cambodia and Laos. The exodus of refugees from these two countries, many of whom ended up in northeastern Thailand, made northeastern villagers aware that ordinary Khmer and Lao sought asylum in Thailand even if only temporarily. The stories of killing in Cambodia reinforced the negative view of a communist-led government.

Of greater importance than what occurred in neighboring Laos and Cambodia was the failure of the CPT to offer a vision of a political order that was compelling to villagers. Like the Communist Party of Kampuchea, the CPT also adopted Maoism as well as Marxist-Leninism as the foundation for its ideology, which in the history of the party is characterized as "the correct path for the liberation of all semi-colonial, semi-feudal countries" (Communist Party of Thailand 1978, 161). The CPT, again like the Khmer Rouge, rejected the "revisionism" associated with the reforms begun by Khrushchev in 1956 (163). By aligning itself with the Communist Party of China in the Sino-Soviet rift, the CPT would in the late 1970s lose the support of the Vietnamese and Lao communist parties, which, thus, made logistical support of the insurgency by China more difficult. This difficulty intensified when the Vietnamese military drove the Khmer Rouge, the only remaining ally of the CPT in Southeast Asia, from power in early 1979.

The rigid Maoism of the CPT leadership also alienated many of the students who had joined the insurgency after October 6, 1976.[9] At the time none of the CPT leaders had much charisma within the party. At least two of the student leaders of the *Sipsi tula* movement, Thirayut Boonmee and Seksan Prasertkul, who joined the party in the mid-1970s, might well have evolved into significant leaders if they had been encouraged by the CPT leadership and if conditions had been more conducive (see, in this connection, Wedel and Wedel 1987). Both were well educated and sought to adapt Marxist-Leninism to Thai intellectual predilections as well as to socioeconomic conditions. As Seksan wrote in 1975, "The theory of revolution is not ready-made theory. . . . This applies to revolutionaries in Thailand: they may learn the revolutionary ways of other countries, but they must keep in mind that every struggle and every situation has its own unique character" (quoted in Wedel and Wedel 1987, 147). Seksan and Thirayut were not, however, able to convert their reputations as leaders of the *Sipsi tula* movement into charismatic authority within the CPT.

Although Seksan and Thirayut and other students who joined the insurgency initially attempted to accept the discipline of the party and not question the CPT's line in order to contribute to the overthrow of the right-wing regime that took power in Bangkok after October 1976, they eventually found themselves in conflict with the leaders of the CPT. This conflict was dramatized in a film released in 2002 about Seksan's and Chiranan Pitpreecha's (then his wife) time with the CPT. "The Moonhunter," as the film was called in English, or "Sipsi Tula: Songkhram Prachachon" ("Fourteenth of October—Peoples' War") in Thai, culminates with the break that Seksan and Chiranan (as well as other student leaders such as Thirayut) made with the CPT in the early 1980s. This break was not only over ideology but also due to the strong negative reaction that many had to the excesses of the Khmer Rouge that they began to learn about after its ouster in early January 1979 (Wedel and Wedel 1987, 196).[10]

It must be added that the highly urbanized Sino-Thai Seksan and Thirayut as well as other former students who came from Bangkok had little, if any, firsthand understanding of conditions in the rural areas of Thailand. In this regard they were similar to the old leaders of the CPT who came primarily from Sino-Thai urban dwellers. Because the CPT leaders, old and new, lacked understanding of or empathy with the characteristics of the society and culture of the "peasants" for whom they claimed they were creating a revolution, they failed to lead a revolution that was "peasant" based, their rhetoric notwithstanding.

ISAN VILLAGE CULTURE AND THE FAILURE OF THE "PEASANT REVOLUTION"

Scott, in his analysis of the failure of uprisings of rural people in Southeast Asia who faced severe hardships in the wake of the Great Depression, stressed the necessity of examining the culture of rural people "to discover how much their moral universe diverges from that of the elite" (Scott 1976, 238–39). I would add in regard to Thailand that "elites" must be understood to include also the leadership of the Communist Party of Thailand. The CPT, like the Khmer Rouge in Cambodia, failed to understand or decided to reject the cultural foundations of rural society based on the traditions of Theravada Buddhism.

The center of rural society in northeastern Thailand, as it is in rural communities throughout the Theravada Buddhist world, is the temple-monastery (*wat* in both Lao and Thai). The *wat* is both the residence of members of the Buddhist sangha, that is, monks and novices, and the locus for communal rituals that bring members of village families (even if living far away) together. These rituals center on the offering of alms (Pali, *dana*; Lao and Thai, *thawai than*), consisting of the "requisites" of food, clothing, shelter, and medicine, to members of the Buddhist sangha. By observing the discipline (Pali, *vinaya*; Lao and Thai, *winai*), members of the sangha exemplify the dhamma, the teachings of the Buddha, and through their sermons they also instruct the laity in the dhamma. The sangha, thus, is essential for Buddhism to be perpetuated as a popular religion.

In northeastern Thailand, as elsewhere in Thailand, Laos, Burma, and Cambodia, it has long been the custom (probably since at least the fifteenth century) for a male to enter the sangha for at least a short time. Although in the past boys in the Northeast often entered the sangha as novices (*samanen*) in order to gain a basic education for literacy that had secular as well as religious significance, since the 1930s, with the establishment of government-sponsored compulsory public education, only a small number of boys spend any time as novices.[11] Most men, however, have ordained as a monk for at least one period of the "rains retreat" (Pali, *vassa*; Thai and Lao, *phansa*). The men of Ban Nong Tuen are, I believe, typical of men throughout rural northeastern Thailand. In a survey conducted in 2005, I found that approximately 60 percent of men who were twenty-five years of age and older had spent at least one *phansa* as a monk. There had been some decline since 1963 when I had found in a previous survey that approximately 70 percent of men twenty years of age and older had been monks for at least one *phansa*.[12]

Although few who became or become monks remain in the monkhood for life, there are, even if precise data are not available to demonstrate it, certainly more permanent monks who have come from northeastern villages than from any other sector of Thai society. The sangha in northeastern Thailand has been strongly influenced by the tradition of forest meditation that originated with Achan Man Bhuridatto Thera (1870–1949), a monk subsequently widely recognized as a Buddhist saint (*arhat*), that is, one who is very advanced on his way toward achieving *nibbana* (Sanskrit, nirvana), ultimate salvation (see Taylor 1993; Kamala 1997). Monks residing in the numerous forest monasteries (*wat pa*) in the Northeast—only a few are found in other regions—are widely respected by villagers as exemplifying the Buddhist ideal of detachment (*tat chai*, lit., "to cut off one's heart") from the desires of the world while still living in the world.

In the late twentieth century, forest monasteries have proliferated just as the forested areas of the Northeast have significantly diminished. In the late 1980s forest monks established a temporary residence in the forest of the village guardian spirit (*phi pu ta*) in Ban Nong Tuen, and in the 1990s another forest monk established a permanent forest monastery in what had formerly been the forested area where cremations had taken place but which had been abandoned when a new crematorium was built in the grounds of the village *wat*. This forest monk has led villagers in a reforestation project around the forest monastery. The forest monks in Ban Nong Tuen represented a new Buddhist environmentalism that is village based (see Taylor 1991). Forest monks (*phra pa*) provide a marked contrast with the "forest soldiers" (*thahan pa*) as the communist-led insurgents were known.

The CPT itself said little about the sangha other than criticizing rightist monks (de Beer 1978, 155). Its commitment to doing away with "the culture and education of the imperialists and feudalists" (152) and to eliminating superstitious practices (155) indicates that the CPT leaders considered the Buddhist traditions that were so important in the lives of villagers to be impediments to the revolution. While some villagers joined with or supported the insurgency because of their grievances, their worldview was radically different from that of the leaders of the CPT. Even though the CPT could attract some followers who had significant grievances against the Thai government, it could not lead a "peasant" revolution because it failed to articulate its critique of the class and power structure of Thailand within the worldview of the *chao ban*, the villagers on whose behalf it purported to act.

THE AMNESTY OF 1980

The end of the radical right-wing government headed by Tanin Kraivichien came not because the CPT succeeded in taking power, but because Tanin alienated many in the military leadership. Several generals who had direct experience of rural society through their involvement with counterinsurgency efforts came to recognize that without attending to the underlying causes of grievances among the rural population, the use of force alone would only make the situation worse. In an extraordinary assessment that in many ways echoed that of the CPT, General Chavalit Yongchaiyudh, one of these generals and a subsequent prime minister, said in a speech to Thai students in the United States:

> The conditions in rural society in Thailand is [sic] very distressing and I think all of you know it very well. You might have even seen the people delighted to receive only ten or twenty baht. What is even worse are all the "influences" which are deep rooted in the rural society. You may have seen them; if they are not happy with someone, that one may die, he may get killed.... If someone has no money, then he may get it from them at an exorbitant interest rate and after three or four years he has lost all his land. This is the real condition of oppression and exploitation in the rural areas. (quoted in translation in Suchit 1987, 69)

In 1977, General Kriangsak Chomanand, who had served with Thai troops posted to Korea, Laos, and Vietnam and who had had long experience in counterinsurgency in northern Thailand, where he had developed an understanding of the reasons why people joined an insurgency, led a coup against the Tanin government.[13] During the three years he served as prime minister, he proved to be very pragmatic, even entering into an agreement with China to allow aid to the Khmer Rouge, then fighting Vietnamese forces in return for China's stopping of support for communist insurgents in Thailand.[14] More significant was the shift of policy initiated by Kriangsak, supported by a group of younger military officers who became known as the "Young Turks," men who had experience in counterinsurgency and who supported a more open society (Chai-anan 1982). In September 1978 he granted amnesty to students who had been arrested or charged with communist subversion or lèse majesté after October 6, 1976. He also made a show of patronage towards the labor movement, and he eased restrictions that allowed the press once again to engage in criticism of public policies (see Girling 1981, 220).

In 1979, under Kriangsak's impetus, a new constitution was promulgated. This document was similar to the constitution of 1932, with the potential power of elected members of Parliament counterbalanced by additional representatives appointed by the military and the royal elite (Morell and Chai-anan 1981, 279). He himself demonstrated his commitment to allowing the populace as well as the elite to determine who wielded power by resigning as prime minister in 1980, telling Parliament that he "no longer felt he had the support of the public."[15]

It would be his successor, General Prem Tinsulanonda, then the commander-in-chief of the armed forces and the new favorite of the "Young Turks," who brought the CPT-led insurgency to an end with his promulgation in April 1980 of Ministerial Order No. 66/2523, "Policy of Struggle to Win Over Communism." The proclamation laid the foundation for a new political order.

The decree aimed at eliminating "the revolutionary situation" by combating the insurgency with political means rather than with force. Toward this end, the first two elements in the implementation of the policy stressed the necessity to change the conditions in the countryside that were leading people to join or support the insurgency. A "political offensive" was to be launched "to instill in the people's mind a recognition that this land is theirs to protect and preserve and that it is partly they who are the owners, rulers, and beneficiaries." Even more important, "social injustice must be eliminated at every level, from local to national levels. Corruption and malfeasance in the bureaucracy must be decisively prevented and suppressed. And all exploitation must be done away with and the security of the people's life and property provided" (quoted in translation in Suchit 1987, 91). Those who had joined the insurgency who took advantage of the amnesty were to be assisted "to enable them to make a proper start to their new life in society" (92). In practice, this meant not only that those who left the insurgency would not be prosecuted but also that many rural insurgents would be helped to resettle in areas where they could become farmers again.[16]

The significance of this decree cannot be underestimated. It was drafted by a number of "democratic soldiers," also known as the "Young Turks," who were then associated with the Internal Security Operations Command (ISOC). They included General Chavalit Yongchaiyudh, who in 1986 would become commander-in-chief of the army and subsequently would enter politics as the head of the New Aspiration Party (*Phak khwamwang mai*) that he founded. Most intriguing is the involvement of Prasert Sapsunthorn, an advisor to ISOC, who had formerly been one of the chief ideologues of the CPT (Suchit 1987, 14) and who is said to have been the architect of the army's new stance towards the insurgency (Kelly 1983).

The most immediate consequence of Prime Ministerial Order No. 66/2523 was the return to society of many in the erstwhile student movement who had "gone to the jungle." Some of these ex-CPT supporters became "cadres" in a new movement, that associated with the rise of non-governmental organizations (NGOs).

NON-GOVERNMENTAL ORGANIZATIONS: A NEW MEANS FOR RURAL EMPOWERMENT

The 1976 coup, if it had not been reversed, would have denied any future role in shaping policies to those representing the interests of non-elite people—farmers, laborers, environmentalists, proponents of social welfare and social justice, as well as parliamentarians. The 66/2523 decree, and a supplementary decree issued in 1983, had the effect of permitting the reestablishment of student, farmer, and labor organizations that had been banned after 1976 and the creation of new non-governmental organizations. More importantly, although it is doubtful that this was intended, the decree also sanctioned the expression of at least some grievances through public demonstrations and criticism in the press and in academic writings.

In the atmosphere of the new openness, many of those who had been or might have been attracted to the CPT organized and joined one or another of the rapidly proliferating non-governmental organizations (*ongkon ekachon* or *ongkon phatthana ekachon*, known in both Thai and English as NGOs) (Amara Pongsapich 1992).

Most NGOs trace their genealogy to the Foundation for Rural Reconstruction (*Munithi burana chonnabot*), better known in English as the Thailand Rural Reconstruction Movement (TRRM), founded in 1967 by Dr. Puey Ungpakorn, the highly respected economist who became rector of Thammasat University, a position he resigned from after the 1976 coup.[17] In the 1960s, Meechai Viravaidya, who had just recently returned from study in Australia, also founded the Population and Community Development Association of Thailand (PDA, *Samakhom phatthana prachakon lae chumchon*). TRRM became the prototype for the numerous NGOs whose purpose is to promote rural development by "strengthening the bargaining power of the rural poor and other disadvantaged groups to defend their interests not only in the short-run, but also in the long-run" (Jarin Boonmathya n.d., 2). PDA was founded initially to promote family planning and still continues to do so, but it later added more general rural development objectives. Closely related to these two are the NGOs that work with villagers to improve health conditions in rural areas. Following the 1973 revolution, a new type of NGO was created to focus attention on human rights issues. The Union of Civil Liberty (UCL, *Samakhom sitthi seriphap khong prachachon*), founded in 1973, became the prototype for this type of NGO. In the mid-1980s, yet another type of NGO emerged when some activists turned their attention to the growing problems caused by the rapid decline in forests. The prototype of the environmental NGO was the Project or Foundation for Ecological Recovery, better known in English as TERRA (Towards Ecological Recovery and Regional Alliance, *Khrongkan fuenfu niwet nai phumiphak maenam khong*).

After some uncertainty in the early 1980s about whether they would be allowed to organize, activists began to develop NGOs at a rapid pace in the mid-1980s. By 1988 there were nearly four hundred registered NGOs. In 1985 about one hundred of these organizations created the NGO Coordinating Committee on Rural Development (NGO-CORD).[18] In the early period of the NGO movement, those in NGOs were often depicted by right-wing elements as communists. It is true that some who joined NGOs between 1967 and 1976 had gone to the jungle after October 6 to join the CPT. Most in the movement, however, were inspired by a more diffuse democratic socialism. After the promulgation of Decree 66/2523, many of the resurrected and new NGOs found their ideological orientation in the "Buddhist socialism" of the famous scholar and practitioner, Buddhadasa Bhikkhu (1906–93).

Than (Venerable) Buddhadasa, a monk from Chaiya in Surat Thani Province in southern Thailand, gained increasing recognition from the 1950s on, particularly among the urban laity but also among villagers, for the way he situated Buddhist practice in everyday life.[19] His numerous sermons and writings as well as his "spiritual theaters" in Chaiya and Chiang Mai offered people the view that "*Nibbana* is in *samsara*," that is, that ultimate salvation (*nibbana*) is not to be attained through escape from the realm of sentient existence (*samsara*) but through cultivation of moral behavior and self-awareness while remaining within that realm. Because, he taught, the sources of *dukkha*, "suffering," are social, those who understand the truth of the Buddhist message (dhamma) must engage in service to society. This "social service is a kind of socialism, but not the kind associated with Communism" (Buddhadasa 1989, 173).

In the 1980s, a number of social activists translated the dhammic socialism preached by Than Buddhadasa into social action programs. Among the most well known of these activists are Sulak Sivaraksa and Prawase Wasi. Sulak, a prolific essayist and social critic, founded several NGOs, most importantly in 1980 the Thai Inter-religious Commission for Development. Dr. Prawase, a hematologist long affiliated with Siriraj Hospital, developed the village doctor movement in the early 1980s to train villagers to help themselves in health care. For this work, he received the Magsaysay Award in 1982. Both Sulak and Dr. Prawase spoke out to condemn those in the military and government who in their eyes have been corrupted by power. Although both Sulak and Prawase continued to be prominent, the leadership of the NGO movement was from the 1990s on significantly expanded.

Those in the movement, led by former CPT-supporters and others in the left-wing student movement, adopted the critique of social inequality from leftist ideology. Both leftist and Buddhist-based NGO workers shared, however, a common goal—namely, the empowerment of ordinary people so that their interests would be taken into account in the shaping of public policies. As the large majority of NGO workers were based in the Northeast, they tended to identify the ordinary people with the rural villagers of that region. The goal of empowerment was based on the premise that villagers should have the right to choose courses of action that would benefit themselves even if this meant challenging government regulations or the interests of powerful people backed by the state. The choices villagers actually made in the period after the 1980s were, however, not always in accord with what NGO workers expected them to do. This was a consequence of the new types of economic activity that many from the rural Northeast began to engage in.

7

ENTREPRENEURS, MIGRANTS, AND PROTESTORS:

Northeastern Thai Villagers Seek Development on Their Own Terms

The political upheavals of the 1960s and 1970s did not, as might have been expected, have serious negative consequences for the Thai economy.[1] Between 1960 and 1997 the economy of Thailand grew by an average of more than 7.6 percent per year.[2] "The years 1987 to 1990 stand out as a most remarkable period in Thai economic history. In these four year, the growth rate was at or above 10 per cent per year: double-digit growth. This made Thailand the fastest growing economy of the world at the time" (Jansen 1997, 1). The economic crisis of 1997 dramatically reversed the situation. In 1997 the rate of growth was −0.4 percent and in 1998 it was −8.0 percent (Bank of Thailand 1998). By 1999, however, a recovery was underway as the rate of growth was estimated at the end of the year to have been about 4 percent (*Bangkok Post 1999 Economic Review Year-End Edition*).

Although the primary beneficiaries of the growth of the Thai economy were those in Thailand's expanding urban middle class, the transformation of the economy also had profound effects on the rural society of Thailand, and arguably especially in the Northeast. The impact on the rural Northeast is summed up well by Glassman, who has written that "Thailand has not experienced rapid growth *in spite of* "inegalitarianism." Rather, rapid growth has occurred precisely because a highly internationalized state has positioned itself to achieve such growth through the very activities that lead to inegalitarianism and maldevelopment" (Glassman 2004, 8). Although economic growth opened new types of jobs for rural people, the marked unevenness of economic growth proved to be a major source of the dissatisfaction and increasing disaffection that rural northeasterners felt toward governments that paid little heed to their concerns.

Unlike earlier periods, rural northeasterners did not respond to their situation with passivity. On the contrary, the 1990s proved to be a watershed period for these people. Hundreds of thousands sought to better the economic conditions of their families through increased migration, not only to Bangkok and other areas of economic growth in Thailand but also in increasing numbers overseas. Others joined movements to challenge the Thai government's efforts to appropriate natural resources in the region—notably water and forests—for use by government and private enterprises that were not rooted in the Northeast. These movements, combined with the growing sophistication of migrants, laid the groundwork for a new national politics in the early twenty-first century.

A SMALL RURAL WORLD IN THE EARLY 1960s

I begin here by tracing how rural people have adapted to the developing economy of Thailand, with primary reference to the village of Ban Nong Tuen in Tambon Khwao, Muang District, Maha Sarakham Province where my wife, Jane, and I carried out long-term fieldwork. Our original fieldwork, conducted in 1963–64, coincided with the beginnings of what has been termed the "development era" (*samai kan phatthana*) in Thailand initiated during the premiership of Field Marshal Sarit Thanarat (1957–63). Through subsequent research in this village in the early 1980s and 2004–5, as well as numerous visits, the most recent being in 2011, I have been able to observe closely the socioeconomic changes that have occurred over nearly a half-century there. Ban Nong Tuen lies in the Isan rural heartland—the provinces of Khon Kaen, southern Udon, Kalasin, Maha Sarakham, Roi Et, Yasothon, western Ubon, northern Surin, Si Sa Ket, Buri Ram, Chaiyaphum, and northern Khorat. In this region the vast majority of people have long based their livelihood on the cultivation of glutinous rice in rain-fed fields. They traditionally supplemented their diet with fish caught in the Chi and Mun Rivers, but few in this central Isan region, unlike villagers living near the Mekong, depended primarily on fishing for their living. They also differ from villagers in the more hilly areas of the region—Loei, eastern Kalasin, Sakon Nakhon, and parts of Nakhon Phanom and Mukdahan—where lowland wet-rice cultivation is more difficult. Much of what I have documented for Ban Nong Tuen is very similar to what has occurred in the vast majority of rural communities in the heartland of the Northeast.[3]

In the early 1960s Ban Nong Tuen was a somewhat remote (from Bangkok) quiet rural community whose economy was nearly self-sufficient. The primary social unit of the village was a household which usually consisted of a husband and wife and their unmarried children, but which, following local custom, could also include a son-in-law, since men settled in the homes of their wives after marriage (Keyes 1975b). Like all rural communities in Northeast Thailand at the time, Ban Nong Tuen was a village of children and young people. Families lived in houses built of locally available materials, with the exception of the corrugated iron roofing used for many of the houses.

In our first household census, we found that there were 119 households in Ban Nong Tuen with a total of 700 people, or an average of 5.9 people per household. Like rural people throughout the Northeast at this time, Ban Nong Tuen villagers had experienced a significant increase in birth rates over the previous decades. For the decade prior to 1920 the rate of population growth for the whole of northeastern Thailand was approximately 2.0 percent per annum; it rose to 2.7 percent per year for the period of the 1920s and increased again to 3.3 percent for the decade between 1930 and the 1940s, the rate declined to 2.9 percent and then rose again to 3.1 percent in the 1950s and 3.4 percent in the 1960s.[4]

Villagers lived a life defined primarily by relations between kinsmen for producing the basic necessities of life and between fellow villagers for addressing moral and religious concerns. In 1963–64, villagers in Ban Nong Tuen were engaged primarily in producing for their own consumption. Rice was cultivated using labor-intensive methods. Water buffaloes were used for plowing and harrowing of fields. Rice seed was first planted in seedbeds and then the shoots were pulled up and transplanted in the fields. Supplementary foods included some garden crops, bamboo shoots and other plants, and insects collected from the forest. The most important source of protein in the diet came from fish that were either caught by men in nearby streams or reservoirs or raised in ponds.

Women not only worked alongside men in the fields but also assumed responsibility for converting raw food, especially rice, into cooked food for consumption. At the time most village women milled rice paddy through the use of a foot-operated mortar and pestle mill. The staple was glutinous rice that women steamed in the morning for consumption during the day and then prepared fresh again at night.

The village was not only self-sufficient in foodstuffs, but also in almost all goods used by householders. Women spun, wove, and designed almost all clothing for their families from cotton and silk raised locally. Men, in addition to their work in the fields and in fishing (and a very limited amount of hunting), devoted their energies primarily to producing utensils out of bamboo and rattan. They were also responsible for building and repairing houses.[5] Village houses were made out of wood from trees cut in the forest, woven bamboo, and leaves for roofing. Among the few items purchased by villagers were corrugated iron roofing and the iron used for metal tools. The latter was purchased by the four village blacksmiths who made almost all the metal tools used by villagers. In short, the economic characteristics of Ban Nong Tuen, like those of most Isan villages in the 1960s, exemplified what would today be termed a sufficiency economy.

These characteristics were closely interwoven with the religious characteristics of the village. The village was a "moral community" united by common worship of village spirits at the "navel of the village" (*bue ban*) and ancestral spirits (*phi pu ta*) who resided in their own forested area on the edge of the village.[6] Offerings were made annually at these shrines. More importantly, villagers were united in their support of the local *wat* or Buddhist temple-monastery. As already noted in the previous chapter, a substantial majority of village males ordained as monks at the age of twenty for at least three months and often for two "rains retreats" (*phansa*). Some boys also spent time as novices at

Plowing a rice field with water buffalo in Maha Sarakham Province, 1963
(Charles Keyes)

Harvesting rice with an "iron buffalo" in Maha Sarakham Province, 2005
(Charles Keyes)

the *wat*. The monks and novices—the members of the sangha—were central for the observance of the annual ritual cycle. This, together with the agricultural cycle, gave meaning to most villagers' lives from birth, through adolescence, courting, marriage, and concluding with ageing and death.

Neither Ban Nong Tuen nor any other village in Isan has ever been a totally self-contained world even in earlier times. A few village men, after having first been ordained in the local *wat,* had gone on to pursue religious studies at religious centers in the region or even in Bangkok. Since the 1930s government schools had been established in most Isan communities and by the 1960s nearly every child completed four years of primary education in a curriculum devised by the Ministry of Education in Bangkok. While some villagers, mainly women, lost effective literacy after a few years, others used their literacy and numeracy for productive ends, especially in interactions with the world beyond the village. Such interactions had been relatively few prior to the 1960s, but from the 1960s on, rural Isan would become increasingly incorporated into the Thai national eceonomy and the global economy.

VILLAGERS EMBRACE CAPITALISM

In the 1960s villagers wholeheartedly embraced a new orientation toward the world—namely development (*kan phatthana*).[7] This term, and what has come to be called the "development era" (*samai phatthana*) in Thailand, is usually associated with government policies introduced when Field Marshal Sarit Thanarat was the country's military dictator. There is no question but that some of the development programs introduced by the government from the 1960s on—especially road building, rural electrification, and support for industrialization—greatly facilitated growth not only of the national economy but also the economy of rural northeastern Thailand. It was, nonetheless, actions taken by villagers themselves that brought the radical changes to rural lifestyles that they came to associate with development.

Even in the early 1960s Ban Nong Tuen, like other Isan villages, was poor but not totally self-sufficient economically. Some cash was generated through the sale of rice, a few other agricultural and craft products, and through some wage labor outside of the village. Nonetheless, total cash income per household (not per capita) in 1963 was only about 2,800 baht, then equivalent to US$133. Cash was used not only for such items as metal tools and corrugated iron roofing, but also for health care, and especially to support the *wat* and the monks and novices. The main cash crops, while still bringing in very small amounts of income to villagers, were *khao chao*, the dominant variety of rice in Thailand but different from the glutinous rice consumed by villagers, along with tobacco and kenaf, a jute-like fiber crop. Rice was raised in paddy land while tobacco and kenaf were raised on land that was too high for paddy cultivation.

By the 1960s villagers were aware that the economy of Thailand, and especially of Bangkok, was booming and new job opportunities were being created for those who left their villages and traveled to Bangkok or other urban centers. An increasing number of young men from Ban Nong Tuen, like their counterparts throughout rural Isan, made their way to Bangkok to take up unskilled jobs for extended periods. In a survey carried out in 1963 I found that about 30 percent of men over the age of twenty from Ban Nong Tuen had spent several months or even years working in jobs in Bangkok. While most who engaged in migrant work in the 1960s remitted or saved little money, some became the first entrepreneurs of the village. Ngao Khamwicha, whose family we became a part of during our fieldwork, told us he had earned enough from working for six years in Bangkok to open the first shop and the only rice mill in the village.

Ngao had been able to save sufficient money for this investment by working for six years in a Sino-Thai noodle factory in Bangkok. By choosing to work the night shift and thereby avoiding the temptations of Bangkok nightlife, Ngao demonstrated that he knew how to *ot thon*, or to withstand desire for immediate gratification. His ability had been cultivated during his six years spent as a novice and then as a monk. In short, he embodied what I term a Buddhist version of the Protestant ethic.[8] This ethic would enable many northeasterners, both men and women, to improve the conditions of their lives and those of their families as they took advantage of the new opportunities created by an expanding Thai economy.

Villagers initially did not only seek work away from the farm as the means to generate cash income but from the mid-1960s into the 1980s also devoted increasing time and effort to expanding cash cropping. They, like other villagers in the Chi River watershed planted more land in such crops as kenaf, cassava, tobacco, and non-glutinous rice. As a consequence there was a significant reduction in forested land in Ban Nong Tuen, as there was throughout the Northeast. Some villagers, including several in Ban Nong Tuen, also expanded pig and cattle production. By the mid-1990s, however, most villagers had concluded that cash-cropping and husbandry of animals for the market were not a good use of their time and energy because the profits were so small. As a result, as the following graph demonstrates, they began to restrict their agricultural work to producing rice for home consumption.

By the late 1970s villagers had not only deemphasized cash cropping but had also begun to turn to other sources of income generation even in the village. The following table shows the dramatic changes in sources of cash income between 1963, 1980, and 2005.

FIG. 7.1 Percent of Households in Ban Nong Tuen Planting Crops Other Than Rice

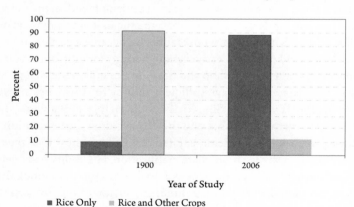

Year of Study

■ Rice Only   ■ Rice and Other Crops

TABLE 7.1 Sources of Cash Income, Ban Nong Tuen, Amphoe Muang, Maha Sarakham, 1963, 1980, and 2005

Sources of Household Income	% Households Gaining Income from Source		
	1963	1980	2005
Sale of cash crops	90.8	63.0	59.8
Sale of livestock	57.5	47.2	22.6
Sale of products from home enterprises	55.8	40.9	8.8
Modern enterprises (rice mills, convenience stores, repair shops, food stands)	2.5	7.1	10.9
Rentals and interest	5.8	6.3	0.4
Wage labor			
out of village (urban)	22.5	50.4	55.2
in village (farm)	4.2	26.0	17.6

Sources: Surveys carried out in 1963, 1980, and 2005

As this table shows, by the early twenty-first century non-agricultural work had become the most significant source of cash income for villagers. The money villagers brought back from urban or overseas work was increasingly invested not in agriculture but in small enterprises such as convenience stores, repair shops, and food stands as well as rice mills.

TABLE 7.2 Average Household Income in Current Baht, Ban Nong Tuen, Amphoe Muang, Maha Sarakham, 1963, 1980, and 2004

	1963	1980	2005
Baht	2,767.00	14,793	39,966
Baht value in dollars	20.80	20.63	39.00
Dollar equivalent	133.03	717.06	1024.77

Sources: Surveys carried out in 1963, 1980, and 2005

A combination of remittances from non-farm work and investments in the local economy led to a substantial increase in rural incomes in the Northeast by the first decade of the twenty-first century. As table 7.2 shows, average household cash income in current baht in Ban Nong

Tuen increased from 2,767 baht (US$133) in 1963 to 14,793 baht (US$717) in 1980 at a time when nearly half of all households were gaining some income from non-farm work. By 2005 the amount, again in current baht, had increased to nearly 40,000 baht (US$1,024).

For Maha Sarakham Province as a whole, in 2004 the average household income was 10,031 baht per month, which translates into about US$3,200 per year.[9] In another village in Maha Sarakham Province studied by Rigg and Salamanca (2009), median household income in 2008 was about 150,000 baht (approximately US$3,750), up from less than 50,000 baht in 1982/83. Similar figures are reported from a long-term study in the village of Don Deng, located fifteen kilometers south of Khon Kaen city. Studies there found that average household income had increased from 50,006 baht in 1981 to 148,328 baht in 2002 (Funahashi 2009).[10] For the Northeast as a whole the average was 9,333 baht/month or US$2,947/year. This compares to a national average in 2004 of 14,778 baht/month (about US$4,667/year) and a Bangkok average of 29,696 baht/month (about US$9,378/year).[11] Thus, although incomes of northeastern rural households, including those in Maha Sarakham, had clearly increased since 1980, they were still in 2004 only about a third of those of people in Bangkok.

Cash incomes of rural northeastern households increased dramatically over the latter part of the twentieth and early twenty-first centuries because of both the increased employment of village men in non-agricultural work and a similar increase in the employment of women. Rural women were able to seek jobs away from their home villages because they were significantly less bound to child rearing than they had been in the past.

One of the most profound changes—indeed a revolutionary change—in village life took place when Thai women, very much including village women, began to adopt birth control methods. In the early 1960s when Jane and I first carried out fieldwork in Ban Nong Tuen, it was a village of children as the following table shows.

The average family had four children and for the Northeast as a whole the population growth rate in the 1960s was 3.4 percent per annum.[12] In a survey carried out in 1963, I discovered that not only did no woman in the village practice any form of birth control; no one in the village had

FIG. 7.2 Population Distribution by Age, 1963

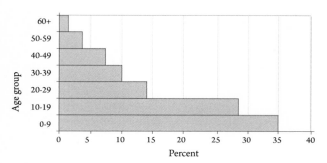

any knowledge of birth control methods other than illegal and dangerous abortions.[13]

By the late 1960s some birth control programs had been instituted in the Northeast by the Population and Community Development Association (PDA), albeit despite the official pro-natalist policy of the government. Word of the possibility of birth control began to spread among villagers, and in 1972, when I next spent some time in Ban Nong Tuen, I discovered that birth control practices had become quite popular.

In the survey made in 1980 in Ban Nong Tuen, I found that in 82 out of 127 households there was at least one woman practicing birth control or someone (usually a woman, but sometimes a man) who had been sterilized. That some form of birth control had been adopted by 64.5 percent of the households in the village is a remarkable figure, given the relatively young average age of the adult population. I also found that most younger couples whom we talked with had determined to have no more than four children and many had decided to have only two children. The adoption of birth control methods by many village women from the late 1960s through the 1970s had led to a significant decline—as the following chart shows—in the percentage of children in the total population of Ban Nong Tuen.

Ban Nong Tuen villagers were typical of villagers throughout northeastern Thailand in embracing family planning. Data from a Thai government source (Thailand, National Economic and Social

FIG 7.3 Population Distribution by Age, 1980

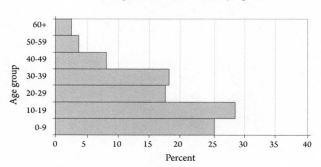

Development Board 1980) supports the finding that there was a marked decline in population growth rate in the Northeast during the last part of the 1970s. The population of the Northeast was estimated to have grown only 1.9 percent in the year from 1978 to 1979 and only 2.1 percent for the previous year (1977–78).

By the mid-1980s few women in Ban Nong Tuen, like rural women throughout the region, were having more than two children. In a survey carried out in 2005, 80 percent of women of childbearing age preferred to have two or fewer children. The dramatic change in population in Ban Nong Tuen can be seen in the following chart showing the population distribution in 2005.

FIG 7.4 Population Distribution by Age, 2005

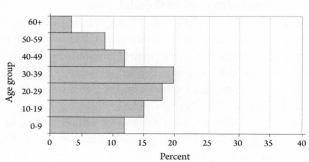

First grade in a village school, Maha Sarakham Province, 1963 (Jane Keyes)

First grade in a village school, Maha Sarakham Province, 2005 (Jane Keyes)

Village women came to understand that if they had too many children neither the children nor their parents could enjoy improved standards of living. By restricting family size village women sought to ensure that their children would have better lives because family resources could then be deployed to pay for higher education and thereby ensure that an adult child would be able to get a well-paying non-farm job, including those overseas. More education was especially valued as a prerequisite for better jobs, and more education required more resources.

For villagers to enter successfully into the capitalist economy of Thailand, they needed basic literacy in standard Thai and basic numeracy. These skills they acquired from government-sponsored primary schooling. Ban Nong Tuen, like most villages in northeastern Thailand, had had a government school since the mid-1930s, and since the late 1940s almost every villager had completed four years of compulsory primary education. From schooling villagers learned to see themselves as "Thai" even though culturally and linguistically they were "Lao." This identification together with competence in standard Thai and in the fundamentals of arithmetic learned in school enabled many villagers to interact in a Thai-dominated world (see Keyes 1991a).

By 1980 Ban Nong Tuen children were all educated up to the by then required primary level of the sixth grade and some continued on to even higher grades. Many villagers came to recognize that additional education was the primary means for gaining better non-agricultural jobs. As the following table shows based on my survey in the village, by 2005, 40 percent of all those currently attending school were studying at levels higher than the basic primary (*prathom*) grades.

TABLE 7.3 Ban Nong Tuen Students Currently in School
by Type of Schooling and Sex, 2005

Type of Schooling	Male	Female	Total
Kindergarten	10	16	26
Primary (*prathom* 1–6)	77	57	134
Secondary (*mathayom* 1–6)	33	27	60
Vocational	20	17	37
University/college	5	6	11
Total	145	123	268

Higher education not only made it possible for villagers to find better jobs; it also made villagers more knowledgeable about the wider world in which they now lived. Because Ban Nong Tuen was only about fifteen kilometers away from the town of Maha Sarakham, a town that had become a center for education in the Northeast, the high attendance of villagers at schools above the primary level was somewhat atypical for Isan villages. Since the 1980s, however, throughout the region increasing numbers of villagers have pursued education beyond the primary level.

MIGRANTS IN SEARCH OF DEVELOPMENT

The expansion of jobs in Thailand's non-agricultural economy increased rapidly from the 1950s on, especially in Bangkok. Faced with limited opportunities to increase incomes substantially through agricultural production, more and more villagers—including women as well as men—began to migrate to Bangkok in search of wage employment. Writing of rural Ubon Province in 1960, Klausner noted that "many villages have almost their entire youth group, from [ages] fourteen or fifteen to twenty, outside the village" (Klausner 1972, 105). As table 7.1 above shows, in the survey I carried out in 1963 in Ban Nong Tuen I found that a little less than a quarter (22.5 percent) of all villagers over the age of twenty had spent some time working in non-agricultural jobs, mainly in Bangkok. Most of those who had had such experience were in the age group 20–30 and all but one were males (Keyes 1966a, 313–14). By the 1970s at least half of the adult population of the Northeast, including both men and women, had migrated to or were in Bangkok for temporary employment (Fuller, Peerasit, Lightfoot, and Sawaeng 1983).[14] The percentage of villagers going to work outside the northeastern region continued to increase, and by the 1980s it had become a normal expectation that nearly every man and woman born in rural communities in Isan would spend from several months to several years working away from their home villages.

By the 1970s more and more young women as well as young men left their villages for extended periods, or even forever, to find work in Bangkok or elsewhere. As Mary Beth Mills has shown in her study of young women factory workers who came from another village in Maha Sarakham, these women were attracted not only by the possibility of adding to their family's income but by the chance to emulate urban women in "becoming modern" (*than samai*) (Mills 1997). In villagers' eyes, "development" increasingly came to mean acquiring the material goods—clothing, household furnishings, motorbikes, radios, televisions, and even houses—that they associated with urban rather than rural life. They found that only by working outside the village could they acquire sufficient money to become "modern" and "developed."

Although most northeastern village women still find work for extended periods in the vicinity of Bangkok, today some can now work in factories that have been recently established in the Northeast. In the 1990s the Population and Community Development Association (PDA), Thailand's largest non-government organization, began a project called T-BIRD, Thai Business Initiative in Rural Development, to encourage companies to establish factories in areas closer to the sources of labor than in the Bangkok area (Tasker 1994). In subsequent years, and especially in the period when Thaksin was prime minister in the early part of the twenty-first century, the government began to offer incentives through tax reductions and other ways to companies, many of them from Taiwan or Hong Kong, to establish factories upcountry. Many were set up in the Northeast. In 2005 in Maha Sarakham I learned from an interview with the provincial industrial officer that there were four major knitwear factories and one major fishnet factory that foreign companies had established in the province.[15] Women from Ban Nong Tuen worked at four of these factories. These new opportunities notwithstanding, village men and most young village women still were more likely to seek work in Bangkok than in the Northeast.

The significance of migration to Bangkok is indicated in statistics from a government survey carried out in 1996. The survey identified over a half million migrants from the Northeast living in the greater Bangkok Metropolitan Area, with northeasterners accounting for 65 percent of all migrants to the city. An additional 140,000 migrants from the Northeast were identified as living in the highly industrialized provinces of Nakhon Pathom, Samut Sakhon, Nonthaburi, and Samut Prakan located near Bangkok and another 60,000 were living in the

Village girl preparing thread
for weaving, Maha Sarakham
Province, 1964 (Jane Keyes)

Village girl working in a factory
in rural Maha Sarakham
Province, 2005 (Jane Keyes)

eastern seaboard provinces of Rayong, Chon Buri, and Chachoengsao, where port facilities and additional industries are located. The study also shows that while total male migrants exceeded female migrants in all three areas, female migrants exceeded male migrants in the age group from 15–24 years of age.[16]

In the 1970s men and a few women from rural northeastern Thailand began to be recruited for work outside of Thailand. Beginning in the late 1970s recruiters persuaded tens of thousands of men to take up job opportunities in Saudi Arabia and other Gulf States. These men found work primarily in construction and transportation. A much smaller number of women also went to the Middle East where they found work as domestics.[17] In 1982, there were over 100,000 guest workers from Thailand in Middle Eastern countries, the overwhelming majority of them men from northeastern rural communities.[18]

Because Saudi Arabia, which was the destination of the vast majority of Thai who worked in the Middle East, banned the import of Thai workers in the mid-1980s following still unresolved issues regarding the theft of jewelry from the Saudi Royal family and the murder of Saudi diplomats in Bangkok sent to investigate the theft,[19] Thai migration to the Middle East declined significantly from that time on. The first Gulf War led to a further sharp reduction in job opportunities in the Middle East. By the mid-1990s there were only about 20,000 Thai workers in the Middle East, over half of whom were working in Israel (Supang and Germershausen 2000, 9, table 1). Just as jobs began to dry up in the Middle East, however, even greater numbers became available in Taiwan and, to a lesser extent, Singapore and Japan (see Tsay 2001).[20] By the mid-1990s, Taiwan had become the major destination for northeasterners working overseas. In 1995 over 180,000 workers from Thailand, again the vast majority from the Northeast, were working in East Asian or Southeast Asian countries, with over two-thirds of these going to Taiwan (Supang and Germershausen 2000, 9, table 1; also see Kusol 2001).

Job opportunities in Taiwan have been particularly attractive to young men (aged 18–45) from Ban Nong Tuen. In September 2000 when I visited the village I learned that 40 to 50 villagers were currently working or had worked in Taiwan—a very high number, accounting for about 10 percent of the adult population of the village. From the survey carried out in the village in 2005, I found that 26 men from the village were on two- to three-year contracts to work in Taiwan. Another 34 men had already worked there.

Work overseas, in contrast to work in Bangkok, entails up-front investments and willingness to undergo hardships for a prolonged period of time. The typical Thai guest worker is a married village man who can afford the 70,000 baht or more demanded by recruiters for visas, transportation, and fees for the recruiters themselves.[21] They have to be willing to leave their families and forego many pleasures (this was especially true in the Middle East) for three or more years.

As Supang Chantavanich and Germershausen (2000, 7) observe, "the living conditions of overseas Thai workers are rather harsh, and there is a notable lack of welfare and protection." Yet, despite these conditions (which are well known to prospective migrants before they leave), the initial financial costs, and the strains on family relationships, many men still see working abroad as the only way in which they can acquire sufficient wealth to improve the living conditions of themselves and their families. The ability to *ot thon* or withstand desire for immediate gratification that I first observed in 1963–64 in the young village man who had saved enough from his work in Bangkok to open a shop and a rice mill clearly still continues to be a characteristic of many northeasterners who work for long periods away from their families and villages.

It is clear from the few statistics I have cited that migrating in search of non-farm work has become an experience that almost every villager in northeastern Thailand today undertakes at least once and often several times in his or her life. As Rigg and Salamanca (2009, 263–64) found in their own restudy of other villages in Maha Sarakham Province: "migration and mobility have come to be defining features of life and living in Northeast Thailand. Migration is not an aberration—as it is so often presented in policy documents and by officials—but part of the essence of the Northeast in social and economic terms." What is striking is that most migration is still circular. That is, migrants work for several

Villager in Maha Sarakham Province who used monies from working abroad to open a village motorcycle repair shop (Charles Keyes, 2005)

months or even many years and then return to their home villages. Even those who migrate permanently within Thailand (and rarely abroad) usually remit significant amounts of their earnings to their relatives back in their home communities.[22] Nonetheless, because members of households are often gone for extended periods from their home villages, households today transcend the locality of the traditional village; that is, "the household is increasingly defined by its spatial disaggregation" (Rigg and Salamanca 2009, 264). Nonetheless, most continue to identify as *chao ban*, villagers, with the referent now being a larger community of Isan people with whom they work and live.

Even though migration from rural areas such as northeastern Thailand bespeaks a marked inequality between those who control the means of production in the global economy and those whose labor is the foundation of this economy, migrants still are, as Mills observes in her study of women migrants from the Northeast to Bangkok, "conscious agents, making decisions and pursuing goals within—and, at times, despite—their difficult circumstances" (Mills 1999, 11). As she goes on to demonstrate for the rural female migrants with whom she worked, these goals are shaped by a desire to be "modern" (*than samai*).

Migration as practiced by northeastern villagers thus must be interpreted as indicating that most northeastern villagers have made "development" of their rural worlds a personal goal. This is apparent when one reflects on what the monies earned in non-farm employment in Thailand or abroad are used for in the villages from which the migrants come. My many return visits to the village of Ban Nong Tuen have given me a firsthand opportunity to observe the "development" that has come to the village from increased wealth, most of which has been generated from work outside the village.

Those households in Ban Nong Tuen with the largest amounts of disposable cash were either those with members employed outside the village or those that had generated incomes from enterprises that were originally set up from capital accumulated from work as migrants. Over the three decades from 1980 to 2010, the number of "modern" (*than samai*) houses in the village have multiplied. These are houses built in the style of suburban houses in Bangkok with two stories, each of them fully enclosed in contrast to the traditional open, wooden and bamboo northeastern house on stilts. The Ban Nong Tuen villagers who have built these new houses were following the precedent of villagers in many other communities in the Northeast who in the late 1970s and early 1980s began to erect modern houses that were called *ban Sa-u*, "Saudi houses," because the money to build them had been earned by northeastern Thai workers in Saudi Arabia or the Gulf States.

Ban Nong Tuen villagers, like their fellow Isan villagers, are also today conspicuous consumers of commercially produced goods. Since the 1980s most Ban Nong Tuen villagers have worn urban-style commercially manufactured clothing whereas in 1963–64 most wore clothing they produced themselves. Today most women use cosmetics, whereas few did in 1963–64. The styles of dress and housing and of consumption reflect, in part, the images villagers see everyday on the TVs that are in nearly every home. In addition to TVs, there are also many other expensive consumer items such as refrigerators, electric sewing machines, and even a few clothes washing machines and more recently computers. The most common expensive item, next to TVs, are motorcycles. In 1964 a friend who purchased the 50 cc moped that Jane and I had used during our fieldwork acquired the first motorcycle in the village; today nearly every household has at least one motorcycle.

Many of those who have acquired wealth from work outside the village have used some of it not for consumption but for investment in new local enterprises. Whereas in 1963–64 there had been only one very small shop and one rice mill in Ban Nong Tuen, today the many enterprises include food stalls, small restaurants, vehicle repair shops, tailoring shops, beauty shops, a bakery, convenience stores, as well as numerous rice mills. At the most patronized convenience store modeled on a 7-Eleven store, the most popular item for sale were cellphone cards used primarily for villagers to stay in contact with relatives working elsewhere in Thailand or abroad. The shops also sell all sorts of sundry consumer goods such as packaged foods, bottled drinks, medicines, small farm equipment, hardware, electrical goods, and some clothing. Several households own small trucks used for transporting goods or people to and from local markets. In addition to investing in local enterprises, some villagers in Ban Nong Tuen also invest in agriculture, purchasing small tractors or other equipment that they hire out. Others invest in a traditional form of wealth—namely cattle—albeit usually of a newer and more expensive breed.

As the houses and the many manifestations of participation in a commercial economy indicate, in Ban Nong Tuen villagers, like most of their fellow villagers throughout Isan, are no longer what they once were, namely "peasants." The term "peasant" or the Thai equivalent *chao na*, insofar as it is understood to mean people dependent primarily on subsistence-based production, is no longer appropriate for talking about people who have so patently embraced "development" or "progress" (*khwam charoen*). Ratana Tosakul Boonmathaya (1997, 238) has shown how villagers in rural Khon Kaen, like those in Ban Nong Tuen, committed themselves to the pursuit of progress that, in the words of an eighty-eight-year-old village man, has meant improvement in living conditions in his village. The achievement of such progress or development has come, as villagers in Ban Nong Tuen have discovered, not through remaining *chao na*, not even through planting commercial crops, but in leaving their villages to seek employment in places that have already been "developed."

What is particularly noteworthy is that most migrants, whether they work in Thailand or abroad, return to the village. If men or women leave before marriage, they may well end up marrying someone who is not from the village. Women who do so typically will bring their husbands to live with them in the village. Men (and some women) who leave after marriage see their work as essential in providing support for their families. Their incomes as well as remittances sent back before they return makes it possible for their families to have suburban-style homes and to have many consumer goods associated with the middle class.

Most of those born in Ban Nong Tuen who end up spending much, most, or even all of their lives away from the village, still continue to retain a sense of membership in a moral community that is manifest in the village. Today the *wat* in Ban Nong Tuen consists of entirely new structures—ordination hall (*bot*), ritual center (*wihan*), and residences for monks and novices (*kuti*)—that have entirely replaced those existing in the early 1960s. Almost all these new structures have been financed through merit-making rituals organized by villagers working in Bangkok or abroad. Some men return to the village to ordain at the *wat*, while more become lay followers after they retire. The village today has two monastic establishments. In addition to the traditional *wat*, since the 1980s one or two forest monks have found places to reside either in the forest associated with the *phi pu ta*, the tutelary spirit of the village, or in what was formerly the forested area, known as the *pacha*, "haunted forest," where cremations and burials took place.

While most visitors to the village today would first be impressed by its new houses and new enterprises, the forest monastery and the traditional *wat* stand as reminders that villagers do not only value capitalist development. They remain attached also to a different economy—one rooted in their Buddhist traditions. Although today Ban Nong Tuen, like most other villages in northeastern Thailand, is far from the nearly self-sufficient agricultural community we first encountered in the early 1960s, most people born there still retain a deep attachment to their village identity. Today, however, *ban hao*, "our village," also includes fellow northeasterners wherever they live.

The expansion of the "village" to subsume the Isan region also became manifest in region-wide protest movements that grew in significance in the 1960s. These movements were initially rooted in conflicts with the government over natural resources that were important for the livelihood of villagers in several parts of the region. Conflicts over forests and water would, however, morph into region-wide movements that had radical implications for the future of the Thai polity.

FOREST POLITICS

Beginning in the 1950s, Thailand's forests began to decline rapidly in size; between 1961 and 1985, lands formally classified as "forest" decreased from 53 percent to 29 percent (Hurst 1990, 46). The area of forested lands has since stabilized with the total being approximately what it was in 1985.[23] While the decline initially occurred because of rapid population expansion and a concomitant conversion of forests into fields for cultivation of rice and other crops, it was markedly intensified as commercial interests were given free rein by successive governments to cut teak and other tropical hardwoods for export and to create plantations of commercial trees (rubber, fruit, and, most recently, eucalyptus) and as large and medium dams were built to generate hydroelectric power for the expanding cities with their new industries.

As forests declined, governments in Thailand increased the authority of the state over remaining forestlands (Vandergeest and Peluso 1995; Peluso and Vandergeest 2001). From the late 1960s on, this authority began to be challenged by growing numbers of peoples who faced marked difficulties in pursuing livelihoods if they were denied access to lands, now officially recognized as under state control, even if they had long lived on these lands. State authority in the 1970s began to be further challenged by urban peoples who became concerned about environmental degradation. These challenges laid the groundwork for environmentalist movements in the 1980s.[24]

In the mid-1980s a Buddhist ecology movement involving a number of monks emerged. It has sought to promote a relationship to forests based on the premise that forests are a resource for communities that live among them rather than domains to be allocated for exploitation by commercial interests (see Chatsumarn 1990; Sulak 1990; Stott 1991; Taylor 1991, 1996; Sponsel and Poranee 1995; and Darlington, 2000, 2013). This movement has been most visibly identified by the practice of "ordaining" trees—that is, placing a monk's yellow robes around trees to mark them as belonging to a sacred realm that should be beyond human-made policies and laws.

Despite the fact that such highly symbolic actions served, through the media attention they received, to promote the idea that the use and conservation of forests is a moral concern, this idea was strongly resisted by the Royal Forestry Department (RFD). The department had been compelled to accept a ban in 1989 on logging instituted by the democratically elected government under Chatichai Choonhavan following devastating flooding that was determined to have been caused by the marked decline in forested areas. In 1991, this government was overthrown in a military coup led by General Suchinda Kraiprayoon. The Suchinda government appropriated the rhetoric of forest conservation but instituted a policy that had the opposite effect.

The program that came to be known by its initials in Thai as *Kho Cho Ko*[25] ostensibly aimed at resettling poor people who were living illegally in what were designated as "degraded forest reserves" on other land outside of these reserves. In fact, the real objective of the program was to ensure continued dominance of and exploitation of government-designated reserve forests by the "strategic group" that promoted the interests of a military and bureaucratic elite.[26] In 1991 and 1992, the military-led government moved aggressively to implement the program. What the military junta had not anticipated was that a significant "counter-strategic" group made up of the villagers who were to be displaced, backed by some NGOs and especially by some activist Buddhist monks, would strongly resist these efforts. The result was a series of conflicts that ended only in 1992 after the military junta was compelled by large urban protests to resign and the king appointed an interim government charged with returning power to a parliamentary government.

One of the most significant conflicts took place in the Dong Yai Forest located in southern Nakhon Ratchasima (Khorat) and Buri Ram Provinces in northeastern Thailand. Here, a well-respected monk, Phra Prachak Kuttajitto, had founded a forest monastery in support of long-standing claims by local villagers for the right to use lands in this recently designated forest reserve.[27] These villagers, backed by Phra Prachak, maintained that they were the true conservationists seeking to preserve the forest against the rapaciousness of timber companies and other interests striving to "develop" forest reserves for commercial purposes. From the government point of view, however, these villagers and Phra Prachak and his clerical associates were all deemed to have broken the law by encroaching on forest reserves.

The government overtly manipulated local sangha authorities to join them in insisting that Phra Prachak move his retreat. When he refused to comply, the state dropped all pretenses that the issue could be construed in religious terms. Instead, armed police were sent in to destroy the retreat and to evict Phra Prachak and his followers from the forest. Phra Prachak, deeply depressed by the situation, including lack of support from the sangha, decided to leave the monkhood. As a layman, he found himself even more vulnerable to an arbitrary use of state authority when he was charged with gambling and became the object of a nation-wide manhunt. Clearly, some elements representing the state sought to make an example of Prachak to demonstrate that he lacked any moral authority to challenge the state's control of the forest.[28]

While the resistance led by Prachak appeared to have failed, the broader resistance to the *Kho Cho Ko* program benefitted from the end of the military regime in Bangkok. The interim government headed by Anand Panyarachun that had been installed with the backing of King Bhumibol after the resignation of General Suchinda suspended the program because of the widespread protests against it. As Pye (2005, 218) concluded, "The lesson from *Khor Jor Kor* was that the grass-roots mobilisation and protests can win." This success was also more-or-less repeated in the case of protests against a dam planned and built under the jurisdiction of the Electricity Generating Authority of Thailand (EGAT), another Thai government agency that favored Bangkok-centered commercial interests over rural concerns.

"DAMMED" DEVELOPMENT

From 1965 on, beginning with the Nam Pong (Ubolrat) Dam, the government built a series of hydroelectric dams in the Northeast on the Chi and Mun Rivers or their tributaries. These dams represented an effort involving Thailand, Laos, Cambodia, and Vietnam (and later China) to use the Mekong River and its tributaries for economic development purposes. In Thailand, dams were seen primarily as the source of new hydroelectric power to enable the country to industrialize. A few dams were also seen as a means to improve irrigation, primarily for agro-business. Responsibility for planning for dam construction and use was divided between two agencies—the newly created Electrical Generating Authority of Thailand (*Kan faifa fai palit haeng prathet Thai*, better known in both English and Thai as EGAT) and the older Royal Irrigation Department. Both agencies were staffed primarily by technocrats who were recruited because of their presumed ability to design projects that would contribute to economic growth.

During the 1960s and 1970s when a number of dams were built in northeastern Thailand, some villagers living in riparian communities saw their lives dislocated by these projects yet found themselves powerless and voiceless to protest against the government (see Ingersoll n.d., 1969; Johnson 1982; also see Jerachone 1979). They had no choice but to comply with government orders to move from the areas flooded and to accept the meager compensation offered them for the losses of their lands and homes. Although these dam projects were ostensibly undertaken in part to improve irrigation for market-oriented agriculture, very few villagers in the Northeast ever realized economic benefits from them. In 1978/79 after most of the dams had been completed, only 7.2 percent of the cultivated land of the Northeast lay within irrigated areas (Thailand, National Economic and Social Development Board 1980).

Although the electricity generated from these projects was initially consumed almost entirely by users in Bangkok and the surrounding areas where new industries were being established, some was eventually utilized to provide rural electrification in Isan. In the late 1970s and early 1980s the government was successful in extending electricity to almost every village in the Northeast. Unfortunately, the implementation of this policy was sometimes marred by official arrogance, as I personally observed in 1980 when electricity was brought to Ban Nong Tuen. The EGAT official who came to the village to determine where poles carrying the lines for electricity should be placed was dressed in a long-sleeve white shirt and polished shoes that would have been more appropriate for an office in Bangkok. He constantly resorted to using a snifter to keep the village smells out of his nostrils. He ordered villagers to cut down a long row of old tamarind trees lining one side of the main village road. When villagers protested that these trees offered not only fruit but shade during the hot season, he retorted that the decision had already been made (presumably by him or his agency) that the poles must go on that side of the road. Villagers complied reluctantly, and their homes, like those throughout Isan, were soon linked to the national electrical grid.

Of all the protests by northeastern villagers against government-sponsored development projects, none has been so prolonged or attracted more attention than the protest against the Pak Mun Dam, located in Khong Chiam District, Ubon Ratchathani Province, on the Mun River about 5½ kilometers upstream from the confluence of the Mun and the Mekong. Although the protest might be interpreted as being anti-development, it actually entailed a more complex reaction to development.

Although the Pak Mun project was first proposed in the 1960s, it was not until 1985 that EGAT placed the Pak Mun project high on the agenda of its proposed projects. Even though by this time democratically elected governments had assumed much of the power of the state once controlled by the military, most leaders of the political parties were as strongly committed to promoting "development" predicated on industrialization as the military leaders before them had been. Rural people were seen primarily as the source of labor for new industries rather than as people whose ways of life should be maintained and fostered. By the late 1980s rural people in northeastern Thailand had, however, become considerably less compliant and more sophisticated than in the past. They found they could now turn to NGOs as well as to certain academics, some newspapers, and even a few elected representatives for support of their concerns.

The decision in 1989 by the government of General Chatichai Choonhawan to approve the building of the Pak Mun Dam generated significant protests and it remained a major focus of protests thereafter. In 1991, the World Bank granted a loan to the Thai government to build the dam after the bank concluded that adequate attention had been given to the environmental impact of the project—a position strongly contested by those who protested the dam being built. Despite large-scale protests by local villagers, NGOs, many academics, several newspapers, and international environmentalist groups, construction began on the dam in 1991 with the destruction of the Kaeng Ta Na Rapids. Construction was completed in 1995. Because protests continued throughout the construction phase, the government agreed to compensate those whose land was inundated and those whose livelihood as fishermen was seriously eroded once fish were unable to travel upstream from the Mekong. This compensation, however, was never deemed adequate by the displaced villagers involved, especially as it became apparent after the dam was built that the fish ladders associated with the dam were an almost total failure.

The economic crisis that began in Thailand in 1997 made the situation for those impacted by the dam even more dire, as many who had formerly found employment in urban areas returned to the ruined rural communities from which they had come. Worse yet, the government led by Chuan Leekpai and the Democrat Party that assumed office in the wake of this crisis reneged on a new compensation package for the displaced villagers that had been approved by the preceding government of General Chavalit Yongchaiyudh.

On March 23, 1999, more than three thousand rural people occupied the land next to the dam.[29] They founded a settlement they named Ban Mae Mun Man Yuen, the "village of the sustainable Mun River."[30] These villagers, affiliated with the Assembly of the Poor (*Samatcha khon chon*), a loosely organized coalition between rural people and some nongovernmental organizations (NGOs) opposed to the Pak Mun Dam and other government-sponsored development projects, protested against the maintenance of a hydroelectric dam that had caused them and their kinsmen serious economic hardships.[31] In May 2000, members of the settlement actually took over the dam. This action did not lead—as many thought it would—to the government moving in with force to evict the occupiers. On the contrary, it ushered in a prolonged public debate about the cost-benefits of projects such as the Pak Mun Dam.

Although the protestors initially demanded increased compensation for the loss of land and of livelihoods caused by the dam, after the occupation of the dam they shifted to calling for the dam to be decommissioned.

The Monument of the Poor at the Pak Mun Dam, Ubon (Charles Keyes, 2000)

The varieties of fish that were once plentiful in the Mun River but had seriously declined since the dam had been built would only return once the sluices were opened. Some also wanted to see a restoration of the ecology as it existed before the dam had been built. EGAT countered that the dam generated a significant amount of electricity that, if eliminated, would require an increase in electricity production by plants using oil. It also claimed that the fish ladders that had been built with the dam were adequate or could be modified to ensure an adequate flow of fish. Finally, they claimed that compensation had already been more than generous. EGAT was supported by the World Bank's Operations Evaluation Department that had concluded the previous year that the dam had been a success (Atiya Achakulwisut 2000). Local villagers and their NGO supporters, with the backing of the World Commission on Dams (WCD), continued to maintain that quite the opposite was true.[32]

In July 2000, following recommendations of a panel set up by the government to mediate the dispute between the protestors and EGAT, the sluice gates were opened temporarily (*Bangkok Post*, June 22 and July 7, 2000). Because the protestors realized they had won only a tactical victory, most of them left the protest village at Pak Mun to go to Bangkok where they joined other Assembly of the Poor protestors at a makeshift settlement near Government House (July 12, 2000). Here, they sought to keep up the pressure on the government.

In November 2000 the WCD report was released and, as anticipated, proved highly critical of EGAT and the World Bank. It found that that the dam had caused serious problems for people depending for fishing and agriculture on the Mun River. In anticipation of the release of the WCD report, the World Bank prepared a critique that rejected the WCD's findings. EGAT also rejected the findings. On November 21, 2000, "gangsters" attacked remnants of Ban Mae Mun Man Yuen and burned its houses. EGAT initially admitted responsibility for the attack, and then denied it (*Bangkok Post*, November 21, 2000). Over the ensuing two months, the protest was eclipsed by campaigns to elect a new parliament in January 2001. The opposition Thai Rak Thai (Thai Love Thai) Party of Thaksin Shinawatra gained an overwhelming majority of seats in northeastern Thailand, including all seats in Ubon Province. The very strong support given by northeastern villagers to Thaksin's party seemed to indicate that they believed that Thaksin would be more sensitive to the problems of the Northeast than Chuan Leekpai, the previous prime minister.

The Thaksin government did intervene to try to resolve the conflict. After some study, the government reached an agreement with the Assembly of the Poor that the sluice gates of the dam would be opened for four months during the rainy season, from June to October. Although EGAT resisted this agreement and some local villagers supported EGAT, the agency was compelled to comply with Thaksin's order to open the sluices. Meanwhile, two studies, one by Ubon Ratchathani University and the other by the National Economic and Social Development Board were undertaken to determine the relative costs and benefits of keeping the dam fully operative as EGAT advocated, shutting it down completely as some critics argued should be done, or allowing the sluices to be open for part of the year as the compromise called for (*Bangkok Post*, June 21, 2001). After the long debates about the dam, in 2003 EGAT agreed to open the gates of the dam for four months a year and in 2005, after considerable resistance on EGAT's part to implement this decision, the gates were supposed to be opened "permanently" for four months a year. Sombat Rasakul, in August 2005, wrote that it was the protests that finally compelled the government to implement this decision. "It may seem strange that the concrete monstrosity on the Moon River which cost the nation billions of baht was built just to let the water run freely. But this is the reality in a country where the right to public participation is never recognised by the government until the people demand it" (Sombat 2005).

In 2007, the government put in power by the military junta that removed Thaksin from power reversed the decision and ordered that the sluice gates be permanently closed. Prime Minister Surayud Chulanont informed a new group of protestors who came to Bangkok that "the decision was based on recommendations by the Internal Security Operations Command" (Subhatra 2007). Although protests resumed after the government led by Abhisit Vejjajiva and the Democrat Party came to power, this government also refused to open the sluice gates for more than four months a year (*The Nation*, August 18, 2011).

Chris Baker (2000, 8) wrote that the Assembly of the Poor with which the Pak Mun protestors were affiliated "is at heart a classic peasant struggle over rights to resources of land, water, and forests." In other words, the conflict over Pak Mun might be interpreted as one involving anti-development "peasants" against a pro-development state. Baker goes on, however, to say that the Assembly of the Poor "differs radically from peasant movements of earlier eras. Peasants are not what they were."

This conclusion foreshadowed new protests not just about Pak Mun but more fundamental questioning by northeastern villagers about the inequalities and injustices that have their roots in government-sponsored "development" policies. This new questioning re-surfaced with a vengeance in the period after the military junta relinquished power and a deeper political crisis emerged.

DEVELOPMENT: STATE OR PEOPLE CENTERED?

The development theory that became dominant in the 1950s and that was subsequently adopted by "developing countries" around the world was predicated on the assumption that through a combination of public and private investment in industry the economy would expand. A corollary of this theory was that while dislocations might occur in the process, the expansion of industry would eventually open sufficient new jobs for the majority of the society for its members to benefit from it. A second corollary was that only those with the necessary technical training and/or sufficient capital could make the decisions as to what investments to make. Associated with the adoption of the goal of pursuing "development," "a discourse was produced," as Escobar (1988, 429) has noted, "that instilled in all ['developing'] countries the need to pursue this goal, and provided for them the necessary categories and techniques to do so."

In Thailand both the government goal of guided "development" and the foundations for a new "development" discourse were enshrined in the first national development plan promulgated in 1962 under the government of military dictator Sarit Thanarat. Although since 1962 there have been a number of political upheavals with democratically elected governments in power for extended periods, this approach has remained the basis of development policy up to the present day. All Thai governments have seen their role as using public monies to invest in projects determined by technocrats such as those working for agencies like the Electricity Generating Authority of Thailand that will serve the needs of the industries in which private investment is being made (see Suehiro 1989; McVey 2000).

Marxist theory—or, rather, the Marxist theory adopted in states dominated by communist parties—shared with development theory the goal of industrialization but saw government rather than private firms as the source of investment capital. Although communist parties have often seen it as essential to their efforts to gain power to forge alliances with rural peoples, once in power they have instituted development policies that also favor industrial development. In Thailand, the Communist Party of Thailand attempted in the 1960s and 1970s to mount a challenge to the military-private capitalist alliance that has controlled the Thai state, but they failed dramatically. This failure was due, in part, as discussed in chapter 6, to the inability of the CPT to promote an alternative to the development ideology of the Thai state that was convincing and compelling to the peasantry, and especially to the peasantry in northeastern Thailand, where the party had its primary bases. In the wake of the collapse of the CPT in the early 1980s, however, there emerged new and eventually much more successful alternatives to Thai government development policies. These alternatives have been championed not only by non-governmental organizations working in alliance with academics, the press, and a few elected politicians, but more importantly, as I have tried to show, by local people acting individually and collectively.

To understand why some villagers joined the Assembly of the Poor in their protest against government-dictated development projects and many more villagers have chosen to become migrants in the search for work with greater economic benefits than those that can be realized through exclusive pursuit of agricultural occupations, we need to bring in the notion of *agency*. At root, this term points to the fact that the actions of individuals can never be explained entirely with reference to the social forces that impinge on them from the outside. However much these forces may shape the worlds in which an individual lives, the individual still makes choices on how to respond to, or react to, or resist these forces.

Rural northeastern Thai people today exercise their agency in very different conditions from those that prevailed prior to the middle of the twentieth century. Elson (1997) is correct in arguing that by the middle of the twentieth century rural people in Thailand as well as elsewhere in Southeast Asia were no longer "peasants" in the classic sense. That is, they were no longer producing primarily for their own needs with modest surpluses being used to meet social (primarily religious) needs and for taxes or rents levied by political lords or economic landlords. At the same time, Baker (2000) is correct in criticizing Elson for characterizing the "post-peasant" rural population of Thailand as engaged primarily in commercial farming. Although commercialization of farming has been very significant in central Thailand (see Arhiros and Moler 2000), this has not been the case in northeastern Thailand. Baker (2000, 9) has identified "the processes which finally integrated Thailand's smaller peasants, upland colonists, and rural labourers into a commercial economy" as being quite different from Elson's commercialization of rice farming. "The two main processes are the growth of rural–urban labour migrations, and the expansion of communication." Because of education, experience from travel, and information acquired from the now ubiquitous TV and radios in villages, both the villagers who have joined Assembly of the Poor and subsequent protests and those who engage in migration in search of labor have, in Baker's (2000, 11) terms, a "sophisticated appreciation of the wider (national) political economy."

This sophistication, or as I suggest in the concluding chapter, "cosmopolitanism," has made for much more nuanced choices on the part of those who remain rooted to one degree or another in rural communities in northeastern Thailand. As Ratana Tosakul Boonmathaya (1997) has shown in her study based on fieldwork in another part of the Northeast, rural people in northeastern Thailand have been strongly influenced by the discourse on "development" (*kan phatthana*) that originated with the Thai government. But they have reworked this discourse with reference to their own cultural traditions. Both the critique of development adopted so vigorously by the Assembly of the Poor protesters and the pursuit of development by migrants are grounded in a moral economy shaped by rural culture. In an article analyzing the hunger strike undertaken by Pak Mun protesters in July and August 2000, Atiya Achakulwisut and Vasana Chinvarakorn (2000), two reporters for the *Bangkok Post*, interviewed Sa-nguan Puebkhunthod, one of the protesters. Sa-nguan had been hospitalized after being beaten "by riot police for trespassing on Government House" when she joined the "desperate attempt by the Assembly of the Poor to air their grievances." Sa-nguan then joined other villagers in a hunger strike. The reporters quote her as follows:

"They trampled us as if we were not humans," the frail villager from Chaiyaphum said. "I saw a 70-year-old grandmother being hit until her head was bleeding." She pointed out that these incidents took place during last month's Buddhist holidays. Instead of religious ceremonies, July 16 and 17 witnessed a bloody confrontation between Isan villagers and the establishment as the former tried to break into Government House in a desperate bid to urge the Prime Minister Chuan Leekpai to help them. . . . "We didn't want to harm anybody. . . . The only thing we wanted to say was that our suffering is real, and that we were not hirelings trying to pressure the government," the mother of six said.

The reporters asked whether the hunger strike that Sa-nguan and other protesters joined violated Buddhist teachings. "To many Buddhists, fasting, which torments the body, could be considered a form of violence that should perhaps not be condoned." They turned to a highly respected Buddhist monk, Phra Paisal Visalo, about this apparent contradiction with the Buddhist ethic that moral action should lead to a reduction of *dukkha*, suffering, rather than increase it. They report that the monk told them, "Lord Buddha himself, in one of his previous incarnations, allowed himself to be eaten by a pair of tigers and thus prevented further killing. . . . The crux of the matter is the act must be done, not for one's own self-interest, but for the benefit of the public."

Atiya and Vasana also interviewed the Buddhist scholar Santisuk Sophonsiri who cast "the on-going strike as a battle against injustice, with the villagers seeking to wake society up from the malaise of spiritual lethargy. Santisuk viewed the poor as divine messengers who resort to using their own bodies to remind the public of the coming crisis—that disintegration of rural communities, and natural resources, will sooner or later entail the downfall of all" (all quotes from Atiya and Vasana 2000).

This view of the body as a vehicle for a moral statement contrasts strongly with the rational choice view that sees the body as a site of desire for goods and services that can be acquired only through the pursuit of "development." The one who fasts finds a model in the Buddhist monk whose life is supposed to exemplify the ability of humans to control desire (*tanha*) in the pursuit of *nibbana*, that is, transcendence of the world of suffering. Yet just as monks in the Theravadin tradition do not abandon the world in their pursuit of *nibbana*, so, too, those who protested against the Pak Mun Dam were not seeking to withdraw from the modern world to retreat within peasant communities. Mae Sompong Viengchan, another woman protestor who was interviewed at length, said that, "The villagers are not against development. We're against violating rights" (Sompong 2000, 49). In other words, the protests over forest policy and the Pak Mun Dam, and as Somchai Phatharananunth (2006) has shown, other protests in the Northeast, have been predicated on a moral critique of how government imposes an elitist and urban-centered approach to development on villagers for whom development is still shaped by their Buddhist-derived ideas of moral community.

For the vast majority of villagers in northeastern Thailand, like those in Ban Nong Tuen, whose new houses and other conspicuous changes in lifestyle indicate that they have pursued development with the intent of effecting improvements in their standards of living, Buddhist-derived ideas of a moral community still remain strong. This is evident in the many new temple buildings funded by villagers' donations throughout rural northeastern Thailand. It is evident in the fact that many village men in northeastern Thailand continue to enter the Buddhist sangha as novices and monks, and in the fact that both resident and non-resident villagers provide ongoing support for these local monks. The village *wat* continues, thus, to serve as a gyroscope for maintaining northeastern villages as moral communities.

Such "communities" have been expanded to include the region as a whole, as is evident in the significance of *phra thudong*, wandering ascetic monks who reside in forested areas, albeit these areas have shrunk significantly in the second half of the twentieth century. *Phra thudong*, following traditions of forest monasticism that have long been associated with the Northeast because of villagers' support of forest monks (see Kirsch 1967; Taylor 1993; and Kamala 1997), and influenced by the recent Buddhist ecological movement, have sought out those forests preserved because of traditional beliefs in spirits and converted them to Buddhist forest domains. Villagers have readily accepted this conversion not only because of the high respect they give to *phra thudong*, but also because they have been influenced by NGOs and others who have been highly critical of the consequences of deforestation. The support provided for forest monks such as those who have established themselves in Ban Nong Tuen constitutes an implicit critique of government efforts to exercise control over all forest lands for purposes of national development.

Such a criticism was explicitly manifest in Ban Nong Tuen in September 2000. When I visited the forest monastic dwelling located in the decommissioned "haunted forest," that is, the former cremation grounds, I was taken by a villager to a sign at the edge of the grove. The sign announced that a reforestation project was being undertaken in this area in a cooperative effort between villagers and faculty from a nearby university who had learned of Ban Nong Tuen from my writings.

The support offered by villagers for forest monks as well as for the *wat* that remain at the center of rural communities throughout the Northeast is indicative of the way in which local Buddhist culture has influenced northeastern villagers' understanding of "development." Northeastern villagers continue to find in their Buddhist traditions a compelling message for their lives, something that is no longer true of many urban dwellers who have little, if any, contact on a regular basis with Buddhist monks and rites. Villagers remain very much aware that whether they seek to gain monies through work outside of their communities or join in protests against actions by powerful representatives of government and business, such pursuits are conditioned by their moral understandings derived from community-centered Buddhism.

Even in an era of development, northeastern villagers and those who have permanently or temporarily migrated away from the village continue to maintain the value of belonging to a moral community that is summed up in the expression *ban hao*, "our village." Again, I quote from the eighty-eight-year-old Khon Kaen villager interviewed by Ratana (1997, 238), who said that in addition to improvements in living conditions, "progress is to retain our tradition and our community life, which means to preserve the spirit of sharing and helping each other. Also, it means to lead our lives according to Buddhist preaching. This is progress in our community life."

Just as northeastern villagers have reworked the discourse on "development" first introduced by the Thai government to be meaningful with reference to their own experiences, so too they have—as the protests over forests and the Pak Mun Dam clearly demonstrate— used their own understandings to challenge government policies they find inimical to their own interests, and especially those policies they recognize have been imposed on them without any consultation. Protests over access to local resources have, however, been the choice of only a small proportion of northeastern villagers. A far larger number are keenly aware that they cannot pursue "development" for themselves and their families by remaining tied to local means of production, especially agricultural production. They are, at the same time, very much aware that they are at a disadvantage compared with urban Thai to compete for well-paying non-farm jobs. While very large numbers have proven very willing to take relatively low-paying jobs not only in Thailand but also abroad, in doing so they have become even more conscious of the unequal world that is Thai society. Both protestors and migrants have continued to find that their "villages"—even when they are not permanently resident in them—still provide them with a positive sense of belonging to a moral community in contrast to the larger Thai society in which "development" has the primary meaning of having greater opportunity to consume more and more.

Just as northeastern villagers rejected the vision of the political order proffered by the Communist Party of Thailand, those who have acquired a new sense of being "villagers," who have become sophisticated or cosmopolitan because of their experiences working away from their natal communities for extended periods or through joining together to challenge the Thai state's encroachment on their traditional rights over natural resources, have also rejected the elite vision of "development." That rejection became increasingly manifest in a broad political movement in which "rural" northeasterners have asserted their right to shape the policies that can further their own morally based vision of development.

8

SILENT PEASANTS NO LONGER:
Northeastern Villagers and The
New Politics of Thailand

In the century between the 1902 millenarian movement known as the *phu mi bun* uprising and the 2001 election victory of the Thai Rak Thai Party led by Thaksin Shinawatra with strong support from northeastern and northern Thai voters, the peoples living in the rural areas of northeastern Thailand underwent a radical transformation. The transformation entailed the evolution of traditional peasants into Thai citizens with increasingly sophisticated understandings of their interest situations. These situations changed through time, but a constant theme remained the fraught relations between villagers and agencies of the Thai state. In the aftermath of the 1902 uprising, while rural people in northeastern Thailand became legal citizens of the nation-state of Thailand, they lacked and have until recently continued to lack the means whereby they could exercise their full rights as citizens. That is, they have found themselves constantly being subjected to what Agamben (2005) has termed a "state of exception," meaning, in this case, being subject to the rules of law and order instituted by the sovereign power of the Thai state without any right to question these rules.

The bureaucracy and military in Thailand were created without constitutional safeguards to ensure that they would be accountable to the populace, and these institutions have often intruded into the lives of villagers in negative ways. At various times in the modern history of Thailand efforts have been made to enshrine such safeguards in constitutions, beginning with the revolution of 1932, following which the first constitution was drafted. However, for the next eighty years each successive constitution was tossed aside following a military coup.

The principle of constitutional democracy, however, was never purged from Thai political life. The most successful recent attempt to ensure constitutional authority for the Thai political system took place in 1997. In 1992 a broad-based, but basically Bangkok-centered, movement successfully challenged the military's return to power. This movement, combined with the Asian economic crisis of 1997 that began with the collapse of the Thai baht, created conditions that made it possible for NGOs to push for a broadening of democracy that resulted in the crafting of a new constitution. Because this one entailed consultations with many different groups in the society, the 1997 constitution became known as the "people's constitution." The constitution specified that sovereign power "belongs to the Thai people" and is exercised by "the King as Head of State" "through the National Assembly, the Council of Ministers and the Courts in accordance with the provisions of the Constitution."[1] In short, this constitution appeared to be the final realization of the vision of parliamentary democracy first espoused by those who had overthrown the absolute monarchy in 1932. There is no question but that it further facilitated the development of politics based on electoral competition rather than on the dictums of the military or bureaucracy. The political empowerment of ordinary people—including those with roots in the rural countryside of northeastern Thailand— made possible the rise in the early twenty-first century of Thaksin Shinawtra, the most successful populist politician in modern Thailand.

THAKSIN AND THE EMPOWERMENT OF RURAL PEOPLE

As Pasuk Phongpaichit and Baker (2009, 226) in their definitive biography of Thaksin have said, "Since Thailand began to flirt with democratic policies over seven decades earlier, no politician had dominated the public life of the nation in the same manner." The scion of a Sino-Thai merchant family from Chiang Mai, Thaksin's first career was in the Royal Thai Police. He then turned to business and became successful in telecommunications, his ventures eventually becoming subsumed under the Shin Corporation. In 1994 he entered politics, first as a member of the Palang Dhamma ("Power of the Buddha's Teachings") Party headed by Chamlong Srimuang, a former general turned politician who had been elected mayor of Bangkok and who had assumed the leadership of the 1992 revolt against military rule. This was an unusual alliance as Thaksin was not a member of the Santi Asoke sect with which Chamlong was closely associated; Chamlong would later turn against Thaksin for his alleged corruption and publicly express regret that he had ever been aligned politically with him.[2] Chamlong went on to become a leader of the anti-Thaksin People's Alliance for Democracy and in this role would become deeply antagonistic to the populist politics that under Thaksin empowered northeasterners and northerners.

In 1998 Thaksin founded the Thai Rak Thai (Thai Love Thai) Party (TRT), a party that itself or in its new avatars as Phalang Prachachon (People's Power) Party and then as the Pheu Thai (For Thai) Party has dominated Thai electoral politics for over a decade. Thaksin's first government, formed after the TRT succeeded in gaining the most seats in Parliament in the 2001 election, initiated several populist policies that were subsequently to become the hallmark of the party. By 2004 Thaksin had put into place a number of such policies, with debt alleviation, the 30-baht health scheme, and the million baht fund for loans in every village being among the most significant and especially important for those living in rural communities. By the time of the next (2005) election, Thaksin had acquired a reputation among rural people, especially in the Northeast and North, surpassing that of any other political leader.

At the time of the February 2005 election Jane and I were engaged in a restudy of Ban Nong Tuen. We observed the enthusiastic turnout for the election, with many villagers returning to vote from working in Bangkok and elsewhere in Thailand; some of these returnees traveled in Bangkok taxis. After the landslide victory of Thai Rak Thai in this election, we were told by several villagers whom we interviewed that— to paraphrase their views—in the past politics were always controlled by people in Bangkok; today they could see that the votes of ordinary villagers had helped elect a government.

Election poster for a Thai Rak Thai candidate associated with Thaksin Shinawatra in a village in Maha Sarakham Province (Charles Keyes, 2001)

Villager voting in Maha Sarakham Province (Charles Keyes, 2005)

Like some other populist political figures—for example, Juan Perón in Argentina and Hugo Chavez in Venezuela—Thaksin clearly took advantage of his power.[3] There is little question but that he used his power to benefit himself, his family, and cronies financially and to run roughshod over human rights in his war on drugs that had led to a large number of extrajudicial killings. He also not only failed to contain a growing insurgency in the Malay area of southern Thailand but also made the situation much worse by deploying excessive force in seeking to suppress the insurgents. In the end, however, it was the suspicion that Thaksin was challenging the charisma of the king that proved the most critical for fueling the growing opposition to him. The king himself in his birthday speech in December 2003 warned Thaksin to heed criticism (Pasuk and Baker 2009, 228). From at least this point on, whisperings about Thaksin seeking to supplant the king in charismatic authority began to grow in pro-royalist circles.

At the end of 2005, Chamlong Srimuang, who since abandoning party politics had become best known as the lay leader of the Santi Asoke fundamentalist Buddhist movement, together with the media tycoon Sondhi Limthongkul, launched a protest movement to seek to force Thaksin's ouster from office. This movement was christened the People's Alliance for Democracy (*Phanthamit prachachon phuea prachathipatai*), or PAD for short, and its followers came to be known as the "Yellow Shirts" (*Suea lueang*) because they adopted for their signature dress the color associated with the day of birth of the king (Monday). The Yellow Shirts drew their primary support from the Bangkok middle class and the military, royal, and bureaucratic elites. They even gained some support from the labor unions for workers in government-owned industries who were very concerned about Thaksin's proposed privatization of these industries as well as from some NGOs concerned about the Thaksin government's violation of human rights. Because their main support was primarily from among the urban middle and upper classes, the Yellow Shirts were deeply suspicious and often hostile to the people of the rural areas who comprised the base for Thaksin's electoral appeal.

During the period from late 2005 through 2006, the Yellow Shirts staged almost continuous demonstrations against the Thaksin government. In September 2006, the leaders of the military, backed by advisers to the king, decided to intervene and staged a coup while Thaksin was out of the country. The images in the media following the coup, with people in Bangkok offering flowers and welcoming the military forces, suggested that the coup was widely accepted. In retrospect those welcoming the coup were primarily from among Bangkok's middle class—that is, from among those who supported the PAD's challenge to Thaksin. What was not evident in the reports of the media at the time was the very different view held not only by people in northeastern and northern Thailand but also by many in the urban working class, most of whom had roots in the rural Northeast.

THE RED SHIRTS

By the end of 2006 opposition to the military takeover began to be organized, most significantly by a group calling itself the United Front for Democracy Against Dictatorship (*Naeo ruam prachathipatai totan phadetkan haeng chat*). The UDD would subsequently become better known as the Red Shirts (*Suea daeng*), signified in the color of shirts and jackets that members wore. The Red Shirts drew their support from northeastern and northern Thailand and from the working class in Bangkok, most of whom had roots in the rural Northeast. This alliance perpetuated one that had formed the basis for the electoral support of the Thai Rak Thai Party and its successors.[4]

The military junta that took power in September 2006 threw out the 1997 constitution and oversaw the writing of a new one designed to constrict the power of an elected parliament. On August 20, 2007, the electorate in Thailand was asked to vote on whether or not to adopt this new charter. Although the referendum passed with 57 percent of the total vote, the vote also demonstrated the "limits of ideological domination"[5] with 44 percent of the total population of the country not going to the polls and, most notably, with 62 percent of the population of northeastern Thailand and a substantial majority of northerners voting against this military-backed revised social contract.[6] This dissent reflected the very different view of what constituted the basis of political legitimacy held by northeasterners and northerners as compared with the view of supporters of the new constitution.

In December 2007 a new election for Parliament under the authority of the new constitution was held and to the shock of the Yellow Shirts, the junta, and the outgoing government, the People's Power Party or Phak Palang Prachachon, the successor to Thai Rak Thai, won the greatest number of seats and was able to form a government with Samak Sundaravej as prime minister. Such a government was not acceptable to the Yellow Shirts and their backers in the military, bureaucracy, and palace. Legal actions led to Samak being forced to resign and the People's Power Party to be disestablished. A new successor party to Thai Rak Thai, the Pheu Thai Party, still commanded sufficient seats to form a government under Somchai Wongsawat, but this government was allowed to have only a very brief existence.

Throughout 2008 the Yellow Shirts staged increasingly disruptive protests against what were claimed to be governments headed by Thaksin's surrogates. These protests culminated in the PAD takeover of Bangkok's airports on November 28, 2008. Yellow Shirt pressure together with a number of problematic judicial actions paved the way for the Democrat Party, the largest anti-Thaksin party in Parliament, to form a new government at the end of 2008. This government, led by Abhisit Vejjajiva, would remain in office until new elections were held on July 3, 2011.

There can be no question but that the success of the extra-parliamentary Yellow Shirt protests was a stimulus to the Red Shirt movement. If free elections could be held, the Red Shirt leaders said, then the people's will would result in the formation of a democratic government organized by the Pheu Thai Party. Arguing that the Abhisit government came to power through non-democratic means, beginning in 2009 the Red Shirts started mobilizing to pressure the Abhisit government to resign and call new elections. While the Red Shirts had significant support in northern Thailand, most of those who joined the Red Shirt rallies in Bangkok in 2009–11 were from the Northeast or from among migrant workers from the Northeast working and living in and around Bangkok.

The first significant anti-coup protest took place in April 2009. Protestors gathered first in Pattaya where an ASEAN summit was to be held. Taxis driven by Red Shirt supporters blocked several prime ministers (from China, New Zealand, Japan, and South Korea) from leaving their hotels and then protestors stormed the hotel where the conference was to be held. An embarrassed Abhisit government felt compelled to cancel the summit. The protest then shifted to Bangkok, where thousands of protestors had gathered. These protests became violent, with protestors confronting security forces with an improvised arsenal that included slingshots as well as guns, and the security forces using tear gas and live ammunition. Although the government was able to restore order by late April, the Red Shirts retreated only to prepare more systematically for future challenges to what they considered an illegitimate government.

On March 12, 2010, tens of thousands of Red Shirts once again began streaming into Bangkok, most of them again coming from the rural Northeast; within the city the size of the protests waxed and waned as tens of thousands of workers joined after work hours. The protestors demanded that the Thai government headed by Prime Minister Abhisit and his Democrat Party dissolve Parliament and set a date for a new election. A few days later, on March 19, another event took place a long way from Bangkok in an agricultural area in southern Israel. There a worker recruited from Thailand was killed by a rocket fired from the Gaza strip. Although this story was given only limited attention in the Thai press, *The Nation*, a Thai English-language paper, reported that the Thai who died was one of thirty thousand Thai working in Israel.[7] Although these two events—demonstrations on the streets of Bangkok and the death of a Thai migrant worker in Israel—may seem totally unconnected, they were in fact inextricably connected.

Thai workers in Israel, like the protestors in Bangkok, are also overwhelmingly from northeastern Thailand. That literally millions of people born in rural communities in northeastern Thailand in the late twentieth and early twenty-first centuries joined the global labor force working not only in Bangkok, but in the Gulf States, Israel, Taiwan, Singapore, Japan, and even in Europe and North America makes such people very different from the images that most middle-class Bangkokians hold of them. Because Isan villagers have become workers in a global labor system, they can been seen as cosmopolitans (*khon mi khwam ru kiaokap thua lok*), not simply as traditional rice farmers, even though most still retain their identity as "villagers" (*chao ban*).[8]

Despite the fact that the Red Shirts, after having moved in mid-April 2010 from their original location near central government offices to Ratchaprasong/Silom in the central business district, were seriously disrupting normal life in the city, the Abhisit government delayed using significant force to disperse them. One reason for this appears to be the fear that doing so would result in even more bloodshed than had occurred on April 10, when a violent confrontation first took place. The government was reported to have also feared that it could not depend entirely on the security forces, as many army recruits had roots in northeastern villages and at least some in the police were loyal to Thaksin, a former police officer. By mid-May, however, military units that the Abhisit government could depend on had been brought in to clear the Red Shirt protestors from the central business district.

The Thai forces moved on the Red Shirts in Ratchaprasong on May 19, 2010. After the Red Shirt leaders surrendered, some of the women and children at the protest site took refuge in nearby Wat Pathumwanaram. Six people, including a nurse, were shot dead at the *wat*. With these deaths, the total number of those killed in the conflict between April 10 and May 19 was eventually pegged at ninety-two.[9] Of these, eleven were soldiers and the rest were civilians.[10] The total number injured was at least eighteen hundred, by far the majority of them civilians, and the civilians, in turn, were overwhelmingly Red Shirt supporters. As of 2013, even with a Pheu Thai government in power, investigations into the causes of the deaths and injuries have been stymied by the non-cooperation or stalling tactics of military leaders.

After the military moved to end the protest rally, a number of hard core followers of the Red Shirts, some apparently following advance planning, set fire to several buildings in the central business district, with the most serious damage being the destruction of the Central World Plaza of Bangkok, the second-largest shopping mall in Southeast Asia. Moreover, some Red Shirts mobilized followers upcountry to attack and burn provincial office buildings in Udon, Khon Kaen, Mukdahan, and Ubon in northeastern Thailand.

The army, the Ministry of Interior, and the metropolitan police were able to reestablish order throughout the country. The aftermath of the bloody events of April–May 2010 in some ways echoed the forceful repression of the *phu mi bun* uprising a century earlier. As in 1902, the leaders of the protests in 2010 were arrested and as in 1902, the followers of the 2010 movement went back to their villages, although in the more recent case they were sent home on government-arranged trains and buses. The outcome of the end of the protests in 2010 was, however, very different from the suppression of the 1902 uprising. The primary reason lies in the fact that the 2010 protestors were not "ignorant" peasants, but were Thai citizens with sophisticated understandings of rights and justice.

NORTHEASTERN THAI "RURAL" SOCIETY: IMAGES AND REALITY

In 1948, Phya (Phraya) Anuman Rajadhon (also known by his pen name Sathian Koset), the foremost scholar of Thai culture of his time, published "The Life of the Thai Farmer" (*Chiwit chao na*). This was one of the earliest accounts I have found of rural life in northeastern Thailand.[11] Phya Anuman (born in 1888) was the son of a Chinese migrant to Thailand and, thus, had much in common with the Sino-Thai who subsequently became the dominant element in the Bangkok middle class. His account of village life in the northeastern province of Khorat, based on the notes of a monk from that province (Anuman 1961, 3), offers the perspective, thus, of an urban Sino-Thai who himself lacked any roots in the Thai countryside. It was, nonetheless, an account that foreshadowed anthropological research that attempts to present the rural Isan world from the native point of view.

I had read "Life of the Thai Farmer" before embarking in 1962 on my first ethnographic research in northeastern Thailand.[12] Rereading it after the events of 2010 I was struck by the continuity between the image of rural northeasterners presented there and the images still held by many Bangkok middle-class people today.

Life in the city [*nai muang*] and life in the country [*nok muang*] offer sharp contrasts. One is close to nature; the other is remote from nature. One is the source of food and health; the other is a place where people gather to share their food and disease germs. To say only this much makes it appear that in the city there is only evil [*khon leo*], not to be compared with the country. Actually if one were to speak of the good points, the city has many advantages over the country, because the center of progress [*khwam charoen*] is the city. If this progress spreads to the country in appropriate proportions, one can say that the nation, both city and country, achieves prosperity. If the city is selfish to too great a degree—seeking to accumulate wealth and provide entertainment and comfort for itself, becoming remote from nature and never glancing toward the country—the progress of the city will be like a light that flares up only for a moment and then goes out for lack of fuel, that is to say, food. (Anuman 1961, 7; Thai words from Anuman Rajadhon 1965, 129–30)

To summarize, people living in the outer areas (*nok muang*)—that is the rural areas—make their living from agriculture, and while their work is essential for the people of the city (*nai muang*) and while their proximity to nature has its benefits, the country people (*khon bannok*) lack "progress" (*khwam charoen*). As I have shown above with primary reference to the village of Ban Nong Tuen, the view of Isan villagers as living as peasants outside the world of urban dwellers may have been true a half century or more ago, but it has not been true for at least several decades.

By the late twentieth or early twenty-first century most people born in villages in northeastern Thailand, like those in Ban Nong Tuen, were far more dependent on cash income from work outside the village or from local enterprises such as shops, rice mills, vehicle repair shops, cafes, and food stands that had been started with capital from work outside their natal villages than they were on the sale of agricultural products. As a consequence of work experience in Bangkok, elsewhere in Thailand, or abroad, together with access to information gained through new media, those born in villages in northeastern Thailand have come to see themselves as belonging to much larger worlds than those defined by the perimeters of their home communities.

Despite this, most continue to identify as villagers and even as agriculturalists. Maureen Hickey, in her dissertation on Bangkok taxi drivers (Hickey 2010), recorded a conversation with a long-time driver who was born—like many Bangkok taxi drivers—in a village in Roi Et Province in the Northeast. He told her that although he makes his living as a taxi driver, he does not identify as one. Instead, he said, "I am a villager [chao baan]. I am a farmer [chao naa]" (Hickey 2010, 170). Such identities are embraced by many of those born in villages in northeastern Thailand even if they have migrated temporarily or permanently to work in Bangkok or even in as distant a place as Israel where the Thai worker mentioned above was killed.[13]

Such migrants remain "farmers" because they often return home to assist with farming either for short periods or for longer ones once they "retire" from off-farm work. Migrants who are kinsmen or from the same village may reside together in Bangkok or overseas, retaining ties with those in their home village through remittances and even receiving support from those in these communities. In 2006 in Bangkok I had a conversation with a taxi driver who told me that he was one of four siblings, two women and two men (including himself). The two men and husband of one of the women were in a taxi cooperative and they and their families had apartments close together. The remaining members of the family maintained their home farm where they produced—with some periodic assistance from the other siblings—enough rice to supply all family members both in the village and in Bangkok.

As I found in a survey conducted in Ban Nong Tuen in 2005, by that date no family any longer produced rice to sell; rather, family members consumed all that they produced. This mode of what I call "social insurance" agriculture entailed much less labor than had traditional rice farming. Instead of using water buffaloes for harrowing and plowing fields, small hand-operated Japanese-made tractors or, in some cases, larger rented tractors were being used. Fields were now seeded by the broadcast method rather than by the more labor-intensive transplanting method that had been used traditionally. Most families also hired equipment for harvesting from one or another village owner rather than doing this work by hand. The money needed to carry out these new modes of rice production came primarily from the earnings of family members who worked outside the village.

I was struck in looking at videos of the Red Shirt demonstrators (most of whom came from northeastern Thailand) in Bangkok in March and early April 2010—that is until the violence began on April 10— by how similar the gatherings were to Isan temple fairs (*ngan wat*).[14] The music being played at these demonstrations was primarily Isan "country-Western" (*luk thung*) style music with roots in traditional *molam*. The demonstrations brought the northeastern village first to the administrative centers of Bangkok, and then to the economic centers.

The cosmopolitan nature of rural northeasterners is not understood or, if it is understood, not appreciated by those in Bangkok who still assume that "rural" people have (or should have) the same characteristics of subsistence-based agriculture that Phya Anuman described a half century ago. Images generated from this assumption have been incorporated into many movies, TV programs, and newspaper articles ever since. Unlike Phya Anuman, these more recent depictions lack his sensitivity to the native point of view, that is, to understanding the reality of the northeastern "village" as actually experienced by those who live in it.

Monks at a Red Shirt protest, May 2010 (reproduced by permission from EPA)

A somewhat benign view of villagers as bound by traditional peasant values is presented in a glossy publication issued in 2011 by the Abhisit government. The booklet is entitled *Khit pho di* (lit., Thinking, Sufficient, Good), which is glossed in the book as *chumchon ruam phalang khit, rop ru mosom pho praman, phuea chiwit thi di yangyuen*—"thinking of cooperative community labor, knowing what is modest and appropriate, so the good life is sustainable" (emphasis in original). The booklet contains a number of stories that illustrate how villagers have followed the king's philosophy of sufficiency economy in local cooperative efforts. While the stories are of real people, this booklet presents rural society as many urban people would like it to be, not as it really is (Thailand, Samnak nayok ratthamontri 2011).[15]

The post 2006-coup government made "sufficiency economy" the basis for government policies towards the rural peoples of the country. As Walker observes: "The mismatch between sufficiency economy rhetoric and local economic practice suggests that the current preoccupation with sufficiency economy may not really reflect a concern with rural development at all" (Walker 2010, 260). Instead, he concludes: "the primary objective of the sufficiency economy campaign was to publicly construct a moral connection between royal virtue, the sufficiency economy philosophy and the new political regime in which electoral power would be constrained" (261). Some advocates of the moral basis of power consider the Red Shirt push to make electoral power be the basis for the polity as rooted in greed and/or ignorance.

In late 2009 Dr. Chirmsak Pinthong, professor in the Faculty of Economics at Thammasat University, a former senator and a member of the commission that drafted the post-coup constitution, published in the Thai newspaper *Naeo Na* an influential op-ed piece entitled "*Rao kamlang yu nai yuk 'songkhram klang muang'!*" (We are living in an era of "civil war"!).[16] General Prem Tinsulanonda, a former commander-in-chief of the army, an unelected prime minister in the 1980s, the head of the king's Privy Council and the *éminence grise* of the royalist right wing in Thailand, strongly recommended that his followers read this piece. It could, thus, well be taken as the manifesto of the opposition to the Red Shirt movement. In it Chirmsak characterizes the movement as being made up of those who sell their souls for advantage or who are ex-communists who promote class warfare. He sees the followers (mainly northeastern) of the movement as the "ignorant poor" (*khon yakchon rue khon thi khao mai thueng khomun khaosan phiangpho*). He thus echoes assertions made by other right-wing leaders that the rural supporters of Thaksin are "stupid" (*khon ngo*).

This theme was repeated over and over again by right-wing media and on many blogs in 2009–10. On March 29, 2010. For example, *The Manager*, owned and edited by Sondhi Limthongkul, one of the leaders of the Yellow Shirts, ran the following cartoon.

The cartoon carried the caption "System for usage of city streets in Bangkok. Monday–Friday: Let cars drive. Saturday–Sunday: Let buffalos march." Water buffaloes are depicted in the popular media as stupid beasts. Images of buffaloes, referring to the Red Shirts, were conspicuous in the Yellow Shirt counterdemonstrations.

The "stupid" peasants who were vilified in the Bangkok-centered media became in very large numbers the followers of the Red Shirts. Although the prevailing interpretation of the movement among spokesmen for the middle class and the establishment in Bangkok was that the movement had been organized and funded primarily to

Cartoon stigmatizing the Red Shirt protestors published in *The Manager* magazine, March 29, 2010 (reproduced by permission)

enable former prime minister Thaksin Shinawatra to return to power, the northeasterners living both in the region and in Bangkok have more sophisticated understandings of why they became supporters. Thomas Fuller, a reporter for the *New York Times*, traveled to the Northeast to interview some supporters of the Red Shirts and in an article published on April 19, 2010, wrote: "Supporters of the red shirts in the northeast, while acknowledging that Mr. Thaksin remained a key inspiration for the movement, said it had taken on larger goals. "This is not for Thaksin, this is for democracy," said Chaisawat Weangwong, a forty-two-year-old rice farmer. Mr. Chaisawat offered a basic definition of democracy: "The majority chooses the winner" (Fuller 2010).

The "village" that Red Shirts set up in the heart of Bangkok's commercial district came to an end on May 19, 2010, when army units finally moved to carry out the order of the government to clear the district and Red Shirt leaders asked their followers to go home, after which they themselves surrendered. In the aftermath of the worst civil conflict Bangkok has ever seen, the northeasterners who had come to Bangkok or had commuted from their homes in the city retreated back to their home villages and middle-class Bangkokians once again resumed their urban lives.

Nonetheless, as Phya Anuman recognized so long ago, the city still depends on the village, but in 2010 it was no longer for food or even for labor but for votes in elections. Despite some of the rhetoric and symbolism, the demonstrators in Bangkok in 2009–10 did not seek the violent revolutionary overthrow of the Thai political system. Their primary demand throughout their demonstration was for new and free elections; that is, they sought the right to have a legitimate voice in a parliamentary democracy of the type first envisaged in the overthrow of absolute monarchy in 1932 but which had been thwarted many times by those (mainly in the military) who preferred a "guided democracy" at best and authoritarian dictatorship at worst.

Pasuk and Baker (2012, 227) have concluded that the Red Shirt movement in Thailand in 2009–10 was similar to revolts elsewhere of "the dispossessed against an old political establishment." However, in Thailand, for historical reasons that have been laid out here, for the people of the northeastern region the movement faced "fierce opposition, strengthened by old institutions." The movement has also been linked inexorably to Thaksin Shinawatra, "a modernist and business advocate who became a populist; a man with contempt for democracy who became its defendant; a corrupt moneybags who profited from the "double standards" and then railed against them" (Pasuk and Baker 2012, 226). The equivocal leadership of Thaksin and the continued power of old institutions notwithstanding, the people from which the Red Shirts emerged, very much including the cosmopolitan villagers of northeastern Thailand, persisted in their quest to have a voice in a democratic polity.

RURAL PEOPLE MAKE THEIR VOICES HEARD

Although many observers were highly doubtful of an election being held in the wake of the 2010 events, Prime Minister Abhisit, after having consulted not only with leaders of his Democrat Party but also with key members of the military and monarchical elite, dissolved Parliament in May 2011 and called for elections to be held on July 3. Abhisit was attempting to use the elections to achieve the long-standing goal of elite-centered Thai politics of an order based on "consensus, reconciliation, normalcy, unity and integration" (Chairat 2012, 90). The rules that applied for the election also were deemed favorable for the Democrat Party to gain a marked increase in the number of seats it held in Parliament. For northeasterners and northerners the memory of the protests had, however, only intensified their feelings of injustice. Moreover the rural base of the Pheu Thai Party, the successor to the Thai Rak Thai Party that Thaksin had founded, continued to see this party as representing their interests better than the Democrat Party did. As polls began to show that Pheu Thai would win a majority of seats, some in the establishment worked out an "accommodation" with Thaksin (see Crispin 2011a, 2011b) that entailed a commitment to forego any military resistance to the formation of a government by the Pheu Thai.

The Pheu Thai Party also had a telegenic leader to lead it into the election. Since Thaksin was in exile owing to his conviction for improper use of government power in a land deal involving his former wife, his younger sister Yingluck Shinawatra picked up the mantle of leadership.

Although Yingluck had previously devoted herself to business rather than politics, her name recognition, her being the first woman ever to aspire to being prime minister, her espousal of the same populist policies as her brother, and her very well-managed campaign led to Pheu Thai winning a clear majority of seats in Parliament. This was only the second time in Thai history that a party had won such a majority, the previous time being Thai Rak Thai's victory in 2005.

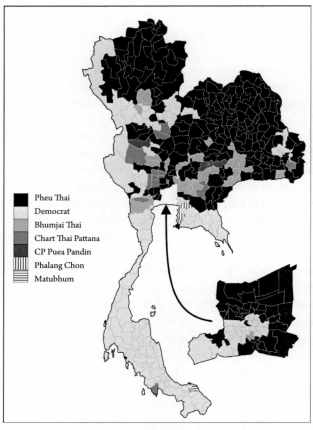

July 2011 election results (courtesy Pasuk Phongpaichit and Chris Baker)

The results of the election, graphically shown on maps such as the one above, demonstrate that the support for Pheu Thai was overwhelming in both northeastern and northern Thailand as well as in the suburbs of Bangkok, the latter area being heavily populated by working-class people with roots in rural, northeastern Thailand. In the immediate post-election period, the military and others who had strongly opposed Thaksin still allowed Pheu Thai not only to form a government, but also to undertake to lead the country.

The competing approaches to political authority represented by Pheu Thai and its Red Shirt allies on one side and the military with monarchical support on the other will not disappear simply because Pheu Thai won a majority of seats in Parliament. The 2011 election, like all elections since 2001, demonstrates, nonetheless, that the assumption that Thailand should be ruled by those whose authority comes from control of force, even if backed by the charisma of the king, has been successfully challenged by those who base their authority on the will of the people as expressed through voting. The majority of the "people" whose voices have been strongly expressed through the election as well as in the Red Shirt demonstrations are overwhelmingly those with roots in rural northeastern Thailand.

I am very much aware that the Red Shirts also have deep roots in rural northern Thailand as well as in rural northeastern Thailand, but the "rural" in the North is, I suggest, different from the "rural" of the Northeast. Andrew Walker (2012, 39ff) has shown that in the North the politicized villagers who supported the Red Shirts are more likely to be what he terms "middle-income peasants" whose economic base remains agriculture (albeit commercial agriculture) rather than work outside of rural areas and especially work abroad as is the case for rural northeasterners. The northerners as well as northeasterners both share a sense of having been relegated too long to the margins of the Thai political order. Their combined support of the Red Shirt movement and their votes for Pheu Thai represent a challenge to the Bangkok-centered elite view of sovereignty as deriving from the monarchy, at least as this institution is interpreted by the elite rather than on behalf of the people.[17]

In the early twenty-first century, the Thailand first shaped by the integration policies of King Chulalongkorn in the late nineteenth century is in the process of being transformed into a pluralist polity in which diverse interests are accommodated through a democratic system, that is, a constitutional system in which legitimacy is predicated not solely on the decisions of those who govern, but also on the voices of the governed (see Kalyvas 2005). Rural northeasterners who emerged from being peasants to become cosmopolitan villagers and who in the twenty-first century joined to support the Red Shirt protests and vote in favor of parties committed to parliamentary rather than guided democracy played and will continue to play a major role in the reshaping of the Thai polity to accommodate all citizens of the country.

NOTES

PREFACE

1. I use the real name of the village in contrast to some scholars who use a pseudonym for the rural community in which they have worked. I do so because several Ban Nong Tuen villagers in the 1970s were perplexed after seeing a paper I had published as to why I had used a pseudonym not only for the village but also for those villagers I mentioned in the paper. They told me that felt they were not being allowed to have their own identity. Since then I have used the name of the village in all my publications and in 2011 Thomas Fuller, a reporter for the *New York Times*, put the village on the map in an even more prominent way than my own writing had done with a front page article in the NYT (Thomas Fuller 2011). Officially, the Ban Nong Tuen that we first came to know in the early 1960s was subsequently divided into three *muban*, a term usually glossed as "village," but those living in all three have continued to worship at one Buddhist temple monastery (*wat*) and to propitiate common ancestral spirits together. I have therefore continued to use the name for what remains a unified community.

CHAPTER 1   RURAL ISAN

1. My estimates are based on Brown (1965), Smalley (1994), and Grabowsky (1996).

2. The term has been used with reference to political systems in Southeast Asia that consist of a central kingdom surrounded by satellite vassal principalities. The first scholar to recognize this type of socio-religio-political structure appears to have been Robert Heine-Geldern (1942, reprinted as Heine-Geldern 1956). Tambiah (1977) refers to this model as a "galactic polity" (also see Wolters 1982). The *monthon*

system introduced in the late nineteenth century was, however, in a real sense the antithesis of this model, as the new "circles" replaced autonomous *hua muang* and were administered directly from the capital through royally appointed governors.

3. Originally two names were used for *monthon* in the Northeast—Udon, meaning north, and Isan, meaning northeast. In the area that is today northern Thailand there was another *monthon*, Phayap, whose name means northwestern. Udon Thani subsequently was used as the name of a province in the Northeast. Although the name Phayap continued to be used for some purposes (albeit not official ones) to refer to northern Thailand, the people of northern Thailand themselves never embraced the term for their own identity, preferring to call themselves *khon muang*, which echoes a premodern referent to the autonomous domains of the region.

4. None of the principal cities in the Northeast—most notably Khorat (Nakhon Ratchasima), Khon Kaen, and Ubon Ratchathani—share with Chiang Mai or Nakhon Si Thammarat the characteristic of once having been the seat of a semi-autonomous kingdom. Khorat is, in some ways, a successor to Phimai, a provincial center under the Angkor Empire. However, since its founding in the seventeenth century it was an outpost of the Siamese empire. Ubon only became significant after the nearby semi-autonomous Lao principality of Champasak was attached to French Laos. Khon Kaen, like many other towns in the Northeast, was once the seat of a *hua muang*, but it became significant only as an administrative-commercial center under Siamese rule. The one place that has some similarity to Chiang Mai is That Phanom near the Mekong River in the northeastern corner of the region because it is the site of a major Buddhist shrine. Although it was and still is revered by Lao, it was never associated with a significant political center.

5. Although at least 85 percent of the population of the northeastern region are related to the lowland Lao, there are also Khmer-speaking and other Mon-Khmer-speaking people in the southern part of the region, people of Chinese descent in the market towns, and speakers of other Tai languages in pockets throughout the region. Although most of those of Chinese descent identify as *khon Isan*, the Khmer and Khmer-related peoples do not.

6. Kampoon's novel is based on his own childhood experience in what is today Yasothon Province in the central part of the Northeast. Susan Kepner, in her introduction to the translation of the book (Kampoon 1988, 12), says the novel "is set in the 1930s," that is, at the time when Kampoon, who was born in the 1920s, was a young boy.

7. One reason the film was not popular was because the dialogue was in Lao, which necessitated having Thai subtitles.

8. Prajuab, an Ubon schoolteacher who in the 1950s worked with the first community development program in the Northeast supported by UNESCO, wrote an autobiographical account of her life (Prajuab 1958) and then reworked this in a

novel (Prajuab 1971). Research in the 1950s also focused on the Ubon area where the TUFEC (Thailand-UNESCO Fundamental Education Centre) work was centered. See Madge (1957) and Klausner (1972, 2000). In the 1960s studies were made by foreign and Thai researchers, including myself, in many different parts of the region (see Amyot 1964; Keyes 1966b, 1975a, 1975b; Kirsch 1967; Jancis F. Long, Millard F. Long, Kamphol, and Sawart 1963; Lux 1962, 1969; Mizuno 1968, 1971; Suthep 1968; Tambiah 1968a, 1968b, 1969, 1970; and Yatsushiro 1968). Also see my review essay on northeastern rural society in the 1960s (Keyes 1975a).

9. There were two such shrines, one at the center (*lak ban*) or "navel" of the village (*bue ban*), and the other in a small forest preserve on the edge of the village. The former was associated with an unnamed (at least in Ban Nong Tuen) deity who connects the village to a cosmic order, while the second was dedicated to *phi pu ta*, the ancestral spirit of the village.

10. Wimonphan Pitthawatchai (1973) provides a good description in Thai of the *hit sipsong*. Tambiah (1970) presents a detailed account of the ritual cycle in a village in Udon Province.

11. Prior to establishment of government schools in the mid-1930s, most males also served for several years at the *wat* as novices (*nen/samanen*), but ever since a government school was established only a few boys from poor families have become novices for any length of time.

12. As a graduate student at Cornell University, I immersed myself in the theoretical literature on peasant society in preparation for my field research in Thailand. Most influential on my thinking was the work of Robert Redfield (1956) and Eric Wolf (1956). Wolf's (1966) book on peasants also helped me reshape my thinking as I wrote my dissertation.

13. Even though the leader of the coup, General Sonthi Boonyaratglin, was himself a Thai-speaking Muslim, the new government was no more successful in ending the conflict in the south than the previous democratically elected government. In no small part this failure is a consequence of deep-seated prejudices by Thai Buddhists regarding Malay-speaking Muslims living within Thailand (see Keyes 2008/2009). The best analysis to date of this conflict is by McCargo (2009).

14. On the ironic use of *phrai* by the Red Shirt leaders and their followers, see Macan-Markar (2010) and Voranai Vanjaka (2010).

CHAPTER 2 THE FOUNDATIONS OF ISAN

1. This chapter is based, in part, on the first chapter of *Isan: Regionalism in Northeastern Thailand* (Keyes 1967).

2. A comparison of the 1960 and 2010 censuses shows that the percentage of the population living in the Northeast has declined from about 34 percent in the 1960 census to 31 percent in 2010. Since, as discussed below, a sizeable percentage of those

who remain officially registered as living in northeastern communities actually live for extended periods outside the region, the actual percentage of the population of Thailand who today reside in the region is certainly much less than 31 percent. Many officially registered as living in the Northeast are actually permanent or semi-permanent residents of the Bangkok Metropolitan Region.

3. I use the term *Tai* to designate any people speaking a domestic language belonging to the Tai or Daic language family. Such people are found from Assam in the west to Hainan Island in the east, and from southern China in the north to Malaysia in the south (LeBar et a1. 1964, 187–244). Consequently, Tai does not simply refer to people who are living within the present-day kingdom of Thailand. The term *Thai* is used to refer to all citizens of Thailand no matter what language they first learn to speak. Here I refer to the Thai of the central region of Thailand as central Thai. Some of my discussion of the ethnolinguistic composition of the population of northeastern Thailand is based on Brown (1965) and Smalley (1994).

4. In 2000 the Khmer-speaking population of Thailand was approximately 1.4 million, of which most were in the northeastern provinces of Buri Ram, Si Sa Ket, Surin, and Khorat. In addition there are four hundred thousand people who call themselves Kui and whom the Thai formerly called Suai (meaning "tribute"). The Kui, who live in Buri Ram, Surin, Si Sa Ket, Ubon, and Roi Et Provinces, speak a language closely related to that of the Khmer. These data are from *Ethnologue*, the website of the Summer Institute of Linguistics (see http://www.ethnologue.com/ show_country.asp?name=TH). On the Khmer of northeastern Thailand, see Denes (2006) and on the Kui, Komatra (1998) and Cuasay (2002).

5. Skinner (1957, 84) recorded that the Chinese who moved into northeastern Thailand as well as northern Thailand were primarily speakers of Hainanese and were, thus, already different from the Teochiu, Hokkien, and Cantonese who settled in Bangkok. The best study to date on the development of what I term a Sino-Isan, as distinct from a Sino-Thai, identity is a dissertation on the public culture of Khon Kaen by Kaewta Chantharanusorn (2008).

6. I have sometimes also called the northeasterners "Thai-Lao." By this term, I mean the Lao who live in Thailand.

7. *Phasa Isan* has two referents. The first is the standardized spoken Isan language used on the various radio stations in the Northeast. The second refers to the written language used by publishing houses that print traditional northeastern literature. This language employs Siamese (rather than Lao) script, slightly modified for the different dialects, and northeastern vocabulary.

8. I do not attempt here a detailed reconstruction of the ethnohistory of the Khorat Plateau prior to the arrival of Tai-speaking people but seek only to provide some background for understanding the evolution of the distinctive identity of the region. Since the 1960s there have been a number of major archaeological research projects on the Khorat Plateau. As a result of this research it is now known that

settlements in the region, such as the famous site of Ban Chiang, were increasing "greatly from a period beginning in the fourth or early third millennium BC" (Higham 1988, 92). Rice cultivation may have developed independently in the region (White 1995) and metallurgy (first in bronze followed by iron) evolved more-or-less independently of outside influences (Higham 1996, 2004; but also see a revised view in Higham and Rachanee 2012). Subsequently the indigenous peoples who were speakers of Mon-Khmer languages adopted Buddhist and Hindu-Buddhist practices. By the ninth century much of the region was connected to the expanding Angkorian empire. The Siamese conquest of Angkor in the fifteenth century left something of a political vacuum that would not be filled until the Lao and Siamese empires began to expand. Srisakara Vallibhotama (1990) has brought together much information about the cultural history of the ancient Khorat plateau.

9. The spelling Lan Xang derives from a French transliteration of the spoken version of the name, while Lan Chang is based on the spelling in Lao (and Thai). Lan Xang has become the accepted spelling in both English-language and French-language works about Laos.

10. That Ayutthaya should be the capital of a Tai-speaking kingdom thus gives rise to some puzzling questions. Professor O. W. Wolters developed a very intriguing and plausible theory that the founding of Ayutthaya represented the merging of the fortunes and objectives of a Chao Phraya Valley Tai kingdom lying to the west of Ayutthaya (Suphan Buri) with those of the Mon kingdom of Lavo (Wolters 1966). Also see Charnvit Kasetsiri (1976).

11. This account of the conquests of Fa Ngum is based on Maha Sila Viravong (1964, 26–34). Although the reliability of this source is open to some question, the other main source (Le Boulanger 1931, 41–51) provides sufficient collaboration to justify the claim that almost all of northeastern Thailand was brought within the domains of Fa Ngum's kingdom.

12. Gerrit van Wusthoff, a Dutch visitor to Vientiane in 1641–42 and the first Westerner to travel up the Mekong from Cambodia to Laos, made a stop at That Phanom, but neither he nor a Father de Leira, a Jesuit who was in Vientiane between 1642 and 1647, recorded any additional information about Vientiane's influence on the Khorat Plateau (Lévy 1959, 61).

13. Several pieces of evidence support the thesis that Ayutthaya did not exercise political control over any part of the Northeast prior to the beginning of the seventeenth century. In a listing of all known archaeological sites in Thailand (Chin 1957), there is not one site that was built by Ayutthaya prior to the founding of Nakhon Ratchasima. In his history of the provinces of Ubon, Si Sa Ket, Surin, Roi Et, Maha Sarakham, and Kalasin, Amorawong Wichit dismisses the pre-seventeenth-century history of the Northeast in the following terms: "The lands of Monthon Lao Kao [i.e., the area comprising the above mentioned provinces] before 1638 was a

jungle inhabited by forest people who traced their lineage from the Khom [i.e., the Khmer of the Angkorian empire]" (Amorawong 1963, 22). Finally, in my examination of the histories of each northeastern province given in booklets prepared for the twenty-five-hundred-year anniversary of Buddha's enlightenment, I could again find no reference to Siamese control over northeastern areas prior to the founding of Nakhon Ratchasima.

14. The dating of the foundation of the "shrine of two friendships" at Dan Sai is open to some question. In the inscription found at the site (Finot 1915), the date given is AD 1560 and the two kings in question are given as Thammikarat of Vientiane and Maha Chakkraphat of Ayutthaya. Maha Sila's version of the Lao annals claims that this stele was erected in 1670 during the reign of one Suryawongsa Thammikarat (Sila 1964, 76–77) and that in 1485 a treaty by Ayutthaya and Lan Xang had been signed at the same place (47). The name of the Siamese king or kings is not given in Maha Sila's version. In neither Wyatt's nor Wood's history of Siam is any reference made to this treaty having been concluded during the reign of King Chakkraphat (r. 1548–69) (Wyatt 1984, 92ff; Wood 1924, 112–23). The Buddhist shrine of Phra That Si Song Rak in Dan Sai commemorates the signing of the treaty, but the town and district are far better known today as the locus of a distinctive festival honoring local spirits known as *phi ta khon*.

15. Wood, unfortunately, does not cite a source for his information and I have not found confirmation of the 1610 Lan Xang attack on Ayutthaya in any other source. Nonetheless, there is no question that by the mid seventeenth century, there was a marked shift in the relative power of Lan Xang and Ayutthaya.

16. For the detailed history of the events culminating in the founding of the three Lao kingdoms see Maha Sila Viravong (1964, 83–5, 106–8); Archaimbault (1961); Le Boulanger (1931, 131–35); and Toem Singhatthit (1956, 1:352 passim).

17. Nakhon Ratchasima (Khorat) had already proven itself to be a somewhat reluctant part of the Siamese kingdom. In 1691 and again in 1639 revolts against Ayutthayan rule had broken out at Khorat, although each time the rebellion had been put down (Wood 1924, 220, 222; Manit 1962, 18–19).

18. For the detailed description and analysis of the events leading up to and including this invasion of Vientiane see Wyatt (1963, 14–21) and Wenk (1968, 94–100).

19. During the reign of King Taksin (1767–82) the Siamese capital was on the Chao Phraya River at Thonburi. After Taksin was replaced by General Chakkri, the capital was moved to the opposite bank of the river in Bangkok.

20. The kings of the Bangkok dynasty founded by Chakkri are often referred to as Rama I, Rama II, etc. King Chakkri was Rama I and the present king, Bhumipol Adulayadej, is Rama IX.

21. On the controversial story of Thao Suranari see Saipin Kaew-ngarmprasert (1995) and Keyes (2002a).

22. For a good summary of the events leading immediately up to the Vientiane revolt of 1827 see Wyatt (1963, 27–31). For a summary of the Thai version of the revolt see Vella (1957, 80–89) and Toem Singhatthit (1956, 1:149–59). An older Lao interpretation of the revolt is given by Maha Sila Viravong (1964, 111–35). Two Lao historians, Mayoury Ngaosyvathn and Pheuiphanh Ngaosyvathn (1988a, 1988b, 1989) have offered a revisionist perspective on the Siamese-Lao war of 1827–8, seeing Chao Anu as a Lao nationalist hero who challenged Siamese imperialism.

23. In a document prepared at the height of a period of Thai irredentism in 1941, the Thai government listed as losses to the French 87,000 square kilometers in the Sipsong Chao Thai (or Sipsong Chu Thai) region in present-day northern Vietnam, 175,000 square kilometers in Cambodia, and 207,500 square kilometers in Laos (Thailand, Department of Publicity, 1941, no page). Of these areas only the Lao areas, less the territory of Luang Prabang, and the provinces of Battambang, Siem Reap, Sisophon [Banteay Meanchey], and Melouprey [Preah Vihear] in Cambodia were fully integrated into the Siamese kingdom at the time of the treaties with the French. The Siamese claim to the Sipsong Chao Thai rested solely on the fact that the region was populated mainly by Tai-speaking people. Cambodia and Luang Prabang were vassals. Bangkok also lost to Britain some vassals in the Malay states but did not lose any territory that was fully a part of the kingdom at the time.

24. Some northern parts of Cambodia were also ceded to France in the Treaty of 1904. In 1907 the rest of Cambodia, the provinces of Siem Reap, Battambang, and Sisophon, were transferred from Siamese to French control. On the fixing of the boundary between Siam and French Laos, see Breazeale (2002); also see Thongchai Winichakul (1994) for a broader discussion of the fixing of the boundaries of modern Thailand.

25. Among other aspects, these variations are evident in the dialect differentiations that Brown found in the Northeast (Brown 1965).

26. The term *muang* does not have any one English gloss for it may mean a principality, city, province, or country, but in all cases it is a political entity larger than a village (*ban*). Siamese officials applied the term *hua muang*, in which the word *hua* means head, to small principalities comprising a single important center and subordinate *muang* and villages.

27. The Ayutthayan *hua muang* included, besides Khorat (Nakhon Ratchasima), Surin, Sangkha, and Khukhan in the southern part of the Northeast on the Cambodian border. All three were created at the same time (1760) in consequence of services rendered by the Suai [Kui] (a Mon-Khmer minority group) leaders of these areas to the king of Ayutthaya (*Changwat Surin* 1957, 8). In fact, the actual

inclusion of these territories within the Siamese kingdom did not come until after the founding of the new dynasty at Thonburi/Bangkok.

28. The listing of the names of the *hua muang*, their founding dates, and the nature of their tributary position can be found in Toem Singhatthit (1956, 1:510–34). The lack of certainty as to how many of these *hua muang* lay in what is today northeastern Thailand is a consequence of the difficulty in locating about seventeen of the names on maps of the area. At least three of these "Lao" *hua muang* were situated in what is present-day Cambodia and another one was in the province of Lomsak that today is a district in northern Thailand.

29. An expanded description of the structure of the *hua muang* can be found in Toem Singhatthit (1956, 1:488–507) and Bunchuai Atthakon (1962).

30. The standard work on the integrative reforms instituted under King Chulalongkorn is by Tej Bunnag (1977). Paitoon Mikusol (1995) provides more detailed information than presented here on the institution of these reforms in northeastern Thailand.

CHAPTER 3 BUDDHIST MILLENIALIST ROOTS OF ISAN POLITICAL CULTURE

1. This chapter is based primarily on Keyes (1977) and also draws on Keyes (1973b).

2. Since Pali is the sacred language of Theravada Buddhism I use Pali forms such as *kamma* rather than Sanskrit forms like *karma*.

3. On Buddhist millennialism in Burma, see Mendelson 1960, 1961a, 1961b, 1963a, 1963b, 1963c, 1964; Sarkisyanz 1965; Spiro, 1970, 162–87; and Rozenberg 2005, 2010; for Sri Lanka, Malalgoda 1970; and for the Karen, Stern 1968 and Hinton 1979.

4. Beliefs in the imminent manifestation of Maitreya are also found in Thailand. In 1968, during my research in Mae Sariang, northwestern Thailand, the district Buddhist abbot showed me a tract that told of the coming of Phra Si An—i.e., Ariya Maitreya. In 1973 I obtained several pamphlets describing a Maitreya cult in Thonburi, the twin city of Bangkok. Newspaper accounts in 1974 (*Thai Rat*, February 9 and 10; *Bangkok Post*, February 10; *Sayam Rat*, February 11) carried a story about a husband and wife living in Kumphawapi District, Udon Province, northeastern Thailand, who claimed that Phra Si An had already been born. In September 1976, I received (from Edward Fallon, then a graduate student at the University of Wisconsin engaged in research on northeastern Thai history) a booklet entitled *Phra Si Ariya Mettraiya (Phra Si An)*, compiled by Un Mahachokchai (Khon Kaen, 1976). It describes a woman in Chiang Khan District, Loei Province, northeastern Thailand, who has been accepted by numerous villagers in adjacent areas as being an incarnation of the Maitreya Buddha. On other Maitreya beliefs in Thailand, see Pornpen Hantrakool and Atcharaphon Kamutphisamai (1984).

5. The term *saksit* is derived from two Sanskrit terms, *śakti*, creative power associated with the consort of Śiva, and *siddhi*, extraordinary powers usually acquired through meditative or Tantric practices. In Lao and Thai usage, *saksit* means an endowment of supernatural power and is usually associated with one who has been a monk (thus, male rather than female as in the Indian original) and has practiced asceticism and meditation.

6. My understanding of millennialism is based on the work of Worsley 1968, Talmon 1969, and Cohn 1970.

7. While I have not pursued the question, it may be that gold leaf serves as a medium whereby the merit of persons and the Buddha himself can be tapped.

8. The story is taken from "Rueang Phra Khru Wat Chalong" (Concerning the Phra Khru of Wat Chalong), which is contained in Prince Damrong's *Nithan borankhadi* (Historical anecdotes) (1961 [1935], 12–21).

9. The Chiang Tung Shan actually share much the same cultural, linguistic, and religious traditions with the Northern Thai (Yuan, Khon Muang). The ethnoreligious identity that links the Chiang Tung Shan (who are also known as Khuen) and Khon Muang persists for many to the present day (see Cohen 2000, 2001).

10. The major primary source I have used for constructing an account of this uprising is the set of documents collected in a file kept by the Thai Ministry of Interior and now available for study through the National Archives in Bangkok [hereafter NA-B], catalogued as M.2.18, "*Rueang phi bun*" (Concerning the *phi bun*), under the Ministry of Interior (*Krasuang mahatthai*) records of the fifth reign (reign of King Chulalongkorn). A short account of the uprising, by Prince Damrong Rajanubhab (who was minister of interior at the time and who figures prominently in the archival records) appeared in his book (1961 [1935], 352–58). Toem Wiphakphachanakit (1970, 2:557–87), whose father was a Siamese official in the Northeast at the time of the uprising, has given a detailed account in his *Prawatsat Isan* (History of the Northeast). Some additional details can also be found in two local histories compiled by northeasterners, Bunchuai Atthakon (1962, 76–77) and Phra Thep Ratana Moli (1965, 101–2). It is quite likely that further research will uncover yet other local chronicles containing accounts of the uprising. Paitoon Mikusol's study (1972) *Kan pathirup kan pokkhrong monthon Isan samai thi phrachao boromwongthoe kromluang Sanphasitthiprasong song pen khaluang yai (pho so 2436–2453)* (Provincial reforms in Monthon Isan during the period when Prince Sanphasitthiprasong was high commissioner [1893–1910]), by far the best secondary source, has made extensive use of the archival materials, as well as some other primary sources. Reference here is to the version published as an MA thesis (Paitoon 1972), although it exists in two other published versions (Bangkok: Bannakit, 1974, and Bangkok: Ministry of Education, Instructional Documents No. 149, 1974). Tej

Bunnag's (1967) "Khabot phu mi bun phak Isan ro so 121" (Millenarian revolt in northeastern Thailand, 1902) is a stimulating article that draws upon archival data and on Toem's and Prince Damrong's accounts.

Tej's (1968, see 271–73, 276, 280) doctoral dissertation, "The Provincial Administration of Siam from 1892 to 1915" also contains some discussion of the uprising as well as providing an excellent detailed analysis of the political changes that provided the context within which the uprising took place. In "The 1901–1902 "Holy Man's" Rebellion," Murdoch (1974) has provided an analysis of the uprising based on Tej's article and on an earlier version of my study presented here. He has also taken into account some published French sources (for example, Bourotte 1955; Dauplay 1929; and Le Boulanger 1931) that treat the uprising as it occurred in French-controlled territory. To date, no one has examined any French archival source for possible data on the uprising in either Thailand or Indochina. Ishii (1975), in his brief paper "A Note on Buddhist Millenarian Revolts in Northeastern Siam," has focused on the cultural ideas underlying the uprising, and I have taken up a similar theme in my "Power of Merit" (Keyes 1973b). More recent studies also include those by Chatthip Nartsupha (1984). In addition to the study by Murdoch, those by Gunn (1990) and Gay (2002) provide insights into the Lao Marxist interpretation of the uprising in Laos.

11. I draw here on Mom Amorawong Wichit's (1963, 102) account in *Phongsawadan hua muang monthon Isan* (Chronicle of the provinces in the northeastern circle). Mom Amorawong, a Siamese official posted to Ubon, compiled his chronicles in 1904; they were first published in 1915. Also see Tej (1968, 102–3) and Paitoon (1972, 20).

12. Paitoon observes that Prince Sanphasit especially excluded "artisans" and "rich persons" in order to stimulate economic development. "Rich persons" were determined by the number of large animals (cattle, buffaloes, horses, elephants) a man owned.

13. This monk's birth name was Chan, but like other monks he became known by his religious names. His ordination name was Sirichan, but he became known primarily by the titles conferred on him by the Thai sangha. At the time of the *phu mi bun* uprising, he was known as Phra Yanarakkhit, but later became better known as Phra Ubali.

14. NA-B, V, M.57/15. "Rueang Phra Yanarakkhit wa duai ratchakan nai monthon Isan" (Concerning Phra Yanarakkhit speaking about administration in Monthon Isan), February 10–September 3, 1902. My translation.

15. NA-B, V, M.2.18/11, letter from Prince Sanphasit to Prince Damrong, July 11, 1903; also see Paitoon (1972, 98). Prince Damrong—in a letter to Prince Watthana, High Commissioner of Monthon Udon (NA-B, V, M.2.18/3, April 28m 1902)—was of the opinion that those who first spread the message about the coming of the *phu*

mi bun were followers of Ong Kaeo, a claimant to the status of *phu mi bun* who lived in French Laos. Murdoch (1974, 55), who drew on French sources, identified Ong Kaeo as an Alak tribesman from Southern Laos. Paitoon (1972, 79), drawing on a Siamese source, identifies him as a local Lao official of Saravane who had a Siamese title. While Ong Kaeo was certainly a major figure in the uprising in both French Laos and in northeastern Thailand, he does not appear to emerge until about two years after the first indications of the millennial ideas have begun to be reported in northeastern Thailand.

16. Paitoon Mikusol (1972, 100) gives the titles of the four documents as: (1) *Nangsue Phraya In* (Lord Indra's book), (2) *Nangsue Thao Phraya Thammikarat* (Book of Lord Dharmikaraja), (3) *Nangsue phu mi bun* (Book of the meritful persons), and (4) *Tamnan phuenmuang krung* (Local accounts of the capital).

17. I have consulted versions of the message as reported in the following: a letter from Phraya Suriyadetwiset Ruetthasathiwichai, a Siamese special commissioner sent to investigate the causes of the uprising, to Prince Damrong (NA-B, V, M.2.18/11, August 30, 1902); excerpts from and summaries of documentary sources reported by Paitoon (1972, 100–102), and Tej (1967, 78); composite versions reported by Toem Wiphakphachanakit (1970, 2:559) and Bunchuai Atthakon (1962, 76).

18. Other dates given include the eighth day of the waning of the eighth month, year unspecified (Paitoon 1972, 100) and the middle of the sixth month, year of the Ox [May 2, 1901] (Toem Wiphakphachanakit 1970, 2:559).

19. Thai, *yak*, giant demons.

20. Phraya Suriyadetwiset (NA-B, V, M.2.18/11), my translation.

21. Bad karmic deeds (*bap*) refers to acts defined by the Buddhist dharma as producing ill consequences.

22. *Tat kam wang wen*, lit., "to cut (oneself) loose from karma and free (oneself) from anger."

23. Sacralized water (*nam mon*) consists of water over which ritual mantras have been chanted.

24. In another version of the message it is said that "Maidens who still have no husband should go about to find a husband. The bride price will be figured at one *at* and one *salot* only. If a maiden is unable to find a man who is unmarried, then it is permissible to become the wife of a man who is already married. But (in this case, one) must pay four *at* to the original wife as the price of buying her husband. If (maidens do not take husbands), the *yaksa* will eat them." (Phraya Suriyadetwiset in letter to Prince Damrong, August 30, 1902; NA-B, V, M.2.18/11, my translation).

25. What evidence is available suggests that the followers were primarily from areas along the Mekong and in the Chi and Mun River valleys. The Khmer and Kui-speaking people of the southern part of the region and the Khorat Thai-speaking people of southwestern part of the region may not have been attracted to the movement.

26. NA-B, V, M.57/15, letter from Phra Yanarakkhit to Prince Damrong, dated February 20, 1902; Paitoon (1972, 105).

27. Paitoon speculates that instead of meditating while in caves and in the hills, he was actually plotting rebellion with others.

28. NA-B, V, M.2.18/3, telegram from Prince Sanphasit to Prince Damrong, February 26, 1902.

29. Elsewhere Paitoon (1972, 120) says that 288 men were captured at Ban Sapho. Toem Wiphakphachanakit (1970, 2:564) says that three hundred men were killed and four hundred captured there.

30. Ong Kaeo continued to give the French trouble until 1910, when he was finally killed by trickery (Murdoch 1974, 60).

31. Tej (1967) makes too much, I believe, of the poverty of the northeastern populace being the major cause of the uprising, and also of the importance of economic aid being the major successful effort in effecting a reduction of millennial tendencies.

32. The term *ngo* may have had a somewhat different meaning to those writing about the *phu mi bun* uprising than it does to members of the twenty-first century Thai elite who have again applied the term to northeasterners. However, as the pejorative designation of the uprising as *kabot phi bun* suggests, there can be no question that the term was meant to be denigrating just as it is in contemporary usage. By combining the term *phi* (spirit, ghost) with *bun* (Buddhist merit), those reporting to the Siamese monarch mocked the pretensions of the leaders of the movement. There is a clear continuity in the negative attitudes of Thai elite regarding the rural northeast for over a century.

33. There were also some monks who followed the Mahayana traditions of China or Vietnam as well as some in western or northern Thailand who followed Burmese or Shan traditions.

34. The most extended account of the introduction of reform Buddhism in northeastern Thailand is by Toem Wiphakphachanakit (1970, vol. 2, ch. 10). Taylor's account—the fullest in any English source—draws on Toem as well as a few other Thai sources.

35. Taylor (1993) and Kamala Tiyavanich (1997) are the best sources in English on the evolution of forest monasticism in northeastern Thailand that is traceable to the influence of Achan Man. Also see Keyes (1981).

36. The connection between curing cults and political movements has recently been given some more attention (see Jackson 1999 and Pattana 2013).

37. Ishii took his information from Thai Noi, *Nayokratthamontri khon thi 11 kap 3 phunam patiwat* [The 11th prime minister and three leaders of the coup d'état] (Bangkok, Phrae Phittaya, 1964), 546–49.

38. On the cult in Udon, see *Thai Rath*, February 10, 1974; *Bangkok Post*, February 10, 1974; and *Siam Rath*, February 11, 1974. My information on Loei comes from a personal communication with Edward Fallon, August 8, 1974. On the cult of King Chulalongkorn, see Stengs (2009).

CHAPTER 4 ISAN BECOMING THAI

1. It took until 1955, however, for the rail line to reach Nong Khai, the main port of entry for the Lao capital of Vientiane (*Bangkok Post*, September 23, 1955).

2. When Jane, my wife, and I first went to Maha Sarakham in the center of northeastern Thailand we found that many official communications were still transmitted by telegraph. The only telephones were in the offices of the governor and district officer; others who wished to make calls could, like us, do so only through the local post office. All calls, including overseas calls, had to be routed through Bangkok. Telephone usage did not become widespread until after the introduction of mobile phones in the 1990s.

3. See Tambiah (1968) for a detailed analysis of premodern education in the Thai northeast. Also see Keyes (1966a, 140–2; 1991, 90–95).

4. David Wyatt's *The Politics of Reform in Thailand* (1969) provides a detailed and insightful analysis of political debates and conflicts surrounding the modern educational system during the reign of King Chulalongkorn. Also see Watson (1982).

5. The term "rebelliousness" appears in a flyer circulated in Khorat in 1996 when Saipin's book about the history of Thaoying Mo became a source of controversy (see Keyes 2002a, 113).

6. There is some evidence that the Thai government's fear of communist activities in the Northeast at this time may have been connected with knowledge of the establishment of a Thai communist party in the early 1930s. In 1935 a Siamese delegate, with the improbable name of Rashi, represented a Siamese communist party for the first time at a meeting of the Comintern in Moscow. In a speech he delivered at the meeting he declared: "We, the communists of Siam, here at the Seventh Congress of the CI, for the first time have the good fortune to raise our voice and report that in our small and distant country there already exists a CP, and a revolutionary struggle is already developing. We are not yet a section of the CI, we only request our acceptance into the great world union of communists" (US Department of State, 1950, 28; also see Goscha 1998, 90).

7. *Thau* (*thao*) is a Lao title of respect. *Chin* might perhaps be the Thai and Lao word for Chinese (*Chin*), but this is only speculative. In 2002 Vietnamese long settled in northeastern Thailand erected a shrine in a village in Nakhon Phanom Province in memory of his visit to the region in the 1920s (Hardy 2008, 285). The shrine was built in the area of the Northeast where there is today a concentration

of people of Vietnamese descent rather than in Udon Province, where he actually spent most of his time.

8. During the Vietnamese war against the French in the post–World War II period even more Vietnamese refugees poured into northeastern Thailand. These people tended to be loyal to Ho Chi Minh and thus became a source of worry to the pro-Western government. However, despite the presence of a large number of pro-DRV Vietnamese in the Northeast, I do not believe that the "Vietnamese problem" was a component of the "northeastern problem." There is too much ethnic antipathy between these two peoples for the Vietnamese to have had any major political influence upon the northeasterners. This conclusion is borne out by studies of the Vietnamese in Thailand (Poole 1967, 1970, 1975; Flood 1977). In the late twentieth century after Thailand and Vietnam restored relations, the Vietnamese in northeastern Thailand began to gain new positive attention, especially from Vietnamese in Vietnam who had lived in Thailand or had relatives who had done so (also see Hardy 2008).

9. Using Ingram (1971, appendix D) for exchange rates, the equivalent in the 1930s for these figures would have been US$1.7 to 5.5 million.

10. Again, the following paragraphs on education have been adapted from Keyes (1991a).

11. The educational role of the *wat* was not entirely displaced by the secular school; it still remains possible to this day for a villager to gain an education as a novice that can be utilized for secular (and non-agricultural) purposes at a later stage in his life. For monastic education as a means to effect social mobility by people from rural backgrounds, see Wyatt (1966), Holmes (1974, 90–93), and Tambiah (1976, 288–312).

12. Dararat Mettarikanon (2003) has undertaken a much more detailed account than what I provide here of how northeasterners engaged with the parliamentary system after it was first created.

13. For an English text of this plan see Landon (1939, 260–93) and for a discussion of it see Vella (1955, 373–8). It should be noted that although the plan seems in Western eyes to be straightforward state socialism, within the Thai context it had different connotations. Bureaucratic membership was long aspired to by any Thai who wished to advance socially in the secular world. Thus, making all people employees of the state would confer this status on all.

14. In English language literature the representative body that in Thai is called *ratthasapha* was first called the "National Assembly," but in later literature has been called "Parliament."

15. Information on the origin and activities of prewar representatives in the National Assembly is extremely difficult to find. What data does exist usually relates only to the most prominent MPs.

16. For a brief description of the war and the subsequent negotiations see Vella (1955, 381–84), Landon (1941), and Crosby (1945, 117–21). For a Thai nationalist view written shortly after the war see Maha Sivaram (1941).

17. Direk Jayanama, then deputy minister of foreign affairs, is quoted in an article by Landon (1941, 39) as having given the following justification for Thailand's actions: "As it is evident that the action of the French in compelling Thailand to give up the Thai natural frontier, the Mekong River, renders our frontier devoid of strategic security, the most important object of government must be to secure the return of the Thai original frontier so that Thailand may be in a position to enjoy peace and happiness and need not fear danger from any other power.... If reference is made to the racial principle, it is clearly evident that the fact that Thailand should have the Mekong River as the frontier conforms in all respects to this racial principle. It is already well known that the people who live in that region are of the same race and blood as the Thais." For a fuller account of Nai Direk's role during World War II, see Direk Jayanama (2008).

18. One illustration of the importance of northeastern politicians in the Free Thai Movement can be found in the fact that in 1944 Thawin Udon (Roi Et) was sent as representative of the Free Thai to the Chinese government in Chungking (Smith and Clark 1945–46, 193). Among other northeastern MPs who were involved in the Free Thai Movement were Chamlong Daorueang (Maha Sarakham), Thong-in and his brother Thiam Sirikhan (Sakon Nakhon), Thong-in and his brother Thim Phuriphat (Ubon), Fong Sitthitham (Ubon), Liang Chaiyakan (Ubon), Kwang Thongthawi (Kalasin). The last three were followers of Khuang Aphaiwong more than of Pridi and later joined Khuang in founding the Democrat Party.

19. See, for example, Kurlantzick (2011, 50).

20. An informant from Phetchabun who had been born in the village in Maha Sarakham in which I did research claimed that most of the conscript labor for the Phetchabun scheme was from the Northeast. Whether or not this is true, other villagers believed it was so and, in consequence, held Phibun in low esteem.

21. Information on the activities of northeastern politicians just prior to the end of the war and in the immediate postwar period was taken, unless otherwise indicated, primarily from Thompson and Adloff's file on "Who's Who in Southeast Asia" (1945–50). This file, a microfilm of which exists in the Cornell University Library, is in turn based on press reports appearing in Bangkok in the 1945–50 period. There are many limitations to using this file, but it provided the only primary information available to me on the period. Dararat Mettarikanon (2003) has made use of other sources and her work should be consulted for more details.

22. The prime ministers in this period were Khuang Aphaiwong (August 1944–August 1945 and again from January 1946–March 1946), Seni Pramoj, who had been the Free Thai Movement's leader in the United States during the war (September

1945–January 1946), Pridi himself (March–August 1946), and Pridi's protegé, Thamrong Nawasawat (August 1946–November 1947). Both Khuang and Seni were to break with Pridi after March 1946.

23. Darling has claimed, without citing a source, that "The Cooperative Party [was] composed largely of Free Thai politicians from the poverty-stricken northeastern provinces" (Darling 1965, 47). Another political party, the Constitutional Front, also supported Pridi.

24. Shortly after the war the Khmer independence movement, called the Khmer Issarak, received Thai support and "set up a Committee to co-ordinate their activities in Bangkok" (Lancaster, 1961, 135). After French forces retook Vientiane on April 24, 1946, thus completing their reconquest of Laos, the leadership of the Lao Independence Movement (Lao Issara) fled to Bangkok and set up a government-in-exile there (Dommen 1965, 27). The Viet Minh set up a news agency in Bangkok and a headquarters for the purchase of arms (Tanham 1961, 67). Bernard Fall has claimed that most of the arms purchases made by the Viet Minh in Bangkok were from the United States (Fall 1964, 70, 465n14).

25. At the time Le Hi was the editor of the weekly *Vietnam News Bulletin* published in Bangkok, and Tran Van Giao was then the former head of the Provisional Executive Committee of Cochin-China (Thompson and Adloff 1950, 234–35). The other two officers of the league, both Thai, were Manot Watthitya (assistant secretary) and Sukhit Nimmanhemin (librarian). Although neither of the latter two were themselves northeasterners, both had close ties to Tiang Sirikhan. Representatives of Cambodia, Indonesia, Burma, and Malaya also signed the manifesto proclaiming the objectives of the league (Vietnam Information Service 1947, 7–8).

26. For a controversial (pro-Pridi) assessment of Ananda's death and the subsequent political ramifications, see Kruger (1964). Handley's (2006, 76–79) more recent review of what is (and is not) known about Ananda's tragic death supports the view that the conclusion that Pridi was responsible is not credible and he dismisses the rather bizarre theory of Stevenson (1999, 50ff) that Tsuji Masanobu, a Japanese wartime commander, arranged the assassination. Gilbert King (2011), in a long blog on the Smithsonian web site, has reviewed in some detail what is known about the circumstances surrounding King Ananda's death and does not reach a firm conclusion as to the cause of his death. King opines that "It is also possible that [King Bhumibol], too, remained uncertain of the circumstances surrounding his brother's death."

27. On the founding of the Prachachon Party, Coast has given this description: "In mid-1947 a serious split occurred among the Democrats' fifty-nine Assembly members when Nai Liang Jayakal [Liang Chaiyakan], MP from Ubon, formed the Prachachon, or People's Party, and took it into the Pridi camp. Liang claimed that

his group was not attached to anybody and that only his convictions had caused him to leave the Democrats; the Democrats, however, charged the split had been bought by Pridi" (Coast 1953, 38). However, whether Liang was still pro-Pridi at the time of the 1948 election is doubtful since he was shortly to organize an opposition in the Assembly that assumed pro-Phibun characteristics. Liang Chaiyakan, one of the most durable of the Isan MPs, having been elected in every election in the 1930s and 1940s, switched party allegiances at very opportune times. After the war, he was an organizer of the Democrat Party. When Pridi was firmly in power, Liang broke with the Democrats and joined in supporting Pridi. After the 1948 elections he became a supporter of Phibun and subsequently became a cabinet minister in Phibun's government.

28. Another northeastern MP, Fong Sitthitham, one of the main northeastern leaders of the Democrat Party, was also arrested at this time. Although he was later released, the inclusion in the arrests of a northeastern MP who was not a follower of Pridi reflects the extent to which the government had come to believe that the Isan region was a haven for sedition.

29. Professor Lauriston Sharp, who was engaged in field research in Thailand at the time of the Kilo 11 incident reports that in Bangkok and villages near kilometer 11, there was general shocked disapproval of Phibun and his unpopular police over this incident. For a time some passersby would salute the marker and for months peasants would express disapproval of a person by saying "send him to kilo 11!" However, while not condoning the "dirty business," peasants in nearby Bang Chan expressed the clear stereotype (probably acquired from government radio broadcasts) that the northeastern leaders were "rebellious," "enemies of democracy," and "spreaders of communism." (Lauriston Sharp, personal communication, March 1965). For another contemporary account of the Kilo 11 incident see Roth (1949).

30. The defense counsel for these men was Prayot Iamsila, later an MP from the northeastern province of Khon Kaen.

31. The rai, a standard unit of land measurement, is equal to approximately 3/5 of an acre. Although paddy production increased slightly in both regions in the 1950s, the same disparity between regions continued to hold. In 1960–61 the average yield in the central plains was 231 kilograms per rai as compared with 153 kilograms per rai for the Northeast (Thailand, Ministry of Agriculture 1961, 39).

32. Beginning in the late 1950s kenaf production became a major source of cash income in the Northeast. Although the expansion of kenaf production helped the Isan peasantry narrow the gap between the Northeast and the central plains in commercial agricultural production, the northeastern farm family continued to lag far behind the central Thai peasant family in cash income from farm production.

33. According to Ingram (1971, 337), the exchange rate for 1953 averaged 18.37 baht to the US dollar.

34. This statistic was obtained from Skinner (1957, 305), who in turn was quoting from an Economic and Demographic Survey of Bangkok (Thailand, Central Statistical Office, 1955, table 15–16).

35. That migrants were men from this age group is collaborated by many reports from the 1960s (Textor 1961, 6–7, 12; Klausner 1956, 2:2; Long et al. 1963, 100; and my own research in a village in Maha Sarakham). Also see Meinkoth (1962); Sternstein (1975); Pramote Prasarkul (1978); Hafner (1980); and Fuller, Peerasit, Lightfoot, and Sawaeng (1983). In the 1960 census there is some indication of this in the lower percentage of males in the age group 20–29 in the Northeast (16.3 percent) as compared with similar figures from other regions (17.2 percent in the North, 17.3 percent in the South, and 17.6 percent in the East) and the whole country (17.0 percent).

36. For other information on the phenomena of temporary migration of northeastern villagers to Bangkok in this period, see Textor (1961), Kirsch (1966), Klausner (1956, 1:16, 2:1–3), Kickert (1960, 2), and Long et al. (1963, 100–101). It should be noted that Bangkok has not been the only place that has attracted northeastern villagers in search of wage labor, but only those who have migrated to Bangkok and, to a lesser extent, to other places in the central plains are of interest here. As I discuss in the final chapter in this volume, northeasterners are not only the majority of internal migrants in Thailand, but they also came to constitute the majority of migrant workers from Thailand working overseas.

37. In political campaigns from at least the 1980s, politicians often used the phrase *ban hao* (Thai, *ban rao*), "our village" or "we villagers," when seeking the support of northeastern Thai villagers.

38. I have found mention of at least three different occasions between 1949 and 1957 when Isan representatives in Parliament called a rally of northeasterners in Bangkok: January 1949, December 1950 (both described in Thompson and Adloff 1945–50), and February 1957 (*Bangkok Post*, February 7, 1957).

39. In this period the government controlled rice exports through three organizations (two Chinese and one government controlled). The rice millers in the Northeast complained that they were not being allotted sufficient rolling stock to transport their rice and that they were forced to pay a fee ("security money") for quality control performed in Bangkok. These factors, the rice millers claimed, led to a reduction in profit and created conditions of unfair competition with rice firms in other parts of the country. In November 1948 all sixty-nine rice merchants in the Northeast banded together to protest to the government and finally a compromise was ostensibly reached in February 1949 (*Bangkok Post*, February 14, 1949). However, in July the issue was raised again in the Parliament by several Isan deputies thus suggesting the compromise had not been successful. Sharp made the following observation on this problem: "While the entire dispute may be seen in the large as a

calculated effort to loosen the grip of Chinese rice merchants on Thailand's economy, such incidents have furnished excellent grist for the local political mills of the Northeast and provide a factual basis for their claims of geographic discrimination by the central government" (Lauriston Sharp, unpublished manuscript, 1951).

40. According to Thompson and Adloff's files (Thompson and Adloff 1945–50) the four were Nat Ngoenthap (Independent, Maha Sarakham), Chuen Rawiwan (Sahathai—that is, a follower of Pridi) and Tiang Sirikhan, Nong Khai), Fong Sitthitham (Democrat, Ubon), and Yongyut Phuenphop (Sahathai, Udon).

41. As a major northeastern political leader, Thep Chotinuchit is something of an anomaly. According to a brief biography given by D. Wilson (1959, 314–15), Thep was the son of a government official in the central Thai province of Nakhon Pathom. He was a graduate of the Law Institute in Bangkok and later received an MA from Thammasat University. He was appointed a judge in 1937 and shortly thereafter elected to Parliament from Si Sa Ket. This is the first mention of his connection with Si Sa Ket Province that he was to represent, with an interlude between 1938 and 1947, until Sarit abolished the Parliament in 1958. What his connections with Si Sa Ket were to ensure him the popularity that he enjoyed there is not clear. Although born and educated in central Thailand, and although his brother, Pethai, was an important figure in Thonburi politics, Thep was one of the strongest advocates of northeastern causes. When Thep died in 1974, he was deemed to be a sufficiently significant political figure to merit an obituary in the Bangkok Post (April 8, 1974).

42. It is probable that all of the votes that Thep received were from among the 123 elected MPs since the appointed members of Parliament would undoubtedly have been Phibun supporters.

43. Klaew remained the leader of leftist politicians from the Northeast until his death in 2006 at the age of eighty-eight (The Nation, April 9 and 10, 2006).]

44. There was, however, a small underground communist party whose members were overwhelmingly Sino-Thai from Bangkok and southern Thailand.

45. These assertions are based upon knowledge of the past affiliations of the MPs in question, press reports of their campaigns, and subsequent actions that they engaged in after the election. The "leftists" were joined later by a number of other Isan deputies, primarily among those elected as Independents. However, it is impossible to determine if any of these others had run on a leftist platform or whether they had joined the left after being elected.

46. The Poujadists were a short-lived populist movement in France in the 1950s that espoused the elimination of taxes. The movement took its name from Pierre Poujade, its founder, who was a book and stationery shop owner.

47. Nai Liang was not so popular, however, with an audience of northeastern pedicab drivers whom he addressed in Bangkok just before the election. He promised that if the government parties won the election, the government would

help the northeastern pedicab drivers organize an association and would provide them with welfare housing. One member of the audience asked why the government was only now interested in helping the northeastern pedicab drivers to organize an association. Isan people had been driving pedicabs in Bangkok for more than ten years, and furthermore, why was it only at election time that the government was proposing a program of welfare housing when the drivers had requested such housing a year ago? "It was said that the crowd did not cheer [Liang Chaiyakan] but cheered the northeasterner who had questioned him" (*Bangkok Post*, February 7, 1957).

48. The percentage was not so high in the February 1957 election when 40 percent of those who had been MPs after the 1952 election were reelected. Of the fifty-three representatives chosen in the December 1957 election, thirteen had been elected in both 1952 and February 1957, sixteen had been elected in February 1957 but not in 1952, and eighteen were newly elected in December 1957.

49. Among the twenty-one deputies at this meeting there were six from leftist parties, eight from pro-government parties, and four independents.

CHAPTER 5 MONARCHY, SECURITY, AND DEVELOPMENT

1. In his semi-authorized biography of the king, Stevenson (1999) provides much detail about the tension that existed between the king and Phibun after the king's return.

2. Much has been written about the US support for the Thai military and the counterinsurgency effort in Thailand. See Thak's biography of Sarit (Thak 1979), Fineman (1997), and Glasser (1995). My summary about US bases in Thailand is taken from a Wikipedia article: "United States Air Force in Thailand" (http://en.wikipedia.org/wiki/United_States_Air_Force_in_Thailand); in turn this article is based on information from the *Air Force Historical Research Agency*.

3. William Klausner (personal communication, April 25, 2012) notes that in the 1950s, the term for "development" was *burana* and only later changed to *phatthana*. The root meaning of *burana* is "fulfilled," while that of *phatthana* is "prosperity." The reason for this change has not yet been fully explored by scholars of Thailand.

4. When my wife and I were based in Khon Kaen in 2004–5, we often passed by the monument, but almost never saw anyone looking at it.

5. I first became aware of the role USIS played in making the king and queen better known in an interview I had with the head of USIS in September 1962.

6. This photo is reproduced in Stevenson (1999) with the caption "With a leper, continuing the work of his doctor-father to cure and bring lepers into normal society." I don't think that many who saw this photo in the 1950s and 1960s knew the woman was a leper, but it did convey the sense that the king's touch carried a potency that was more than simply that of a friendly gesture. Handley's (2006) much more

impressive critical biography of the king fails to give adequate attention to the charisma that Thai citizens associate with the king. William Klausner (personal communication, April 25, 2012) recalled that when he was engaged in fieldwork in a village in Ubon, he "witnessed the villagers laying down white cloths for the king to step on when he visited Ubon in 1955. They then took these cloths, imbued with the sacred power of the king, to be worshiped in their homes."

7. One villager noted that the king then spoke Thai with a slight accent, a consequence of his having been educated in Switzerland in a school where French was the medium of instruction.

8. *Molam* means a person with competence (*mo*) in singing (*lam*). *Molam mu* is performed with a troupe (*mu*) as distinct from other forms of *molam* that may be performed by a couple or an individual. For more on the *molam* tradition of the Northeast, see Miller (1985).

9. Leedom Lefferts in a recent paper (2011) has made a case for how the traditional annual ritual of *bun phra wet* in the Northeast at which the *jataka* story is told/enacted of Prince Vessantara (Phra Wet), the last incarnation of the man who became the Buddha, induces the northeasterners to recognize "their relationship with their rulers and become active in legitimating the rulers' rights and responsibilities to them." In other words the story of Phra Wet, like the stories told in *molam mu,* contributed to shaping a worldview in which villagers see themselves as subjects of a Buddhist monarch.

10. Charles Keyes, unpublished fieldnotes, October 31, 1963.

11. I elaborated on this point in my "Power of Merit" (Keyes 1973b).

12. This was before Thai soldiers began to be sent to fight in Vietnam and Laos.

13. They also had firsthand contact with American soldiers since, in conjunction with this exercise, an American Civic Action group constructed a new school only a few kilometers away from Ban Nong Tuen.

14. The main leadership within the pro-government party for repealing the Anti-communist Act came from Thim Phuriphat (Ubon) and Woraphot Wongsanga, a deputy from Udon.

15. In the aftermath of this coup many left-wing northeastern MPs as well as pro-government MPs who had traveled to Russia or China were arrested or went into exile. Among those arrested were Thawisak Triphli (Hyde Park Movement, Khon Kaen), Klaeo Noraphat (Economist, Khon Kaen), Thep Chotinuchit (Economist, Si Sa Ket), Yuang Iamsila (Free Democrat MP elected in February but not December, Udon), Plueang Wansi (independent, Surin), and Phonchai Saengchat (Economist, Si Sa Ket), as well as Banchoet Saichya (National Socialist, Roi Et), who had visited China. Thim Phuriphat and Sa-ing Marangkun (Buri Ram) and perhaps other Isan deputies reportedly found asylum in Laos in Pathet Lao territory.

16. Sarit's death from liver failure was attributed to his heavy drinking.

17. Sarit and his successors found that labeling their presumed enemies as "communist" led to increased military and foreign aid from the United States (see Fineman 1997). In other words, the northeastern problem" was as much a creation of the United States as the Thai government.

18. See, in this regard, the detailed memorandum, "Counterinsurgency in Thailand," prepared by the International and Social Studies Division of the Institute for Defense Analyses, dated June 1968 (http://foia.abovetopsecret.com/Vietnam_War/Thailand/COUNTERINSURGENCY_IN_THAILAND_VOL_1.pdf).

19. Hans Platenius (1963), the World Bank Adviser to the Northeastern Development Committee in the 1960s, offered a detailed appraisal of the development needs of the Northeast, but expressed doubt that the government would actually be able to significantly address these needs. Platenius observed that the centralized form of government in Thailand tended to preclude the design and implementation of policies tailored specifically to regionally specific problems (Platenius 1963, 99ff; also see Harmon 1964).

20. The 1963 film *The Ugly American*, directed and produced by George Englund and starring Marlon Brando, based on a novel by Eugene Burdick and William J. Lederer, contains a sequence on road building in Thailand (albeit disguised as a fictional country, Sarkhan) conveys well the "security" premise on which US loans to Thailand for expanding the road network was based.

21. In 1962–64 Jane and I made much use of local buses to travel from Maha Sarakham to Ban Phai in Khon Kaen Province, the railhead from which we took a train to Bangkok.

22. The Ubol Ratana Dam was completed in 1966 and the Lam Pao Dam in 1968. The Sirindhorn Dam in Ubon Province was completed in 1970.

23. Given the porous character of soils in the Northeast, the deepness of the rivers, and the relative lack of natural embankments in the forms of mountains or hills, the region is not well suited to dam projects.

24. On the Community Development Program, see Thailand, Ministry of Interior, Community Development Bureau, Department of Interior (1961, 1962); Thailand, Ministry of Interior, Community Development Department, Research and Evaluation Division, Department of Interior and American Institutes for Research, Asia/Pacific Office (1970); Titaya (1964); Yatsushiro et al. (1964); Choop (1965); Patya (1968); Keyes (1966a, 97–103).

25. Mobile Development Units were first established in 1962 (see Thailand, Ministry of Defense 1962, as cited in Nairn 1966, 105n). They received significant financial as well as logistical support from the United States military (see Huff 1967).

26. Given that much migration from the Northeast was temporary or circular, it is probable that the number of migrants to Bangkok during this period was under reported and that the proportion may have been higher than the figures given.

27. I used *sat* rather than *chat* in transliterating the word for "citizen" in this quote in order to convey how it was expressed in the local northeastern dialect.

28. The article was published in Thai under the pseudonym of *phusuekhao khong rao*, "Our Special Correspondent," as "Chotmai chak Isan" (Letter from the Northeast) in *Sangkhomsat Porithat* (Social Science Review), in the 1960s practically the only outlet for critical reflection on politics in Thailand (Keyes 1968). The article prompted what was then known as the Communist Suppression Operations Command (later known as the Internal Security Operations Command) to send a team led by a police and army colonel to visit Maha Sarakham and my friend in Ban Nong Tuen was called to the provincial capital. Although "he denied everything because otherwise he would have been a marked man" (Charles Keyes, unpublished field notes, July 14, 1980), all demands for bribes ended and the leader of the bandit group was sentenced to jail. By the time the bandit leader was released over a decade later the situation had significantly changed; not only was he blind, but he no longer had any patrons left in the police or justice system. My intervention clearly had made a difference and, thus, the conclusion of my friend's case was far from typical. To this day many in Thailand who commit criminal acts are able to avoid punishment because of the assistance of police or other officials.

CHAPTER 6 THE FAILURE OF COMMUNIST REVOLUTION

1. This chapter has been adapted in part from Keyes (2011a).

2. The communist-led insurrection in Malaysia had spilled over into southern Thailand where some Sino-Thai had sympathy for the cause led by Sino-Malay. Even after Chin Peng, the leader of the insurrection, fled to southern Thailand in 1960 and continued until 1989 to mount low-level attacks across the border, he found little support for the insurrection among Sino-Thai, much less Thai-Malay, in southern Thailand. Nonetheless, the leadership of the Communist Party of Thailand was in the hands of Sino-Thai throughout the history of the CPT.

3. The only information that I have been able to find on the "Thai Exiles Group" or "Thai Exiles Association" appears, undocumented, in the *US Army Area Handbook for Thailand* (American University 1963, 384–85). This group apparently included several Thai groups living in exile in communist countries. However, for our interests, the most important was the one in Laos: "The Association's activities, in the autumn of 1962 seemed to focus on a plan to unite the Northeastern Region with Laos. Thai police were called on in September to investigate reports that the exile group in Laos was sending some of its members into the region to conduct separatist propaganda among the villagers. In November, Minister of the Interior General

Praphas Charusathien asserted that the bulk of the exiles do not constitute a serious subversive threat, but that a few of them, like Deputy Minister of Education Tim Buriphat [Thim Phuriphat, former MP from Ubon], do have sufficient prestige in the Northeastern Region to bear watching" (American University 1963, 385).

4. The Thai term for "forest fighters," *tahan pa,* incorporates the term *pa,* which traditionally has been used in contrast to *ban* or *muang,* "village" or "polity." The *pa* was historically considered to be the home of people who were wild and dangerous. Communist insurrectionaries who identified as belonging to the "forest army" were, thus, putting themselves beyond the existing (political) order.

5. Charles Keyes, unpublished fieldnotes, September 12, 1972. Another genre of popular music that emerged in this period—*phleng luk thung,* "songs of the children of the rice fields"—with roots in traditional northeastern music—would subsequently become a vehicle for expression of the hardships of life in rural areas, but usually with reference to romance rather than politics.

6. Both Stuart-Fox and Girling are drawing on other sources that they credit.

7. Information on this incident is drawn from a report entitled "Human Rights in Thailand, May–June 1977," put out by Coordinating Group for Religion in Society in Bangkok (1976–78).

8. Charles Keyes, unpublished fieldnotes, July 31, 1980.

9. In this connection see the analysis of the party published most probably by former student leaders in Sweden in 1980. The analysis observes that the flexibility of "middle-ranking cadres" who formulated "local policies from the local situation" contrasted with "the policies adopted by the top leadership" Thailand Information Center 1980, 11).

10. Chiranan's memoirs of her time in the jungle with the CPT, published in 2006, also document this break between the students and the party. In a personal conversation (June 2006), she told me that the students really never knew the CPT leaders, who were surrounded by an aura of mystery (Chiranan 2006).

11. It is still more common for boys in northern Thailand than those in northeastern Thailand to be ordained temporarily as novices.

12. The sources for these data are household surveys carried out in 1963 and 2005 respectively. Another survey carried out in 1980 showed that the decline had begun by that time.

13. After being forced from the premiership, the king appointed Tanin to the Privy Council.

14. See "Obituary of General Kriangsak Chomanan," *The Sunday Times,* January 22, 2004, from online edition, http://www.timesonline.co.uk/tol/comment/obituaries/article1000123.ece.

15. Obituary of Kriangsak Chomanan, *The Economist*, January 8, 2004; online at http://www.economist.com/node/2329646?story_id=2329646.

16. After they returned from the jungle Seksan and Thirayut went abroad for graduate study (something that would not have been possible in the post 9/11 world, as they would have been considered "terrorists") and returned to Thailand to assume academic posts. Today, both are well-known public intellectuals and prominent advocates for Thai civil society.

17. I am indebted to Jarin Boonmathya, a long time NGO worker and organizer, for information on the NGO movement. In addition to conversations, also see Jarin Boonmathya (1986, n.d.). Gohlert (1991) also provides much general information about the NGO movement.

18. In 1991 this organization was given official recognition by the government. This recognition was brokered by Meechai Viravaidya, then minister attached to the office of then prime minister Anand Panyarachun (see *The Nation*, August 21, 1991, and Amara Pongsapich 1992, 11). The creation of a Joint Coordination Committee between the representatives of government agencies and NGOs working on development issues signaled that the NGO movement had evolved in the fifteen years since the October 6 coup from having a very tenuous and marginal place within the Thai political system to being a major force within that system. NGOs prospered in no small part because of the significant financial support they received from foreign foundations such as Ford and Rockefeller and those established by German and Scandinavian governments.

19. Many of Than Buddhadasa's sermons have been translated into English. Particularly noteworthy in this regard are his essays on "Buddhist socialism" (*thammikasangkhomniyom*). See Buddhadasa (1986, 1989). For good introductions to the work of Than Buddhadasa, see Swearer (1979) and Jackson (1988). The collection *Radical Conservatism: Buddhism in the Contemporary World—Articles in Honour of Bhikkhu Buddhadasa's 84th Birthday Anniversary*, compiled by the Thai Inter-Religious Commission for Development and International Network of Engaged Buddhists (Bangkok: The Sathirakoses-Nagapradipa Foundation, 1990), contains pieces by many of those who have sought to put Than Buddhadasa's ideas into practice.

CHAPTER 7 ENTREPRENEURS, MIGRANTS, AND PROTESTORS

1. This chapter draws in part on papers first presented as keynote addresses at the Eighth International Thai Studies Conference, Nakhon Phanom, Thailand, January 9–12, 2002, and the Tenth International Thai Studies Conference, Thammasat University, Bangkok, January 2008, and on Keyes (2014).

2. Data for 1960 to 1993 are from Jansen (1997, 4), and for 1994 to 1997 from Bank of Thailand (1997).

3. The work of Jonathan Rigg (see especially 1991, 1994, and Rigg and Salamanca 2009) and Mary Beth Mills (1997, 1999), who also conducted long-term research in Maha Sarakham Province, as well as that by Ratana Tosakul Boonmathya (1997), and Leedom Lefferts (1974, 2004) in Khon Kaen, confirm my own findings.

4. Population figures used for calculating these percentages have been taken, in part, from Lefferts (1974, 62).

5. In 1966–67 I made a collection of tools used in Ban Nong Tuen for farming, hunting and gathering, utensils for making clothing and for cooking food, and such personal and household goods as clothing, betel-nut boxes, and lanterns, for the Burke Memorial Washington State Museum. In 1972–74, I made a similar collection for the American Museum of Natural History in New York. Photos and descriptions of these artifacts can be seen via the websites of the two museums—see http://collections.burkemuseum.org/ethnology/search.php?lc=seasia (search under source: Keyes) and http://anthro.amnh.org/asia (search under donor: Keyes).

6. High (2009), based on research in rural Laos, discusses the significance of the cult of *phi pu ta* for being the focus of village-based identity even for many who have moved away from their natal communities.

7. See chapter 5 for an explanation of this term.

8. I developed this interpretation further in another paper (Keyes 1983b). Also see Keyes (1990 and 1991b).

9. The difference in average household income between those reported in my survey and in more general surveys is a consequence, in part, of different methods. Nonetheless, the data from the 2005 survey in Ban Nong Tuen regarding household income understate significantly the actual household income primarily because of the failure of many families to report most of the remittances they received from family members working away from the village.

10. Don Daeng village is probably the most studied village in northeastern Thailand. Koichi Mizuno carried out the first study in the village in the early 1960s and continued his work into the 1970 (his 1971 study is the most comprehensive). After his untimely death from cancer, colleagues associated with Kyoto University's Center for Southeast Asian Studies began a series of restudies. Some of the results of their work have been published in English (see Fukui, Kaida, and Kuchiba 1983, 1985, and 1988; and Fukui, et al. 1996).

11. These statistics have been calculated from tables found in United Nations Development Programme, Thailand (2010). The map on page 124 of the 2009 UNDP report mislabels Maha Sarakham Province, but the map itself shows the province to be in the second-lowest rung of average income for the country, with most other

northeastern provinces being in the lowest rung. The 2003 report has a better map that shows that average income in the province at that time was in the middle range for the country (United Nations Development Programme, Thailand, 2003, 97). Comparison of these two reports and the one for 2007 is very revealing as to the perspectives of the Thai governments at the time. The 2003 report, prepared when Thaksin Shinawatra was prime minister, focuses on "the power of empowerment," referring to the increasing role played in Thai society by non-governmental organizations such as the Assembly of the Poor. The 2007 report (United Nations Development Programme, Thailand 2007), prepared in the wake of the coup of 2006, made the king's philosophy of "sufficiency development" the organizing theme. The 2009 report prepared after the ascent to power of the Democrat Party–led government at the end of 2008 was more technocratically focused.

12. Population figures used for calculating these percentages have been taken, in part, from Lefferts (1974, 62).

13. The questions I asked in my survey about family planning in 1963 caused some villagers to realize that less dangerous or intrusive methods of birth control existed. The fact that we lived in Ban Nong Tuen for fifteen months and Jane did not become pregnant stimulated many village women to ask Jane for advice, but as the pill had not yet become available, the only method she could tell them about were IUDs, which were then priced beyond what village women could afford. The interest women showed in family planning in the early 1960s foreshadowed, we realized retrospectively, the significant adoption of birth control methods, the most common of which was tubal ligation, which began to become available from the mid-1960s on.

14. Getting precise data on the most common types of migration in the 1960s and 1970s is very difficult because official statistics did not count as migrants those who had lived for only several months away from their home (Fuller, Peerasit, Lightfoot, and Sawaeng 1983, 37–39).

15. Charles Keyes, unpublished fieldnotes, February 4, 2005

16. These figures are based on Thailand, National Statistical Office, Office of the Prime Minister (1997).

17. Thai women who found domestic work abroad were and remain many fewer than women from the Philippines.

18. Supang Chantavanich and Germershausen (2000, 9, table 1) give a figure of 104,824 migrants in Middle Eastern countries other than Israel and a figure of 362 for Israel; Tsay (2001, 22, table 1) gives a figure of 114,135.

19. Because the Saudi jewel robbery has never been resolved to the satisfaction of the government of Saudi Arabia, the ban on Thai labor in Saudi Arabia continues to the present (see Marshall 2010).

20. In 2011 I learned from Suriya Smutkupt, who had earlier in the year carried out research among Thai migrants in Korea, that a significant number of villagers from the Northeast have recently gone to Korea to work. In 2011 when the Libya crisis developed, it emerged that more than 20,000 Thai, almost all from the Northeast, were working in the country (*Bangkok Post*, March 4, 2011; also see Keyes 2011b).

21. Although "in 1994 the Ministry of Labour and Welfare announced the ceiling fee of 46,000 baht per person . . . private agencies could charge" prospective migrant workers, a study made by the Thai Department of Employment in 1995 found "that a large number of workers paid a fee in the range of 70,000–75,000 baht per person (Somchai Ratanakomut 2000, 129). One villager in Ban Nong Tuen told me he had paid 100,000 baht in 1999 to go to work in Taiwan. Workers who went to Libya had to pay "between 120,000 baht and 180,000 baht for job placement services and signed one-year contracts" (*Bangkok Post*, February 27, 2011).

22. Guest workers, by definition, are not allowed to remain permanently in the countries where they work, although some do remain either as illegal workers or as spouses of local people. Among legal migrants overseas, the most well recognized in northeastern Thailand are those women originally from villages who have become *mia farang*, wives of Westerners. Most of these live in Europe. Patcharin Lapanun's (2013) dissertation is a detailed ethnography of how such transnational marriages have reshaped social relations in one community from which many such women have come.

23. The amount of forested land at the beginning of the twenty-first century has been estimated as being between 25 percent (http://www.fao.org/docrep/003/X6967E/x6967e09.htm) and 32 percent (https://www.earthobservations.org/documents/cop/ag_forest/20090701_thailand/15%20Forest%20Cover%20Assessment%20in%20Thailand.pdf).

24. Even the Siam Society sponsored a symposium in 1987 entitled "Culture and the Environment" that included strong critiques of government environmental policies (see The Siam Society [1989], especially the essays in this volume by Chayan Vaddhanphuti and Shalardchai Ramitanondh). There are many works that trace the development of environmentalist movements in Thailand. See, especially, Hirsch (1993, 1994, 1996, 1997), Hirsch and Lohman (1989), Quigley (1995), Rigg (1995), and Usher (2009).

25. The full name of the program was *Khrongkan chatsan thidin thamkin kae ratsadon phu yak rai nai phuenthi pa sanguan sueam thorom*, "Program to distribute arable land for landless people in the degraded forest reserves." This program has been the subject of two detailed studies by Tjelland (1995) and Pye (2005). The Thai initials are often transliterated as *Khor Jor Kor*.

26. I have adopted the notion of "strategic group" from Pye (2005, 294), who argues that "forest politics" in Thailand have been "the outcome of conscious

strategies of different and competing groups developed and pursued under changing social and political conditions."

27. The conflict in which Phra Prachak became embroiled involved villagers mainly in Pakham District, Buri Ram, and Soeng Sang District, Khorat. For other analyses of the case of Phra Prachak, see Taylor (1993b), Jackson (1997, 91–93), and Keyes (1999).

28. He would subsequently find refuge in a Buddhist retreat (see http://www. whatdoyouthinkmyfriend.com/Misc/phra.html).

29. For chronologies of events relating to the Pak Mun controversy, see Sharma and Imhof (1999) and Atiya Achakulwisut (2000).

30. The name has been variously translated as "Sustainable Mun River Village" and "Longevity of the Mun River Village."

31. A publication I purchased from representatives of the Assembly of the Poor at Pak Mun lists sixteen serious cases negatively affecting villagers in northeastern Thailand that the government was called on to address. These include five dams that had already been built, three in the process of being built, five cases relating to forest reserves or national parks, and three cases relating to the use of common lands. Thirteen of the cases concerned Ubon Ratchathani Province (six in Khong Chiam District, the same district as that in which Pak Mun is located). Of the others, two were in Chaiyaphum Province and two in Si Sa Ket Province (Fai Wichakan Samatcha Khon Chon [Technical Unit, Assembly of the Poor] 2000). The Assembly of the Poor has championed the causes not only of rural people in northeastern Thailand but has also played a role in cases involving rural peoples in other areas as well. On the Assembly of the Poor, see Baker (2000) and Missingham (2003).

32. The World Commission on Dams had been set up in 1997 with support by both the World Bank and International Union for Conservation of Nature (IUCN) to "review the development effectiveness of dams and assess alternatives for water resources and energy development, and to develop internationally-acceptable criteria and guidelines to advise future decision-making in the planning, design, construction, monitoring, operation, and decommissioning of dams." See http://www.dams.org/about/history.htm.

CHAPTER 8 SILENT PEASANTS NO LONGER

1. See the constitution at http://www.admincourt.go.th/amc_eng/02-LAW/laws/ContitutionBE2540-1997.pdf.

2. On Chamlong's career until the late 1990s, see McCargo (1998).

3. Montesano (2010, 280–82) has compared Thaksin to Perón. On the comparison with Chavez, I was struck in watching the news about Venezuela that the

followers of Chavez, like those of Thaksin, came primarily from the non-privileged classes of society, yet Chavez, like Thaksin, used his power in self-serving ways.

4. On the Red Shirt movement in general see Pinyo Traisuriyathamma (2010) and Chairat Charoensin-Olarn (2012); on the movement in the Northeast, see Pattana Kittiarsa (2012a), Elinoff (2012), Somchai Phatharathananunth (2012), Sopranzetti (2012a, 2012b), Taylor (2012); and on the movement in the North, see Pinkaew Laungaramsri (2012).

5. This phrase was coined by Andrew Turton (1984) with reference to an earlier political crisis in Thailand.

6. The provinces of the upper north, with the exception of Mae Hong Son, voted against the constitution with "no" votes ranging from 55 to 70 percent in each province. For data and a map relating to this referendum, see http://www.electoralgeography.com/en/countries/t/thailand/2007-constitutional-referendum-thailand.html.

7. "Thai Killed in Palestinian Rocket Attack," *The Nation*, March 19, 2010; http://www.nationmultimedia.com/home/2010/03/19/national/Thai-killed-in-Palestinian-rocket-attack-30125044.html.

8. I have made a more extended argument for why I use the term "cosmopolitan villagers" in Keyes (2012).

9. The number of deaths have been variously reported from eighty-five to ninety-two. In the parliamentary debate that took place in early June 2009, the opposition claimed that there were even more deaths, with some having been concealed. See Kinan Suchaovanich, "Thai Leader Defends Self at Censure Debate," *Associated Press*, June 1, 2009; http://www.google.com/hostednews/ap/article/ALeqM5g3j-vAVG1fg3kEfnogTiH8_4EXvwD9G2HHH03. Since 2012, the figure of ninety-two has been used by Prime Minister Yingluck and others in her government.

10. The number of eleven military casualties comes from an official Thai government website—http://www.thaiembdc.org/Ann_Doc/Thailandupdate8_10.pdf.

11. I know from my own research in the National Archives in Bangkok that there were also official reports from earlier times. But Phya Anuman's "Life of the Thai Farmer" is, to my knowledge, the first published account. *Phya* (or *phraya*) is a title conferred by a Thai king on a distinguished non-royal person. "Life of the Thai Farmer" was first published in Thai in 1948 as a funerary volume for Mrs. Phiw Chaitnanthana. It was republished in Thai in 1965 in a collection of Phya Anuman's essays. William Gedney, a distinguished linguist specializing on Thai and related languages, published an English translation in 1955 and included this translation in a subsequent collection of translations of Phya Anuman's writings (see Anuman 1955, 1961, and 1965).

12. I also discussed the essay in person with Phya Anuman, whom I had the privilege of meeting and getting to know during my first stay in Thailand (see Keyes 1973a).

13. I cannot confirm from any source I have consulted that this worker was in fact originally from northeastern Thailand, but it is highly likely that he was since most Thai citizens working in Israel were and still are from the Northeast. The significance of northeasterners employed abroad once again made the headlines in most Thai newspapers when in February–March 2011 the upheaval in Libya revealed that there were nearly twenty-four thousand Thai working in Libya (*The Nation*, February 24, 2011). All reports about these workers identified them as being primarily from Nakhon Ratchasima and Udon Provinces in northeastern Thailand (see, for example, *Bangkok Post*, March 9, 2011 and my op-ed piece, "Returnees Have Little to Look Forward To," *Bangkok Post*, March 25, 2011).

14. This "temple fair" character of Red Shirt gatherings in Bangkok totally disappeared following the violent crackdown on April 10, 2010. Subsequent gatherings, even after the success of the Pheu Thai Party in the 2011 election, were "haunted" by the memory of the violence of April 10.

15. The king's philosophy was first presented in a speech in December 1997 in reaction to the economic crisis that had developed that year. He proposed that if his subjects would practice a "sufficiency economy" (*sethakit phophiang*), "even fifty percent, but perhaps only twenty-five percent" the crisis could be made bearable. The king proposed that the people of the country should embrace practices that accentuated practices of cooperation and self-reliance to provide for their basic needs rather than depending on markets that were subject to the insecurities of the global capitalist economy. An English translation of the king's speech can be found on line at http://kanchanapisek.or.th/speeches/1997/1204.en.html. The philosophy is the subject of diverse interpretations in Seri Phongphit, with Rado and Long (2014).

16. http://www.naewna.com/news.asp?ID=193202. The weblog, "Political Prisoners in Thailand," dated January 3, 2010 (http://thaipoliticalprisoners. wordpress.com/2010/01/03/new-chirmsak-on-civil-war/) characterizes Chirmsak as "an important intellectual critic of Thaksin and the red shirt movement" and another weblog, "Bangkok Pundit" (http://us.asiancorrespondent.com/bangkok-pundit-blog, January 3, 2010, characterizes him as a fervent supporter of the PAD (People's Alliance for Democracy), a.k.a. one of the Yellow Shirts.

17. Hewison and Kengkij Kitirianglarp (2010) trace these competing views of sovereignty from the 1932 coup to the present for national politics. Malay-speaking peoples in the far south of Thailand also have challenged the Bangkok elite view of sovereignty, but they have not made common cause with northeasterners and northerners or been seen by these latter as sharing the same political objectives.

Anusorn Unno's (2010) dissertation, "We Love 'Mr. King': Exceptional Sovereignty, Submissive Subjectivity, and Mediated Agency in Islamic Southern Thailand," lays out well how Malay-speaking and Muslim villagers in the province of Narathiwat situate themselves with reference to the "competing sovereignties" of the Thai Buddhist nation-state, the old yet still relevant principality of Patani, and transnational Islam.

REFERENCES

Adas, Michael. 1979. *Prophets of Rebellion: Millenarian Protest Movements against the European Colonial Order.* Chapel Hill: University of North Carolina Press.

Agamben, Giorgio. 2005. *State of Exception.* Translated by Kevin Attell. Chicago: University of Chicago Press.

Akin Rabibhadana. 1969. *The Organization of Thai Society in the Early Bangkok Period, 1782–1873.* Ithaca: Cornell University Southeast Asia Program, Data Paper No. 74.

Amara Bhumiratana. 1969. "Four Charismatic Monks in Thailand." Unpublished MA thesis, University of Washington.

Amara Pongsapich. 1992. "Strengthening the Role of NGOs in Popular Participation." Paper presented at a conference on "Democratization in Asia: Meeting the Challenges of the 1990s," Chiang Mai, December 7–11.

American University. Special Operations Research Office, Foreign Area Studies Division. 1963. *U.S. Army Area Handbook for Thailand.* Washington, June.

Amorawong Wichit (Phatom Khanechon), comp. 1963. "*Phongsawadan hua muang monthon Isan*" [Chronicle of the provinces in the NE circle]. In *Prachum phongsawadan phak 4 lae prawat thongthi Changwat Maha Sarakham* [Collected chronicles, part 4 and local history of Maha Sarakham Province]. Maha Sarakham: Cremation Volume for Phra Sarakhammuni.

Amyot, Jacques. 1964. *Intensive Village Study Project, April–May 1964: Ban Nonlan, Amphur Uthumphonphisai, Si Sa Ket, Preliminary Report.* Bangkok: Department of Social Studies, Faculty of Political Science, Chulalongkorn University, typescript.

Anuman Rajadhon (Sathian Koset). 1965 [1948]. "Chiwit chao na" [Life of the Farmer]. In *Prapheni bettalet* [Miscellaneous Customs] by Sathian Koset, 129–94. Bangkok: Samakhom Sangkhomsat Haeng Prathet Thai [Social Science Association of Thailand Press].

————. 1955. *The Life of the Thai Farmer*. Translated by William Gedney. New Haven: HRAF Press.

————. 1961. "The Life of the Farmer." In *Life and Ritual in Old Siam: Three Studies of Thai Life and Custom*, by Phya Anuman Rajadhon, edited and translated by William J. Gedney, 1–60. New Haven: HRAF Press.

————. 1961. *The Nature and Development of the Thai Language*. Bangkok: The Fine Arts Department (Thai Culture, New Series, no. 10).

Anusorn Unno. 2010. "'We Love 'Mr. King'": Exceptional Sovereignty, Submissive Subjectivity, and Mediated Agency in Islamic Southern Thailand." Unpublished PhD dissertation, University of Washington.

Archaimbault, Charles. 1961. "L'Histoire de Champasak." *Journal Asiatique* 294 (4): 519–95.

Aree Sanhachawee. 1970. "Evolution in Curriculum and Teaching." In *Education in Thailand: A Century of Experience*, 95–114. Bangkok: Ministry of Education, Department of Elementary and Adult Education.

Atiya Achakulwisut. 2000. "The Dark Side of Development." *Bangkok Post*, May 2.

Atiya Achakulwisut and Vasana Chinvarakorn. 2000. "Hungry for Justice." *Bangkok Post, Outlook*, August 2.

Aymonier, Étienne. 1895 and 1897. *Voyage dans le Laos*. 2 vols. Paris: Leroux.

Baker, Chris. 2000. "Thailand's Assembly of the Poor: Background, Drama, Reaction." *South East Asia Research* 8 (1): 5–30.

Baker, Chris, and Pasuk Phongpaichit. 2005. *A History of Thailand*. Cambridge: Cambridge University Press.

Bangkok Post. 1999. *Bangkok Post 1999 Economic Review Year-End Edition*, Internet edition. December.

Bank of Thailand. 1997. *Annual Economic Report 1997*. Bangkok.

————. 1998. *Quarterly Bulletin* 38 (34). Bangkok.

Battye, Noel. 1966–67. "Communism and Northeast Thailand During the Administration of Field Marshal Thanom Kittikatchorn, December 9, 1963–September 13, 1966: A Commentary on Some Bangkok, Hanoi, Peking, and New York News Media." Ithaca, mimeo.

Behrman, Jere R. 1968. *Supply Response in Underdeveloped Agriculture: A Case Study of Four Major Annual Crops in Thailand, 1937–1963*. Amsterdam: North Holland Publishing Co. (Contributions to Economic Analysis, 55).

Bell, Peter F. 1969. "Thailand's Northeast: Regional Underdevelopment, 'Insurgency', and Official Response." *Pacific Affairs* 42 (1): 47–54.

Bourdieu, Pierre. 1977. *Outline of a Theory of Practice*. Translated by Richard Nice. Cambridge: Cambridge University Press.

Bourotte, Bernard. 1955. "Essai d'histoire des populations montagnards du Sud-Indochinois jusqu'à 1945." *Bulletin de Société des Etudes Indochinoises* 30:1–133.

Brailey, Nigel J. 1973. "Chiengmai and the Inception of an Administrative Centralization Policy in Siam (I)." *Southeast Asian Studies* (Kyoto) 11 (3): 299–320.

————. 1974. "Chiengmai and the Inception of an Administrative Centralization Policy in Siam (II)." *Southeast Asian Studies* (Kyoto) 11 (4): 439–69.

Breazeale, Kennon. 1975. "The Integration of the Lao States into the Thai Kingdom." Unpublished DPhil dissertation, Oxford University.

————. 2002. "Laos Mapped by Treaty and Decree, 1895–1907." In *Breaking New Ground in Lao History: Essays on the Seventh to Twentieth Centuries*, edited by Mayoury Ngaosrivathana and Kennon Breazeale, 297–336. Chiang Mai: Silkworm Books.

Briggs, Lawrence Palmer. 1951. *The Ancient Khmer Empire*. Philadelphia: The American Philosophical Society (Transactions of the American Philosophical Society, n.s., vol. 41, part 1).

Brown, J. Marvin. 1965. *From Ancient Thai to Modern Dialects*. Bangkok: Social Science Association Press of Thailand.

Buddhadasa Bhikkhu [Phutthathat Phikkhu]. 1986. *Thammikasangkhomniyom/ Dhammic Socialism*. Edited and translated by Donald K. Swearer. Bangkok: Munnithi Komonkhimthong [2529].

————. 1989. *Me and Mine: Selected Essays of Bhikkhu Buddhadasa*. Edited by Donald K. Swearer. Albany: State University of New York Press.

Bunchuai Atthakon, comp. 1962. *Prawatsat haeng phak Isan lae Maha Sarakham bang ton* [Some aspects of the history of the Northeast and Maha Sarakham]. Maha Sarakham: Cremation Volume for Nang Pathuma Atthakon.

Chairat Charoensin-Olarn. 1988. *Understanding Postwar Reformism in Thailand*. Bangkok: Editions Duang Kamol.

Changwat Buri Ram: Ngan chalong 25 phutthasatawat [Buri Ram Province: Twenty-Fifth Century or the Buddhist Era Celebration]. 1957 [BE 2500]. Bangkok.

Changwat Chaiyaphum: Ngan chalong 25 phutthasatawat [Chaiyaphum Province: Twenty-Fifth Century of the Buddhist Era Celebration]. 1957 [BE 2500]. Bangkok.

Changwat Kalasin: Ngan chalong 25 phutthasatawat [Kalasin Province: Twenty-Fifth Century of the Buddhist Era Celebration]. 1957 [BE 2500]. Bangkok.

Changwat Khon Kaen: Ngan chalong 25 phutthasatawat]Khon Kaen Province: Twenty-Fifth Century of the Buddhist Era Celebration]. 1957 [BE 2500]. Bangkok.

Changwat Loei: Ngan chalong 25 phutthasatawat [Loei Province: Twenty-Fifth Century of the Buddhist Era Celebration]. 1957 [BE 2500]. Bangkok.

Changwat Maha Sarakham: Ngan Chalong 25 Phutthasatawat [Maha Sarakham Province: Twenty-Fifth Century of the Buddhist Era Celebration]. 1957 [BE 2500]. Bangkok.

Changwat Nakhon Phanom: Ngan chalong 25 phutthasatawat [Nakhon Phanom Province: Twenty-Fifth Century of the Buddhist Era Celebration]. 1957 [BE 2500]. Bangkok.

Changwat Nakhon Ratchasima: Ngan chalong 25 phutthasatawat [Nakhon Ratchasima Province: Twenty-Fifth Century of the Buddhist Era Celebration]. 1957 [BE 2500]. Bangkok.

Changwat Nong Khai: Ngan chalong 25 phutthasatawat [Nong Khai province: Twenty-Fifth Century of the Buddhist Era Celebration]. 1957 [BE 2500]. Bangkok.

Changwat Roi Et: Ngan chalong 25 phutthasatawat [Roi Et Province: Twenty-Fifth Century of the Buddhist Era Celebration]. 1957 [BE 2500]. Bangkok.

Changwat Sakon Nakhon: Ngan chalong 25 phutthasatawat [Sakon Nakhon Province: Twenty-Fifth Century of the Buddhist Era Celebration]. 1957 [BE 2500]. Bangkok.

Changwat Si Sa Ket: Ngan chalong 25 phutthasatawat [Si Sa Ket Province: Twenty-Fifth Century of the Buddhist Era Celebration]. 1957 [BE 2500]. Bangkok.

Changwat Surin: Ngan chalong 25 phutthasatawat [Surin Province: Twenty-Fifth Century of the Buddhist Era Celebration]. 1957 [BE 2500]. Bangkok.

Changwat Udon Thani: Ngan chalong 25 phutthasatawat [Udon Province: Twenty-Fifth Century of the Buddhist Era Celebration]. 1957 [BE 2500]. Bangkok.

Changwat Ubon Ratchathani: Ngan chalong 25 phutthasatawat [Ubon Province: Twenty-Fifth Century of the Buddhist Era Celebration]. 1957 [BE 2500]. Bangkok.

Chai Anan Samudavanija. 1982. *The Thai Young Turks*. Singapore: Institute of Southeast Asian Studies.

Chairat Charoensin-Olarn. 2012. "A New Politics of Desire and Disintegration in Thailand." In *Bangkok, May 2010: Perspectives on a Divided Thailand*, edited by Michael J. Montesano, Pavin Chachavalpongpun, and Aekapol Chongvilaivan, 87–96. Singapore: Institute of Southeast Asian Studies.

Charnvit Kasetsiri. 1976. *The Rise of Ayudhya: A History of Siam in the Fourteenth and Fifteenth Centuries*. Kuala Lumpur: Oxford University Press.

Chatsumarn Kabilsingh. 1990. "Buddhist Monks and Forest Conservation." In *Radical Conservatism: Buddhism in the Contemporary World-Articles in Honour of Bhikkhu Buddhadasa's 84th Birthday Anniversary*. Thai Inter–religious Commission for Development and International Network of Engaged Buddhists, comp., 301–10. Bangkok: Sathirakoses-Nagapradipa Foundation.

Chatthip Nartsupha. 1984. "The Ideology of 'Holy Men' Revolts in North East Thailand." In *Historical and Peasant Consciousness in South East Asia*, edited by Andrew Turton and Shigeharu Tanabe, 111–34. Osaka: National Museum of Ethnology.

Cheah, Pheng. 2006. *Inhuman Conditions: On Cosmopolitanism and Human Rights*. Cambridge, MA: Harvard University Press.

Chin Yu Di. *Boran wathu sathan thang phraratcha annachak* [Archaeological sites throughout the kingdom]. 1957. Bangkok.

Chiranan Pitpreecha. 2006. *Ik nueng fang fan: Banthuek raem thang chiwit* [Another Blurred Dream: My Memoir of Leaving]. Bangkok: Phraeo Samnak Phim.

Choop Karnjanaprakorn. 1965. *Community Development and Local Government in Thailand*. Bangkok: Institute of Public Administration, Thammasat University.

Close, Alexandra. 1965. "Thailand's Border Alarms." *Far Eastern Economic Review* 48:395–98, May 27.

Coast, John. 1953. *Some Aspects of Siamese Politics*. New York: Institute of Pacific Relations.

Coedès, George. 1966. *The Making of South East Asia*. Berkeley and Los Angeles: University of California Press.

Cohen, Paul. T. 2000. "A Buddha Kingdom in the Golden Triangle: Buddhist Revivalism and the Charismatic Monk Khruba Bunchum." *The Australian Journal of Anthropology* 11 (3): 141–54.

———. 2001. "Buddhism Unshackled: The Yuan 'Holy Man' Tradition and the Nation-State in the Tai World." *Journal of Southeast Asian Studies* 32 (2): 227–47.

Cohn, Norman. 1970. "Medieval Millenarianism: Its Bearing on The Comparative Study of Millenarian Movements." In *Millennial Dreams in Action: Studies in Revolutionary Religious Movements*, edited by Sylvia L. Thrupp, 32–43. New York: Schocken Books.

Communist Party of Thailand. 1978. "A Brief Introduction to the History of the Communist Party of Thailand (1942–1977)." In *Thailand: Roots of Conflict*, edited by Andrew Turton, Jonathan Fast, and Malcolm Caldwell, 158–68 Nottingham: Spokesman.

Conboy, Kenneth, with James Morrison. 1995. *Shadow War: The CIA's Secret War in Laos*. Boulder, CO: Paladin Press.

"A Conspiracy of Hope." 1995. *Seeds of Peace* 11 (2): 32–35. (Reprinted from *The Nation*, April 6, 1995.)

Crispin, Shawn W. 2011a. "Do or Die for Thai Democracy." *Asia Times On line*. April 13. Available at http://www.atimes.com/atimes/Southeast_Asia/MD13Ae01.html.

———. 2011b. "The Deal Behind Thailand's Polls." *Asia Times On line*, June 30. Available at http://www.atimes.com/atimes/Southeast_Asia/MF30Ae01.html.

Crispin, Shawn W., Margot Cohen, and Bertil Lintner. 2000. "Choke Point." *Far Eastern Economic Review*, October 12.

Crosby, Sir Josiah. 1945. *Siam: The Crossroads*. London: Hollis and Carter Ltd.

Cuasay, Peter. 2002. "Time Borders and Elephant Margins: Among the Kuay of South Isan, Thailand." Unpublished PhD dissertation, University of Washington.

Damrong Rajanubhab, Prince. 1954. *Thiao tam thang rotfai* [Travels along the Railway]. Bangkok: Volume distributed for the cremation of Nai Samruat Phanphriya.

———. 1960. *Thetsaphiban* [Provincial Administration]. Bangkok: Cremation volume for Phraya Atthakrawisunthon.

———. 1961 [1935]. *Nithan borankhadi* [Historical anecdotes]. Bangkok: Phrae Phittaya

Dararat Mettarikanon. 2003. *Kanmueang song fang khong: Ngan khonkwa wichai radap prinya ek khong Chulalongkon Mahawithayalai rueang kanruam klum thang kanmueang khong so so Isan pho so 2476–2494* [Politics on the two sides of the Mekong: PhD dissertation at Chulalongkorn University concerning unity of members of parliament, 1933–1951]. Bangkok: Matichon.

Darling, Frank C. 1965. *Thailand and the United States*. Washington: Public Affairs Press.

Darlington, Susan. 2000. "Rethinking Buddhism and Development: The Emergence of Environmentalist Monks in Thailand." *Journal of Buddhist Ethics* 7. Available online at http://www.buddhistethics.org/7/darlington001.html.

———. 2013. *The Ordination of a Tree: The Thai Buddhist Environmental Movement*. Albany: State University of New York.

Dauplay, J. J. 1929. *Les Terres rouges du plateau des Bolovens*. Saigon.

Davis, Sara. 2005. *Song and Silence: Ethnic Revival on China's Southwest Borders*. New York: Columbia University Press.

de Beer, Patrice. 1978. "History and Policy of the Communist Party of Thailand." In *Thailand: Roots of Conflict*, edited by Andrew Turton, Jonathan Fast, and Malcolm Caldwell, 143–58. Nottingham: Spokesman.

Demaine, Harvey. 1986. "*Kanpatthana*: Thai Views of Development." In *Context, Meaning, and Power in Southeast Asia*, edited by Mark Hobart and Robert H. Taylor, 93–114. Ithaca, NY: Cornell University Southeast Asia Program, Studies on Southeast Asia.

Denes, Alexandra. 2006. "Recovering Khmer Ethnic Identity from the Thai National Past: An Ethnography of the Localism Movement in Surin Province." Unpublished PhD dissertation, Cornell University.

Direk Jayanama (Direk Chaiyanam). 2008. *Thailand and World War II*. Chiang Mai: Silkworm Books.

Dommen, Arthur J. 1964. *Conflict in Laos*. New York: Praeger, 1964.

Donner, Wolf. 1978. *The Five Faces of Thailand: An Economic Geography*. London: C. Hurst & Company.

Elinoff, Eli. 2012. "Smoldering Aspirations: Burning Buildings and the Politics of Belonging in Contemporary Isan." In special issue of *South East Asia Research*, edited by Eli Elinoff, *South East Asia Research* 20 (3): 381–97.

Elson, R. 1997. *The End of the Peasantry in Southeast Asia: A Social and Economic History of Peasant Livelihood, 1800–1990s*. Canberra: Australian National University.

Escobar, Arturo. 1988. "Power and Visibility: Development and the Invention and Management of the Third World." *Cultural Anthropology* 3 (4): 428–43.

Evans, Grant. 1998. "Secular Fundamentalism and Buddhism in Laos." In *Religion, Ethnicity and Modernity in Southeast Asia*, edited by Oh Myung-Seok and Kim Hyung-Jun, 169–206. Seoul: Seoul National University Press, GIAS Monograph Series 17.

Fai Wichakan Samatcha Khonchon [Technical Unit, Assembly of the Poor]. 2000. *16 panha khonchon kap thang-ok sangkhom Thai* [16 issues for the poor and the way out for Thai society]. Bangkok: Kangphan Press.

Fall, Bernard B. 1964. *The Two Viet-Nams*. New York: Praeger (rev. ed.).

Feeny, David. 2003. "The Political Economy of Regional Inequality: The Northeast of Thailand 1800–2000." *Crossroads* 17 (1): 29–59.

Fineman, Daniel Mark. 1997. *A Special Relationship: The United States and Military Government in Thailand, 1947–1958*. Honolulu: University of Hawaii Press.

Finot, L. 1915. "La Stele de Dansai." *Bulletin École Française d'Extrême-Orient* 15 (2): 28–36.

Flood, E. Thadeus. 1977. "The Vietnamese Refugees in Thailand: Minority Manipulation in Counterinsurgency." *Bulletin of Concerned Asian Scholars* 9 (3): 31–47.

Fukui, H., Y. Kaida, and M. Kuchiba, ed. 1983. *A Rice-Growing Village Revisited: An Integrated Study of Rural Development in Northeast Thailand. An Interim Report*. Kyoto: Kyoto University, The Center for Southeast Asian Studies.

———. 1985. *A Rice-Growing Village Revisited: An Integrated Study of Rural Development in Northeast Thailand. The Second Interim Report*. Kyoto: Kyoto University, The Center for Southeast Asian Studies.

———. 1988. *A Rice-Growing Village Revisited: An Integrated Study of Rural Development in Northeast Thailand. The Third Interim Report*. Kyoto: Kyoto University, The Center for Southeast Asian Studies.

Fukui, Hayao, et al. 1996. "Transformation of Agriculture in Northeast Thailand." *Tonan Ajia Kenki/Southeast Asian Studies* 33 (4): 521–674.

Fuller, Theodore D., Peerasit Kamnuangsilpa, Paul Lightfoot, and Sawaeng Rathanamongkolmas. 1983. *Migration and Development in Modern Thailand*. Bangkok: the Social Science Association of Thailand.

Fuller, Thomas. 2010. "Whiff of Rebellion Spreads in Thai Hinterland." *New York Times*, April 19.

———. 2011. "Rural Thais Find an Unaccustomed Power." *New York Times*, June 20.

Funahashi, Kazuo. 2009. *Changes in Income among Peasants in Northeast Thailand: Poverty Reduction Seen Through a Panel Analysis*. Shiga: Ryukoko University, Afrasian Centre for Peace and Development Studies.

Gay, Bernard. 2002. "Millenarian Movements in Laos, 1895–1936: Depictions by Modern Lao Historians." In *Breaking New Ground in Lao History: Essays on the Seventh to Twentieth Centuries*, edited by Mayoury Ngaosrivathana and Kennon Breazeale, 281–95. Chiang Mai: Silkworm Books.

Girling, John. 1981. *Thailand: Society and Politics*. Ithaca, NY: Cornell University Press.

Glasser, Jeffrey D. 1995. *The Secret Vietnam War: The United States Air Force in Thailand*. Jefferson, NC: McFarland and Co.

Glassman, Jim. 2004. *Thailand at the Margins: Internationalization of the State and the Transformation of Labour*. Oxford and New York: Oxford University Press.

Gohlert, Ernst W. 1991. *Power and Culture: The Struggle Against Poverty in Thailand*. Bangkok: White Lotus.

Goscha, Christopher E. 1998. *Thailand and the Southeast Asian Networks of the Vietnamese Revolution, 1885–1954*. Richmond, Surrey: Curzon Press.

Grabowsky, Volker. 1996. "The Thai Census of 1904: Translation and Analysis." *Journal of the Siam Society* 84 (1): 49–86.

Gunn, Geoffrey C. 1990. *Rebellion in Laos: Peasant and Politics in a Colonial Backwater*. Boulder, CO: Westview Press.

Haberkorn, Tyrell. 2011. *Revolution Interrupted: Farmers, Students, Law and Violence in Northern Thailand*. Madison, WI: University of Wisconsin Press.

Hafner, James A. 1980. "Urban Resettlement and Migration in Northeast Thailand: The Specter of Urban Involution," *The Journal of Developing Areas* 14 (4): 483–500.

Handley, Paul. 2006. *The King Never Smiles: A Biography of Thailand's Bhumibol Adulyadej*. New Haven: Yale University Press.

Hanks, Lucien M. 1960. "Indifference to Modern Education in a Thai Farming Community." *Practical Anthropology* 7:18–29.

Hannerz, Ulf. 1990. "Cosmopolitans and Locals in World Culture." *Theory, Culture and Society* 7:237–51.

Hardy, Andrew. 2008. "People In-Between: Exile and Memory among the Vietnamese in Thailand–Research note." In *Monde du Vietnam—Vietnam World, Hommage à Nguyen The Anh*, edited by Frederic Mantienne and Keith W. Taylor, 271–93. Paris: Les Indes savants.

Harmon, E. D., Jr. 1964. Comments on Dr. Hans Platenius' Report, "The Northeast of Thailand, Its Problems and Potentialities." n.p., mimeo., March 22.

Heine-Geldern, Robert. 1942. "Conceptions of State and Kingship in Southeast Asia." *Far Eastern Quarterly* 2 (1): 15–30.

———. 1956. *Conceptions of State and Kingship in Southeast Asia*. Ithaca, NY: Cornell University Southeast Asia Program, Data Paper No. 18.

Hewison, Kevin, and Kengkij Kitirianglarp. 2010. "'Thai-Style Democracy': The Royalist Struggle for Thailand's Politics." In *Saying the Unsayable: Monarchy and Democracy in Thailand*, edited by Søren Ivarsson and Lotte Isager, 179–202. Copenhagen: Nordic Institute of Asian Studies, NIAS Studies in Asian Topics 47.

Hickey, Maureen Helen. 2010. "Driving Globalization: Bangkok Taxi Drivers and the Restructuring of Work and Masculinity in Thailand." Unpublished PhD dissertation, University of Washington.

High, Holly. 2009. "The Spirit of Community: Puta Belief and Communal Sentiments in Southern Laos." In *Tai Lands and Thailand Community and State in Southeast Asia*, edited by Andrew Walker, 89–112. Honolulu: University of Hawaii Press.

Higham, Charles. 1988. *The Archaeology of Mainland Southeast Asia*. Cambridge: Cambridge University Press.

———. 1996. *The Bronze Age of Southeast Asia*. Cambridge: Cambridge University Press.

———. 2004. "The Transition from Prehistory to the Historic Period in the Upper Mun Valley." *International Journal of Historical Archaeology* 2 (3): 235–60.

Higham, Charles, and Rachanee Thosarat. 2012. *Early Thailand: From Prehistory to Sukhothai*. Bangkok: River Books.

Hinton, Peter. 1979. "The Karen, Millennialism, and the Politics of Accommodation to Lowland States." In *Ethnic Adaptation and Identity: The Karen on the Thai Frontier with Burma*, edited by Charles F. Keyes, 81–98. Philadelphia: ISHI.

Hirsch, Philip. 1993. *Political Economy of Environment in Thailand*. Manila and Wollongong, Australia: Journal of Contemporary Asia Publishers.

———. 1994. "Where Are the Roots of Thai Environmentalism?" *TEI Quarterly Environmental Journal* 2 (2): 5–15.

———. ed. 1996. *Seeing Forests for Trees: Environment and Environmentalism in Thailand*. Chiang Mai, Thailand: Silkworm Books.

———. 1997. "The Politics of Environment: Opposition and Legitimacy." In *Political Change in Thailand: Democracy and Participation*, edited by Kevin Hewison, 179–94. London and New York: Routledge.

Hirsch, Philip, and Larry Lohmann. 1989. "The Contemporary Politics of Environment in Thailand." *Asian Survey* 29 (4): 439–51.

Holmes, Henry Cobb. 1974. "School Beyond the Village: A Study of Education and Society in Northeastern Thailand." EdD dissertation, University of Massachusetts.

Huff, Lee W. 1967. "The Thai Mobile Development Unit Program." In *Southeast Asian Tribes, Minorities and Nations*, edited by Peter Kunstadter, 425–86. 2 vols. Princeton: Princeton University Press.

Hurst, Philip. 1990. *Rainforest Politics: Ecological Destruction in South-east Asia*. London and New Jersey: Zed Books.

Ingersoll, Jasper. 1969. *The Social Feasibility of Pa Mong Irrigation: Requirements and Realties*. US Department of Interior, Bureau of Reclamation and US Agency for International Development.

———. n.d. *Human Dimensions of Mekong River Basin Development: A Case Study of the Nam Pong Project, Northeast Thailand, 1967–1968*. Draft. (Pre-publication version)

Ingram, James C. 1971. *Economic Change in Thailand, 1850–1970*. Stanford: Stanford University Press.

Ishii, Yoneo. 1975. "A Note on Buddhistic Millenarian Revolts in Northeastern Siam." *Journal of Southeast Asian Studies* 6 (2): 121–26.

Ivarsson, Søren. 2008. *Creating Laos: The Making of a Lao Space Between Indochina and Siam, 1860–1945*. Copenhagen: NIAS Press, Nordic Institute of Asian Studies, Monograph Series, no. 112.

Jackson, Peter A. 1988. *Buddhadasa: A Buddhist Thinker for the Modern World*. Bangkok: Siam Society.

———. 1997. "Withering Centre, Flourishing Margins: Buddhism's Changing Political Roles." In *Political Change in Thailand: Democracy and Participation*, edited by Kevin Hewison, 75–94. London and New York: Routledge.

———. 1999. "Royal Spirits, Chinese Gods, and Magic Monks: Thailand's Boom-time Religions of Prosperity." *South East Asian Research* 7 (3): 245–320.

Jansen, Karel. 1997. *External Finance in Thailand's Development: An Interpretation of Thailand's Growth Boom*. New York: St. Martin's Press.

Jarin Boonmathya. 1986. "Phatthanakan khong ngan phatthana lae nak phatthana khong ongkon ekachon" [Development by NGOs and NGO workers]. Typescript.

———. n.d. [1988?]. "NGOs in Thailand." [Bangkok]: The Village Volunteer Organization for Rural Development.

Jeffrey, Leslie Ann. 2002. *Sex and Borders: Gender, National Identity and Prostitution Policy in Thailand*. Vancouver, British Columbia; Honolulu: University of Hawaii Press.

Jerachone Sriswasdilek. 1979. "An Economic Analysis of Irrigation Development in Nam Pong Irrigation Project, Khon Kaen, Thailand." Unpublished PhD dissertation, Oregon State University.

Jit Poumisak. 1987. "The Real Face of Thai Saktina Today." Translated by Craig Reynolds. In *Thai Radical Discourse: The Real Face of Thai Feudalism Today*, by Craig Reynolds, 43–148. Ithaca, NY: Cornell University Southeast Asia Program, Studies on Southeast Asia.

Johnson, Samuel H., III. 1982. "The Effects of Major Dam Construction: the Nam Pong Project in Thailand." In *Too Rapid Rural Development: Perceptions and Perspectives from Southeast Asia*, edited by Colin MacAndrews and Chia Lin Sien, 172–207. Athens, OH: Ohio University Press.

Kaewta Chantharanusorn. 2008. "Khon chin kap kan phlitsang watthanatham satharana na thetsaban nakhon Khon Kaen" [Chinese and the construction of a public culture in Khon Kaen municipality]. Unpublished PhD dissertation, Maha Sarakham University, Thailand.

Kamala Tiyavanich. 1997. *Forest Recollections: Wandering Monks in Twentieth-Century Thailand*. Honolulu: University of Hawaii Press.

Kampoon Boontawee. 1976. *Luk Isan* [Son of the Northeast] Bangkok: Bannakit.

———. 1988. *A Child of the Northeast*. Translated by Susan Fulop Kepner. Bangkok: Editions Duangkamol.

Katz, Cindi. 2004. *Growing Up Global: Economic Restructuring and Children's Everyday Lives*. Minneapolis: University of Minnesota Press.

Kalyvas, Andreas. 2005. "Popular Sovereignty, Democracy, and the Constituent Power." *Constellations* 12 (2): 223–44.

Kelly, Neal. 1983. "Thailand's Reigning Politician Does Not Want to Be Elected." *Christian Science Monitor*, April 4.

Keyes, Charles F. 1964. "Thailand, Laos, and the Thai Northeastern Problem." *Australia's Neighbours* 4 (17): 1–4.

———. 1966a. "Peasant and Nation: A Thai-Lao Village in a Thai State." Unpublished PhD dissertation, Cornell University, Ithaca, NY.

———. 1966b. "Ethnic Identity and Loyalty of Villagers in Northeastern Thailand." *Asian Survey* 6 (7): 362–69.

———. 1967. *Isan: Regionalism in Northeastern Thailand.* Ithaca, NY: Cornell University Southeast Asia Program, Data Paper No. 65.

———. 1968. "Chotmai chak Isan," [Letter from the Northeast]. *Sangkhomsat Porithat* [*Social Science Review*], Bangkok 6 (1): 89–94. (Published anonymously under the name of *phusuekhao khong rao* [Our special correspondent])

———. 1971a. "Buddhism and National Integration in Thailand." *Journal of Asian Studies* 30 (3): 551–68.

———. 1971b. "Domain, Kinship, and Political Control on the Khorat Plateau." Seattle, mimeo.

———. 1973a. "Phya Anuman Rajadhon and the Study of Culture in Thailand." In *Phya Anuman Rajadhon: A Reminiscence,* edited by C. F. Keyes, W. J. Klausner, and S. Sivaraksa, 31–34. Bangkok: Sathirakoses-Nagapradipa Foundation.

———. 1973b. "The Power of Merit." *Visakaha Puja BE 2516 (1973).* Bangkok: The Buddhist Association of Thailand, 95–102.

———. 1975a. "The Northeastern Thai Village: Stable Order and Changing World." *Journal of the Siam Society* 63 (1): 177–207.

———. 1975b. "Kin Groups in a Thai-Lao Village." In *Change and Persistence in Thai Society: Homage to Lauriston Sharp,* edited by G. William Skinner and A. Thomas Kirsch, 275–97. Ithaca, NY: Cornell University Press.

———. 1976. "In Search of Land: Village Formation in the Central Chi River Valley, Northeast Thailand." *Contributions to Asian Studies* 9:45–63.

———. 1977. "Millennialism, Buddhism and Thai Society." *Journal of Asian Studies* 36 (2): 283–302.

———. 1981. "Death of Two Buddhist Saints in Thailand." In *Charisma and Sacred Biography,* edited by Michael Williams, 149–80. Chico, CA: Scholars Press (Journal of the American Academy of Religion, Thematic Series 48/3–4).

———. 1983a. "Introduction." In *Peasant Strategies in Asian Societies: Perspectives on Moral and Rational Economic Approaches,* edited by Charles F. Keyes. *Journal of Asian Studies* 42 (3): 753–68.

———. 1983b. "Economic Action and Buddhist Morality in a Thai Village." In *Peasant Strategies in Asian Societies: Perspectives on Moral and Rational Economic Approaches,* edited by Charles F. Keyes. *Journal of Asian Studies* 42 (3): 851–68.

———. 1990. "Buddhist Practical Morality in a Changing Agrarian World: A Case from Northeastern Thailand." In *Attitudes toward Wealth and Poverty in Theravada Buddhism,* edited by Donald K. Swearer and Russell Sizemore, 170–89. Columbia, SC: University of South Carolina Press.

———. 1991a. "The Proposed World of the School: Thai Villagers Entry into a Bureaucratic State System." In *Reshaping Local Worlds: Rural Education and Cultural*

Change in Southeast Asia, edited by Charles F. Keyes, 87–138. New Haven: Yale University Southeast Asian Studies.

———. 1991b. "Buddhist Detachment and Worldly Gain: The Economic Ethic of Northeastern Thai Villagers." In *Yu muang Thai: Ruam botkhwam thang sangkhom phuea pen kiat dae Sastrachan Sane Chamrik* [Living in Thailand: Collected Essays in Honor of Professor Saneh Chammarik], edited by Chaiwat Satha-Anand. Special issue of *Ratthasatsan* (*Journal of Political Science*, Thammasat University) 16 (1–2): 271–98.

———. 1999. "Buddhism Fragmented: Thai Buddhism and Political Order since the 1970s." Keynote address presented at Seventh International Thai Studies Conference, Amsterdam, July 1999.

———. 2001. "Fieldwork as History: Letters between Two Researchers in Northeastern Thailand in 1963." In *4 Thatswat phak sanam haeng khwamru/Friends in the Field: 4 Decades of Anthropological and Sociological Studies in Thailand*, compiled by Chumchon Sitkao Mahawitthayalai Khonael, Phuea Ramlukthung Professor A. Thomas Kirsch [Group of Cornell University Graduates to Remember Professor A. Thomas Kirsch]. Chiang Mai: Department of Sociology and Anthropology and Society and Center for Women Studies, Faculty of Social Sciences, Chiang Mai University. 7–23.

———. 2002a. "National Heroine or Local Spirit? The Struggle over Memory in the Case of Thao Suranari of Nakhon Ratchasima." In *Cultural Crisis and Social Memory: Modernity and Identity in Thailand and Laos*, 113–36. Richmond, Surrey, UK: Routledge Curzon.

———. 2002b. "Weber and Anthropology." *Annual Reviews in Anthropology* 31:233–55.

———. 2004. "Thinking about Thailand over Four Decades: The Isan Roots of a *Farang* Anthropologist." Paper presented in conjunction with being awarded an honorary PhD, Maha Sarakham University, December.

———. 2008/2009. "Muslim 'Others' in Buddhist Thailand." *Thammasat Review* 13:19–42.

———. 2009. *Naeokhit thongthin phak Isan niyom nai prathet Thai* [Perspective on Northeastern Thai Regionalism]. Translated by Ratana Tosakul. Ubon Ratchathani: Mekong Sub-region Social Research Center, Faculty of Liberal Arts, Ubon Ratchathani University. (Translation of *Isan: Regionalism in Northeastern Thailand*, with added essay on "Northeastern Thai Ethnoregionalism Updated")

———. 2010. "Opening Reflections: Northeastern Thai Ethnorgionalism Updates." In *Tracks and Traces: Thailand and the Work of Andrew Turton*, edited by Philip Hirsch and Nicholas Tapp, 17–28. Amsterdam: Amsterdam University Press.

———. 2011a. "Communism, Peasants and Buddhism: The Failure of 'Peasant Revolutions' in Thailand in Comparison to Cambodia." In *Community and the Trajectories of Change in Cambodia and Thailand: Anthropological Studies in Honor of May Ebihara*, edited by John Marston, 35–58. Melbourne: Monash Asia Institute.

———. 2011b. "Returnees Have Little to Look Forward To." *Bangkok Post*, March 29.

———. 2012. "'Cosmopolitan' Villagers and Populist Democracy in Thailand." In special issue of *South East Asia Research*, edited by Eli Elinoff. *South East Asia Research* 20 (3): 343–60.

————. 2014. "The Village Economy: Capitalist *and* Sufficiency-Based. A Northeastern Thai Case." In *Exploring Sufficiency Economy: Ethics, Practices, Challenges*, edited by Seri Phongphit with Istvan Rado and Nate Long. Bangkok: King Prajhadipok's Institute.

Keyes, Charles F., Helen Hardacre, and Laurel Kendall. 1994. "Contested Visions of Community in East and Southeast Asia." In *Asian Visions of Authority: Religion and the Modern States of East and Southeast Asia*, edited by Charles F. Keyes, Helen Hardacre and Laurel Kendall, 1–16. Honolulu: University of Hawaii Press.

Khammaan Khonkhai. 1978. *Khru Ban Nok* [Village School Teacher]. Bangkok.

————. 1982. *The Teachers of Mad Dog Swamp*. Translation of *Khru Ban Nok*, by Gehan Wijeyewardene. St. Lucia: University of Queensland Press.

Kickert, Robert A. 1960. *A Pilot Village Study in Northeast Thailand* [Bangkok]: United States Information Service, Report No. 3, October.

King, Gilbert. 2011. "Long Live the King." Past Imperfect, blog on Smithsonian.com. Available at http://blogs.smithsonianmag.com/history/2011/09/long-live-the-king/, last accessed February 2012.

Kirsch, A. Thomas. 1966. "Development and Mobility Among the Phu Thai of Northeast Thailand." *Asian Survey* 6 (7): 370–78.

————. 1967 "Phu Thai Religious Syncretism." Unpublished PhD dissertation, Harvard University.

Klausner, William. 1956. *Progress Reports* (on Work in Nong Khon Village, Ubon Province). n.p., mimeo.

————. 1972. *Reflections in a Log Pond: Collected Writings*. Bangkok: Suksit Siam.

————. 1973. "Wat Isan," *Visakha Puja B.E. 2516* [Annual Publication of the Buddhist Association of Thailand, Bangkok]. 55–58.

————. 2000. *Reflections: One Year in an Isaan Village Circa 1955*. Photographs by William J. Klausner. Excerpts from his collected writings. Bangkok: Siam Reflections Publications Co., Ltd.

Komatra Chuengsatiansup. 1998. "Living on the Edge: Marginality and Contestation in the Kui Communities of Northeast Thailand." Unpublished PhD dissertation, Harvard University.

Krittiya Porasame. 1991. "Villagers Worry about Conservationist Monk." *The Nation*, May 12.

Kruger, Rayne. 1964. *The Devil's Discus*. London: Cassell.

Kurlantzick, Joshua. 2011. *The Ideal Man: The Tragedy of Jim Thompson and the American Way of War*. New York: John Wiley.

Kusol Soonthorndhada. 2001. "Changes in the Labor Market and International Migration since the Economic Crisis in Thailand." *Asian and Pacific Migration Journal* 10 (3–4): 401–27.

Landon, Kenneth Perry. 1939. *Siam in Transition*. Shanghai: Kelly and Walsh.

————. 1941. "Thailand's Quarrel with France in Perspective." *Far Eastern Quarterly* 1:25–42.

Lancaster, Donald. 1961. *The Emancipation of French Indochina*. New York: Oxford.

LeBar, Frank M., et al. 1964. *Ethnic Groups of Mainland Southeast Asia*. New Haven: HRAF Press.

Le Boulanger, Paul. 1931. *Histoire du Laos Français*. Paris: Librairie Plon.

Lefferts, H. Leedom. 1974. "Ban Dong Phong: Land Tenure and Social Organization in a Northeastern Thai Community." Unpublished PhD dissertation, Department of Anthropology, University of Colorado.

————. 2004. "Village as Stage: Imaginative Space and Time in Rural Northeast Thai Lives." *Journal of the Siam Society* 92:129–44.

————. 2011. "Theravada Buddhism and Political Engagement among the Thai-Lao of Northeast Thailand: The Bun Phra Wet Ceremony." Paper presented at the annual meeting of the Association for Asian Studies, Honolulu.

Le Manh Trinh. 1962. "In Canton and Thailand." In *Days with Ho Chi Minh*. Hanoi: Foreign Languages Publishing House.

Lévi-Strauss, Claude. 1953. "Social Structure." In *Anthropology Today*, edited by A. L. Kroeber, 524–53. Chicago: University of Chicago Press.

Lévy, Paul. 1959. "Two Accounts of Travels in Laos in the 17th Century." In *Kingdom of Laos*, edited by by René de Berval, 50–67. Saigon: France-Asie (English edition).

Likhit Dhiravegin. 1993. *Demi Democracy*. Singapore: Times Academic Press.

Lightfoot, Paul. 1980. "Circular Migration and Modernization in Northeast Thailand," Paper presented by the Thai-European Seminar on Social Change in Contemporary Thailand, University of Amsterdam, Anthropological-Sociological Centre, May.

Lightfoot, Paul, Theodore Fuller, and Peerasit Kamnuansilpa. 1983. "Circulation and Interpersonal Networks Linking Rural and Urban Areas: The Case of Roi Et, Northeastern Thailand." Honolulu: East-West Population Institute, Paper No. 84.

Lightfoot, Paul, and Theodore Fuller. 1984. "Circular Migration in Northeastern Thailand." In *Strategies and Structures in Thai Society*, edited by Han ten Brummelhuis and Jeremy H. Kemp, 85–93. Amsterdam: Universiteit van Amsterdam, Antropologisch-Sociologisch Centrum, Publikatieserie Vakgroep Zuid—en Zuidoost—Azië, 31.

Lobe, Thomas. 1977. *United States National Security Policy and Aid to the Thailand Police*. Denver: University of Denver, Graduate School of International Studies (Monograph Series in World Affairs, vol. 14, book 2).

Lomax, Louis E. 1967. *The War that Is, the War that Will Be*. New York: Random House.

Long, Jancis F., Millard F. Long, Kamphol Adulavidhaya, and Sawart Pongsuwanna. 1963. *Economic and Social Conditions among Farmers in Changwad Khonkaen*. Bangkok: Kasetsart University, Faculty of Economics and Cooperative Science.

Lunet de Lajonquière, E. E. 1907. "Le Laos Siamois." *Bulletin du Comité de l'Asie Française* 7 (6): 268–94.

Lux, Thomas. 1962. "Mango Village: Northeastern Thai Social Organization." Unpublished MA thesis, University of Chicago.

————. 1969. "The Thai-Lao Family System and Domestic Cycle of Northeastern Thailand." *Warasan saphawichai haeng chat* [Journal of the National Research Council] 5:1–17.

Lyttleton, Chris. 1994. "The Good People of Isan: Commercial Sex in Northeast Thailand." *Australian Journal of Anthropology* 5 (3): 257–79.

Macan-Markar, Marwaan. 2010. "Anti-Gov't Protesters Use Cultural Taboo as Weapon." Inter Press Service News Agency, April 20. Available online at http://ipsnews.net/print.asp?idnews=51088.

Madge, Charles. 1957. *Survey before Development in Thai Villages*. New York: United Nations Secretariat (UN Series on Community and Development). [Originally issued under the title of *Village Communities in Northeast Thailand*, 1955].

Maha Sivaram. 1941. *Mekong Clash and Far East Crisis*. Bangkok: Bangkok Chronicle.

Malalgoda, Kitsiri. 1970. "Millennialism in Relation to Buddhism." *Comparative Studies of Society and History* 12 (4): 424–41.

Manit Vallibhotama. 1962. *Guide to Pimai and Antiquities in the Province of Nagara Rajasima (Khorat)*. Abridged and translated by M. C. Subhadradis Diskul. Bangkok: The Fine Arts Department.

Marshall, Andrew. 2010. "The Curse of the Blue Diamond." Available online at http://blogs.reuters.com/andrew-marshall/2010/09/22/the-curse-of-the-blue-diamond. Accessed January 2011.

Mayoury Ngaosyvathn and Pheuiphanh Ngaosyvathn. 1988a. *Chao Anu, 1767–1829: Pasason Lao lae asiakane (lueang kao, panha mai)* [Chao Anu, 1767–1829: The Lao People and Southeast Asia (Old Story, New Meaning)]. Vientiane: Samnakphim chamnai S. P. P. Lao.

———. 1988b [BE 2531]. "Chao Anu: Rueang kao panha mai" [Chao Anu: Old Story, New Meaning]. *Sinlapawatthanatham* [Art and Culture] 9 (11): 58–74. Thai summary of Lao book.

———. 1989. "Lao Historiography and Historians: Case Study of the War between Bangkok and the Lao in 1827." *Journal of Southeast Asian Studies* 20 (1): 55–69.

McCargo, Duncan. 1998. *Chamlong Srimuang and the New Thai Politics*. New York: St Martins Press.

———. 2005. "Network Monarchy and Legitimacy Crisis in Thailand." *The Pacific Review* 18 (4): 499–519.

———. 2009. *Tearing Apart the Land: Islam and Legitimacy in Southern Thailand*. Singapore: NUS Press.

McVey, Ruth, ed. 2000. *Money and Power in Provincial Thailand*. Honolulu: University of Hawaii Press.

Meinkoth, Marian R. 1962. "Migration in Thailand with Particular Reference to the Northeast." *Economic and Business Bulletin* 14:2–45.

Mendelson, E. Michael. 1960. "Religion and Authority in Modern Burma." *The World Today* 16 (3): 110–18.

———. 1961a. "A Messianic Buddhist Association in Upper Burma." *Bulletin of the School of Oriental and African Studies* 24 (3): 560–80.

———. 1961b. "The King and the Weaving Mountain." *Journal of the Royal Central Asiatic Society* 48 (3): 229–37.

———. 1963a. "Observations on a Tour in the Region of Mount Popa, Central Burma." *France-Asie* 19 (179): 780–807.

———. 1963b. "Buddhism and Politics in Burma." *New Society* 1 (38): 8–10.

———. 1963c. "The Uses of Religious Scepticism in Modern Burma." *Diogenes* 41:94–116.

———. 1964. "Buddhism and the Burmese Establishment." *Archives de Sociologie des Religions* 9 (17): 85–95.

Migdal, Joel S. 1975. *Peasants, Politics and Revolution: Pressures Toward Political and Social Change in the Third World*. Princeton: Princeton University Press.

Miller, Terry. 1985. *Traditional Music of the Lao: Kaen Playing and Mawlum Singing in Northeast Thailand*. Westport, CT: Greenwood Press.

Mills, Mary Beth. 1997. "Working for Wages in Bangkok, Reworking Gender and Family in the Countryside." In *Women, Gender Relations and Development in Thai Society*, edited by Virada Somswasdi and Sally Theobald, 137–62. 2 vols. Chiang Mai: Chiang Mai University, Women's Studies Center, Faculty of Social Sciences.

————. 1999. *Thai Women in the Global Labor Force: Consuming Desires, Contested Selves*. New Brunswick, NJ and London: Routledge.

Missingham, Bruce D. 2003. *The Assembly of the Poor in Thailand: From Local Struggles to National Protest Movement*. Chiang Mai: Silkworm Books.

Mizuno, Koichi. 1968. "Multihousehold Compounds in Northeastern Thailand." *Asian Survey* 8, 10:842–52.

————. 1971. *Social System of Don Daeng Village: A Community Study in Northeast Thailand*. Kyoto: Kyoto University, Center for Southeast Asian Studies, Discussion Papers No. 12–21.

Moerman, Michael H. 1961. *A Memorandum: A Northern Thai Village*. Bangkok: United States Information Service, Regional Research Office (South East Asia Survey Research Report).

Montesano, Michael. 2010. "Four Pathologies, Late 2009." In *Legitimacy Crisis in Thailand*, edited by Marc Askew, 273–302. Bangkok and Chiang Mai: King Prajhadipok's Institute and Silkworm Books.

Montlake, Simon. 2007. "Making the Cut." *Time*, October 11.

Moore, Barrington, Jr. 1966. *Social Origins of Dictatorship and Democracy: Lord and Peasant in the Making of the Modern World*. Boston: Beacon Press.

Moore, Frank J., Charles T. Alton, H. Leedom Lefferts, Suthep Soonthornpasuch, and Richard E. Suttor. 1980. *Rural Roads in Thailand*. Washington, DC: Agency for International Development (Project Impact Evaluation, no. 13).

Morell, David, and Chai-anan Samudavanija. 1981. *Political Conflict in Thailand: Reform, Reaction, Revolution*. Cambridge, MA: Oelgeschlager, Gunn and Hain.

Morrison, Barrie M. 1979–80. "The Persistent Rural Crisis in Asia: A Shift in Conception." *Pacific Affairs* 52 (4): 631–46.

Murdoch, John B. 1974. "The 1901–1902 'Holy Man's' Rebellion." *Journal of the Siam Society* 62 (1): 47–66.

Mydans, Seth. 2010. "Bangkok Grows Calm, but Social Divisions Remain." *New York Times*, May 20.

Nairn, Ronald C. 1966. *International Aid to Thailand: The New Colonialism?* New Haven: Yale University Press.

Neuchterlein, Donald E. 1965. *Thailand and the Struggle for Southeast Asia*. Ithaca: Cornell University Press.

Nikorn Chanprom. 1991. "Pakham Village Leader Cites 1970 Agreement." *The Nation*, May 24.

Obeyesekere, Gananath. 1968. "Theodicy, Sin and Salvation in a Sociology of Buddhism." In *Dialectic in Practical Religion*, edited by E. R. Leach. Cambridge: Cambridge University Press.

O'Dea, Thomas F. 1957. *The Mormons*. Chicago: University of Chicago Press.

Paitoon Mikusol. 1972. *Kan pathirup kan pokkhrong monthon isan samai thi phrachao boromwongthoe kromluang sanphasitthiprasong song pen khaluangyai (Ph.S.2436–2453)* [Provincial reforms in Monthon Isan during the period when Prince Sanphasitthiprasong was High Commissioner]. MA thesis, College of Education, Bangkok.

Paitoon Mikusol. 1995. "Administrative Reforms and National Integration: The Case of the Northeast." In *Regions and National Integration in Thailand, 1892–1992*, edited by Volker Grabowsky, 145–53. Wiesbaden: Otto Harrassowitz.

Parnwell, Michael, and Jonathan Rigg. 1996. "The People of Isan, Thailand: Missing Out on the Economic Boom." In *Ethnicity and Development: Geographical Perspectives*, edited by Denis Dwyer and David Drakakis-Smith, 215–48. Chichester: John Wiley and Sons.

Pasuk Phongpaichit. 1981. *Rural Women of Thailand: From Peasant Girls to Bangkok Masseuses*. Geneva: International Labor Organisation.

Pasuk Phongpaichit, and Chris Baker. 2009. *Thaksin*. Second Expanded Edition. Chiang Mai: Silkworm Books.

———. 2012. "Thailand in Trouble: Revolt of the Downtrodden or Conflict among Elites?" In *Bangkok, May 2010: Perspectives on a Divided Thailand*, edited by Michael J. Montesano, Pavin Chachavalpongpun, and Aekapol Chongvilaivan, 214–29. Singapore: Institute of Southeast Asian Studies.

Patcharin Lapanun. 2013. "Logics of Desire and Transnational Marriage Practices in a Northeastern Thai Village." Unpublished PhD dissertation, Vrije Univesiteit Amsterdam.

Pattana Kitiarsa. 2012a. "From Red to Red: An Auto-Ethnography of Economic and Political Transition in a Northeastern Thai Village." In *Bangkok, May 2010: Perspectives on a Divided Thailand*, edited by Michael J. Montesano, Pavin Chachavalpongpun, and Aekapol Chongvilaivan, 230–47. Singapore: Institute of Southeast Asian Studies.

———. 2012b. *Mediums, Monks, and Amulets: Thai Popular Buddhism Today*. Chiang Mai: Silkworm Books.

Patya Saihoo (Phatthaya Saihu). 1968. "Botbat khong phatthanakon nai muban phak tawan-ok chiang nuea" [Role of the Community Development Worker in Northeastern Villages]. In *Sangkhomwitthaya khong muban phak tawan-ok chiang nuea* [Rural Sociology of Villages in the Northeastern Region], edited by Suthep Soonthornpasuch, 265–318. Bangkok: Department of Sociology, Faculty of Political Science, Chulalongkorn University.

Peluso, Nancy Lee, and Peter Vandergeest. 2001. "Genealogies of the political forest and customary rights in Indonesia, Malaysia, and Thailand." *Journal of Asian Studies* 60 (3): 761–814.

Pendleton, Robert L. 1943. "Land Use in Northeastern Thailand." *Geographical Review* 33:15–41.

————. 1962. *Thailand: Aspects of Landscape and Life*. New York: Duell, Sloan and Pearce.

Peters, Heather. 1990. "Buddhism and Ethnicity among the Tai Lue in the Sipsongpanna." In Proceedings of the Fourth International Conference on Thai Studies, 11–13 May 1990, 339–52. Kunming: Institute of Southeast Asian Studies, vol. 3.

Phaisan Visalo, Phra. 1990. "The Forest Monastery and Its Relevance to Modern Thai Society." In *Radical Conservatism: Buddhism in the Contemporary World—Articles in Honour of Bhikkhu Buddhadasa's 84th Birthday Anniversary*, 288–300. Compiled by Thai Inter-Religious Commission for Development and International Network of Engaged Buddhists. Bangkok: Sathirakoses-Nagapradipa Foundation.

Philco-Ford Corporation, Education and Technical Services Division, Operations Research Department. 1968. *Thai Local Administration: A Study of Villager Interaction with Community and Amphoe Administration*. Bangkok: United States Operations Mission to Thailand, Research Division.

Phillips, Herbert P. 1967. "Social Contract vs. Social Promise in a Siamese Village." In *Peasant Society: A Reader*, edited by Jack M. Potter, May N. Diaz, and George M. Foster, 346–66. Boston: Little Brown.

Pornpen Hantrakool and Atcharaphon Kamutphisamai, eds. 1984 [BE 2527]. *"Khwamchuea Phra Si An" lae "Kabot Phu Mi Bun" nai Sangkhom Thai* ["Maitreya Beliefs" and "Holy Men Rebellion" in Thai Society]. Bangkok: Sangsan.

Pinyo Traisuriyathamma, ed. 2010. *Red Why, Daeng thammai: Sangkhom Thai panha lae kanma khong suea daeng* [Why Red: Problematic Thai Society and the Emergence of the Red Shirts]. Bangkok: Openbooks.

Platenius, Hans. 1963. *The North-East of Thailand: Its Problems and Potentialities*. Bangkok: National Economic Development Board, October, mimeo.

Poole, Peter A. 1967. "Thailand's Vietnamese Minority." *Asian Survey* 8 (2): 886–95.

————. 1970. *The Vietnamese in Thailand: A Historical Perspective*. Ithaca, NY: Cornell University Press.

————. 1975. "The Vietnamese in Cambodia and Thailand: Their Role in Interstate Relations." In *Indochina: Perspectives for Reconciliation*, edited by Peter A. Poole, 55–69. Athens, Ohio: Ohio University Center for International Studies, Southeast Asia Program, Southeast Asia Series No. 36.

————. 1976. "The Vietnamese in Thailand: Their Continuing Role in Thai-Vietnamese Relations." *South-East Asian Spectrum* 4 (2): 40–43.

Popkin, Samuel. 1979. *The Rational Peasant: The Political Economy of Rural Society in Vietnam*. Berkeley: University of California Press.

Prajuab Tirabutana. 1958. *A Simple One: The Story of a Siamese Childhood*. Ithaca, NY: Cornell University Southeast Asia Program, Data Paper No. 30.

————. 1971. *Little Things*. Sydney: Collins.

Pramote Prasarkul. 1978. "Patterns of Interprovincial Migration in Thailand." *The Eastern Anthropologist* 31 (4): 459–79.

Prateung Laturit. 1991. "Monks Battle to Save the Forests." *The Nation*, February 24.

Pruess, James Brewer. 1974. "Veneration and Merit-Seeking at Sacred Places: Buddhist Pilgrimage in Contemporary Thailand." Unpublished PhD dissertation, University of Washington.

————. ed., and tr. 1976a. *The That Phanom Chronicle: A Shrine History and Its Interpretation*. Ithaca: NY: Cornell University Southeast Asia Program, Data Paper No. 104.

————. 1976b. "Merit-Seeking in Public: Buddhist Pilgrimage in Northeastern Thailand." *Journal of the Siam Society* 64 (1): 169–206.

Pye, Oliver. 2005. *Khor Jor Kor: Forest Politics in Thailand*. Bangkok: White Lotus.

Quigley, Kevin F. F. 1995. "Environmental Organizations and Democratic Consolidation in Thailand." *Crossroads* 9 (2): 1–30.

Quizon, Natalie. 2011. "Foreign Domestic: Filipina Helpers in Hong Kong at the Crossroads of Domesticity and Diaspora." Unpublished PhD dissertation, University of Washington.

Ratana Boonmathya. 1997. "Contested Concepts of Development in Rural Northeastern Thailand." Unpublished PhD dissertation, University of Washington.

Redfield, Robert. 1956. *Peasant Society and Culture*. Chicago: Chicago University Press.

Reynolds, Craig. 1973. "The Buddhist Monkhood in Nineteenth Century Thailand." Unpublished PhD dissertation, Cornell University.

Rigg, Jonathan. 1991. "Homogeneity and Heterogeneity: An Analysis of the Nature of Variation in Northeastern Thailand." *Malaysian Journal of Tropical Geography* 22:63–77.

————. 1994. "Redefining the Village and Rural Life: Lessons from Southeast Asia." *Geographical Journal* 160:123–35.

————. 1995. "Counting the Costs: Economic Growth and Environmental Change in Thailand." In *Counting the Costs: Economic Growth and Environmental Change in Thailand*, edited by Jonathan Rigg, 3–26. Singapore: Institute of Southeast Asian Studies.

Rigg, Jonathan, and Albert Salamanca. 2009. "Managing Risk and Vulnerability in Asia: A (Re)Study from Thailand, 1982–83 and 2008." *Asia Pacific Viewpoint* 50 (3): 255–70.

Ross, Claudia. 1973. "A Song and Dance about Condoms Aids PPAT Drive." *Bangkok Post*, July 8.

Roth, Andrew. 1949. "Siam: Tranquility and Sudden Death." *The Nation* (United States), October: 317–20.

Rozenberg, Guillaume. 2005. *Renoncement et puissance, la quête de la sainteté dans la Birmanie contemporaine*. Geneva: Olizane Press.

————. 2010. *Renunciation and Power: The Quest for Sainthood in Contemporary Burma*. New Haven: Yale University Southeast Asia Studies, Monograph 59.

Rubin, Herbert J. 1973a. "A Framework for the Analysis of Villager-Official Contact in Rural Thailand." *Southeast Asia* 2 (2): 233–64.

————. 1973b. "'Will and Awe.' Illustrations of Thai Villager Dependency upon Officials." *Journal of Asian Studies* 32 (3): 425–45.

Saipin Kaew-ngarmprasert [Saipin Kaeongamprasoet]. 1995 [BE 2538]. *Kanmueang nai anusawari Thao Suranari* [The Politics of the Monument of Thao Suranari]. Bangkok: Matichon, Sinlapawatthanatham Chabap Phiset.

Sarkisyanz, E. (Manuel). 1965. *Buddhist Backgrounds of the Burmese Revolution*. The Hague: Martinus Nijhoff.

Schumacher, E. F. 1973. *Small Is Beautiful: Economics as If People Mattered*. New York: Harper and Row, Perennial Library.

Scott, James C. 1976. *The Moral Economy of the Peasant: Rebellion and Subsistence in Southeast Asia*. New Haven: Yale University Press.

Scoville, Orlin J., and James J. Dalton. 1974. "Rural Development in Thailand: The ARD Program." *Journal of Developing Areas* 9 (1): 53–68.

Seri Phongphit, with Istvan Rado and Nate Long. 2014. *Exploring Sufficiency Economy: Ethics, Practices, Challenges*. Bangkok: King Prajhadipok's Institute.

Sharma, Shefali, and Aviva Imhof. 1999. *The Struggle for the Mun River: The World Bank's Involvement in the Pak Mun Dam, Thailand*. Berkeley, California: International Rivers Network.

Sharp, Lauriston. 1951. "The Northeast." Unpublished typescript.

The Siam Directory. Bangkok: Thai Co., 1947–

The Siam Society. 1989. *Culture and Environment in Thailand: A Symposium of the Siam Society*. Bangkok: The Siam Society.

Sila Viravong, Maha. 1964. *History of Laos*. Translated from the Lao by the US Joint Publication Research Service. New York: Paragon Reprint Corp.

Siriporn Skrobanek, Nataya Boonpakdee, Chutima Jantateero. 1997. *The Traffic in Women: Human Realities of the International Sex Trade*. New York: Zed Books Ltd.

Skinner, G. William. 1957. *Chinese Society in Thailand*. Ithaca, NY: Cornell University Press.

Smalley, William A. 1994. *Linguistic Diversity and National Unity: Language Ecology in Thailand*. Chicago: University of Chicago Press.

Smith, Nicol, and Blake Clark. 1945. *Into Siam's Underground Kingdom*. New York and Indianapolis: Bobbs-Merill, 1945.

Smyth, H. Warrington. 1895. *Notes of a Journey on the Upper Mekong, Siam*. London: The Royal Geographical Society.

Sombat Rasakul. 2005. "Happy Ending to Water Gate Saga." *Bangkok Post*, August 7.

Somchai Phatharananunth. 2006. *Civil Society and Democratization: Social Movements in Northeast Thailand*. Copenhagen: NIAS Press.

———. 2012. "The Politics of Postpeasant Society: The Emergence of the Red Shirt Movement in the Northeast." Paper presented at a conference on "Democracy and Crisis in Thailand," Chulalongkorn University, March.

Somchai Rakwijit. 1976. "Security Situation in Thailand." In *Trends in Thailand*. Singapore: Institute of Southeast Asian Studies.

Somchai Ratanakomut. 2000. "Issues of International Migration in Thailand." In *Thai Migrant Workers in East and Southeast Asia, 1996–1997*, edited by Supang Chantavanich, Andreas Germershausen, and Allan Beesey, 127–39. Bangkok: Chulalongkorn University, Institute of Asian Studies, Asian Research Centre for Migration and UNESCO-MOST Asia Pacific Migration Research Network.

Sompong Viengchan. 2000. *Voice of the River: One Thai Villager's Story of the Pak Moon Dam*. Interview edited and compiled by Jessica Friedrichs, Sofia Olson, Kaia Peterson, and Lydia Shula. Translated by David Streckfuss and Arunee Chupkhunthod. n.p.

Sopranzetti, Claudio. 2012a. "Burning Red Desires: Isan Migrants and the Politics of Desire in Contemporary Thailand." In special issue of *South East Asia Research*, edited by Eli Elinoff. *South East Asia Research* 20 (3): 361–79.

———. 2012b. *Red Journeys: Inside the Thai Red-Shirt Movement*. Chiang Mai: Silkworm Books.

Spiro, Melford E. 1967. *Burmese Supernaturalism*. Englewood Cliffs, NJ: Prentice Hall.

———. 1970. *Buddhism and Society*. New York: Harper and Row.

Sponsel, Leslie E., and Poranee Natadecha-Sponsel. 1995. "The Role of Buddhism in Creating a More Sustainable Society in Thailand." In *Counting the Costs: Economic Growth and Environmental Change in Thailand*, edited by Jonathan Rigg, 27–46. Singapore: Institute of Southeast Asian Studies.

Srisakara Vallibhotama (Sisak Wanliphodom). 1990 [BE 2533]. *Isan, aeng arayatham: Chae lakthan borankhadi phlik chomna prawatsat Thai* [Isan, Basin of Civilization: Archaeological Discoveries which Alter the Face of Thai History]. Bangkok: DK for Matichon.

Stengs, Irene. 2009. *Worshipping the Great Moderniser: King Chulalongkorn, Patron Saint of the Thai Middle Class*. Singapore: NUS Press in association with the University of Washington Press.

Stern, Theodore. 1968. "*Ariya* and the Golden Book: A Millenarian Buddhist Sect among the Karen." *Journal of Asian Studies* 27 (2): 297–328.

Sternstein, Larry. 1975. "Chain Migration to the Primate City: The Case of Bangkok," *Journal of Tropical Geography* (Singapore) 41:70–95.

Stevenson, William. 1999. *The Revolutionary King: The True-Life Sequel to* The King and I. London: Constable.

Stott, Philip. 1991. "*Mu'ang* and *Pa*: Elite Views of Nature in a Changing Thailand." In *Thai Constructions of Knowledge*, edited by Manas Chitakasem and Andrew Turton, 142–54. London: University of London, School of Oriental and African Studies.

Streckfuss, David. 1993. "The Mixed Colonial Legacy in Siam: Origins of Thai Racialist Thought." In *Autonomous Histories, Particular Truths: Essays in Honor of John R. W. Smail*, edited by Laurie J. Sears, 123–53. Madison: University of Wisconsin, Center for Southeast Asian Studies, Monograph No. 11.

Stuart-Fox, Martin. 1979. "Factors Influencing Relations between the Communist Parties of Thailand and Laos." *Asian Survey* 19 (4): 333–52.

Subhatra Bhumiprabas. 2007. "Old War, New Battle for Pak Mun Villagers." *The Nation*, July 16.

Suchit Bunbongkarn. 1987. *The Military in Thai Politics, 1981–86*. Singapore: Institute of Southeast Asian Studies.

Suehiro Akira. 1989. *Capital Accumulation in Thailand, 1855–1985*. Tokyo: The Centre for East Asian Cultural Studies.

Sulak Sivaraksa. 1990. "Building Trust through Economic and Social Development and Ecological Balance: A Buddhist Perspective." In *Radical Conservatism: Buddhism in the Contemporary World—Articles in Honour of Bhikkhu Buddhadasa's 84th Birthday Anniversary*, 179–98. Thai Inter-Religious Commission for Development and International Network of Engaged Buddhists, comp. Bangkok: Sathirakoses-Nagapradipa Foundation.

Supang Chantavanich, and Andreas Germershausen. 2000. "Introduction: Research on Thai Migrant Workers in East and Southeast Asia." In *Thai Migrant Workers in East and Southeast Asia, 1996–1997*, edited by Supang Chantavanich, Andreas Germershausen, and Allan Beesey, 1–9. Bangkok: Chulalongkorn University, Institute of Asian Studies, Asian Research Centre for Migration and UNESCO-MOST Asia Pacific Migration Research Network.

Suthep Soonthornpasuch, ed. 1968. *Sangkhomwitthaya khong muban phak tawan ok chiang nuea* (Rural Sociology of Villages in the Northeastern Region). Bangkok: Department of Sociology, Faculty of Political Science, Chulalongkorn University.

Swearer, Donald K. 1979. "Bhikkhu Buddhadasa on Ethics and Society." *Journal of Religious Ethics* 7 (1): 54–65.

Talmon, Yonina. 1969 [1962]. "Pursuit of the Millennium: The Relation between Religious and Social Change." In *Sociology and Religion: A Book of Readings*, edited by Norman Birnbaum and Gertrud Lenzer, 238–54. Englewood Cliffs, N.J.: Prentice-Hall.

Tambiah, Stanley J. 1968a. "The Ideology of Merit and the Social Correlates of Buddhism in a Thai Village." In *Dialectic in Practical Religion*, edited by E. R. Leach, 41–121. Cambridge: Cambridge University Press (Cambridge Papers in Social Anthropology, 5).

———. 1968b. "Literacy in a Buddhist Village in North-East Thailand." In *Literacy in Traditional Societies*, edited by Jack Goody, 86–131. Cambridge: Cambridge University Press.

———. 1969. "Animals are Good to Think and Good to Prohibit." *Ethnology* 8 (4): 423–59.

———. 1970. *Buddhism and the Spirit Cults in North-east Thailand*. Cambridge: Cambridge University Press (Cambridge Studies in Social Anthropology, 2).

———. 1977. "The Galactic Polity: The Structure of Traditional Kingdoms in Southeast Asia." *Annals of the New York Academy of Sciences* 293:69–97.

Tanabe, Shigeharu. 1984. "Ideological Practice in Peasant Rebellions: Siam at the Turn of the Twentieth Century." In *Historical and Peasant Consciousness in South East Asia*, edited by Andrew Turton and Shigeharu Tanabe, 75–110. Osaka: National Museum of Ethnology.

Tanham, George K. 1961. *Communist Revolutionary Warfare: The Vietminh in Indochina*. New York: Praeger.

Tasker, Rodney. 1994. "Thailand—Home-Town Jobs: Private Firms Create Rural Employment Opportunities." *Far Eastern Economic Review*, April 14.

Tavivat Puntarigvivat. 1998. "Toward a Buddhist Social Ethics: The Case of Thailand." *Cross Currents* 48 (3): 347–65.

Taylor, J. L. 1991. "Living on the Rim: Ecology and Forest Monks in Northeast Thailand." *Sojourn* 6 (1): 106–25.

———. 1993a. *Forest Monks and the Nation-State: An Anthropological and Historical Study in Northeastern Thailand*. Singapore: Institute of Southeast Asian Studies.

———. 1993b. "Social Activism and Resistance on the Thai Frontier: The Case of Phra Prajak Khuttajitto. *Bulletin of Concerned Asian Scholars* 25 (2): 23–16.

———. 1996. "Thamma-chaat: Activist Monks and Competing Discourses of Nature and Nation in Northeastern Thailand." In *Seeing Forests for Trees: Environment and Environmentalism in Thailand*, edited by Philip Hirsch, 37–52. Chiang Mai, Thailand: Silkworm Books.

————. 2012. "No Way Forward But Back? Re-emergent Thai Falangism, Democracy, and the New 'Red Shirt' Social Movement." In *Bangkok, May 2010: Perspectives on a Divided Thailand*, edited by Michael J. Montesano, Pavin Chachavalpongpun, and Aekapol Chongvilaivan, 287–312. Singapore: Institute of Southeast Asian Studies.

Tej Bunnag. 1967. "Khabot phu mi bun phak isan ro so 121" [Millenarian revolt in Isan, 1902]. *Sangkhomsat parithat* [Social Science Review] 5:78–87.

————. 1968. "Khabot ngiao muang Phrae" [Shan Rebellion in Muang Phrae], *Sangkhomsat parithat* [Social Science Review] 6 (2): 67–82.

————. 1977. *The Provincial Administration of Siam, 1892–1915*. Kuala Lumpur: Oxford University Press.

Terwiel, B. J. 1983. "Bondage and Slavery in Early Nineteenth Century Siam." *Slavery, Bondage, and Dependency in Southeast Asia*, edited by Anthony Reid, 118–37. New York: St. Martin's Press.

————. 1984. "Formal Structure and Informal Rules: An Historical Perspective on Hierarchy, Bondage, and the Patron-Client Relationship." In *Strategies and Structures in Thai Society*, edited by Han ten Brummelhuis and Jeremy H. Kemp, 19–38. Amsterdam: Universiteit van Amsterdam, Antropologisch-Sociologisch Centrum.

Textor, Robert B. 1961. *From Peasant to Pedicab Driver*. New Haven: Yale University Southeast Asia Studies (Cultural Report Series No. 9).

Thailand Information Center (Sweden). 1980. "The Communist Party of Thailand and the Conflict in Indochina." *TIC News* 4 (1), October 31.

Thailand, Central Statistical Office. 1955. *Economic and Demographic Survey 1954*, 1st Series (Municipality of Bangkok), 2nd series (Municipality of Thonburi).

Thailand, Committee on Development of the Northeast. 1961. *The Northeast Development Plan, 1962–1966*. Bangkok: The Planning Office, National Economic Development Board, Office of the Prime Minister.

Thailand, Department of Publicity. 1941. *Thailande: Comment des territoires de la Thailande ont été enlevés par la France*. Bangkok.

Thailand, Institute of Public Administration, Thammasat University. 1958. *Khumue chat ongkan khong ratthaban thai, pho so 2500* [Organizational Manual of the Thai Government, 1957]. Bangkok.

Thailand, Khanakammakan phatthana tawan ok chiang nuea. 1961 [BE 2504]. *Phaen phatthana tawan ok chiang nuea pho so 2505–2509* [Northeast Development Plan, 1962–1966]. Bangkok: Suan Wang Phang Phatthanakansetthakit, Samnakngan Satha Phatthanasetthakit Haeng Chat, Samnak Nayok Ratthamontri.

Thailand, Ministry of Agriculture, Division of Agricultural Economics, Office of the Under-Secretary of State. 1955. *Thailand Economic Farm Survey, 1953*. Bangkok.

Thailand, Ministry of Agriculture, Agricultural Statistics Section, Division of Agricultural Economics, Office of the Under-Secretary of State. 1961. *Agricultural Statistics of Thailand, 1960*. Bangkok.

Thailand, Ministry of Communications. 1947. *Ngan chalong rotfai luang, khrop 50 pi* [Fiftieth Anniversary Celebration of the Royal State Railway]. Bangkok.

Thailand, Ministry of Defense. Supreme Command Headquarters. 1962. *The National Security Organization and Conception for Countering Communist Activities in Thailand*. Bangkok, May 29.

Thailand, Ministry of Education. 1961. *Bukkhon samkhan khong chat Thai, Baeprian sangkhom sueksa ton 1, chan prathom pi thi 3* [Important Thai People, Social studies textbook, part 1, 3rd grade]. Bangkok: Khuru sapha.

Thailand, Ministry of Interior, Community Development Bureau, Department of Interior. 1961. *Activities and Accomplishment in the Implementation of a National Community Development Programme, Thailand (1958–1961)*. Bangkok.

————. 1962. *Operational Plan for Thai-SEATO Regional Community Development Technical Assistance Centre, Ubolrajthani, Thailand*. Bangkok.

Thailand, Ministry of Interior, Community Development Bureau, Department of Interior, and American Institutes for Research, Asia/Pacific Office. 1970. *The Impact of the Community Development Program: A Study of Sixteen Villages in Amphoe Nonghan, Changwad Udorn*. Bangkok: Local Affairs Press, Department of Local Administration.

Thailand, National Statistical Office, Office of the Prime Minister. 1952. *Bulletin of Statistics (Bangkok)*, vol. 1.

Thailand, National Economic and Social Development Board, Northeast Regional Development Center, Regional Planning Division. 1980a. *Khomun bueangton phak tawan ok chiang nuea yaek rai changwat* [Basic Statistics of the Northeastern Region, by Province]. Bangkok.

Thailand, National Statistical Office, Office of the Prime Minister/Samnakngan satthiti haeng chat, Samnak nayok ratthamontri. 1997. *Migrant Workers in Bangkok Metropolis, Its Vicinity and Specific Areas / Raeng-ngan khong phuyaithin khao Krungthep Maha Nakhon, parimonthon, lae phuenthi kan phatthana chapho*. Bangkok.

Thailand, Samnak nayok ratthamontri, Samnakngan setthakit phophiang phuea yok radap chumchon (Office of the Prime Minister, Office for Sufficiency Economy for Raising the Standards of Communities). 2011. *Khit pho di* [Thinking, Sufficient, Good].

Thak Chaloemtiarana. 1979. *Thailand: The Politics of Despotic Paternalism*. Bangkok: Social Science Association of Thailand and Thai Khadi Institute, Thammasat University.

Theh Chongkhadikij. 1962. "The Northeast Story." *Bangkok Post*, March 5.

Thep Ratana Moli, *Phra*, comp. ed. 1965. *Urangkha nithan: Tamnan phra that phanom phitsadan* [Legend of the breast bone relic: Chronicle of the That Phanom Shrine, expanded]. Nakhon Phanom, Thailand.

Thompson, Virginia. 1941. *Thailand, the New Siam*. New York: Macmillan.

Thompson, Virginia, and Richard Adloff. n.d., *Who's Who in South-east Asia, August 1945– December 1950*. Microfilm of Filecards, n.p.

————. 1948. *Cultural Institutions and Educational Policy in Southeast Asia*. New York: IPR Secretariat. 37–53.

————. 1950. *The Left Wing in Southeast Asia*. New York: William Sloane Associates (For the IPR Secretariat).

Thongchai Winichakul. 1994. *Siam Mapped: A History of the Geo-Body of a Nation*. Honolulu: University of Hawaii Press.

Titaya Suvanjata. 1964. *Perceived Leader Role of Community Development Workers in Thailand*. Bangkok: United States Operations Mission to Thailand.

Tjelland, Rune. 1995. *Political Brokerage: Rural Activists and Peasant Mobilisation in Northeast Thailand*. Oslo: University of Oslo, Department of Anthropology.

Toem Singhatthit (pseud.). 1956. *Fang khwa maenam khong* [Right Bank of the Mekong]. Bangkok: Samnakphim Witthaya, 2 vols.

Toem Wiphakphachanakit. 1970. *Prawatsat Isan* [History of the Northeast]. Bangkok: Samakhom Sangkhomsat Haeng Prathet Thai.

Tsay Ching-lung. 2001. "Labour Migration and Regional Changes in East Asia: Outflows of Thai Workers to Taiwan." Paper presented at the international workshop on "Labour Migration and Socio-economic Change in Southeast and East Asia," Lund, Sweden.

Turton, Andrew. 1978. "The Current Situation in the Thai Countryside." In *Thailand: Roots of Conflict*, edited by Andrew Turton, Jonathan Fast, and Malcolm Caldwell, 104–42. Nottingham: Spokesman.

————. 1984. "Limits of Ideological Domination and the Formation of Social Consciousness." In *Historical and Peasant Consciousness in South East Asia*, edited by Andrew Turton and Shigeharu Tanabe, 19–74. Osaka: National Museum of Ethnology.

Un Mahachokchai, comp. 1976. *Phra Si Ariya Mettraiya (Phra Si An)*. Khon Kaen, Thailand.

United Nations. Statistical Office of the UN, Department of Economic and Social Affairs. 1955. *Statistical Yearbook*. New York.

United Nations Development Programme, Thailand. 2003. *Thailand Human Development Report 2003*. Bangkok: United Nations Development Programme.

————. 2007. *Human Development Report 2007: Sufficiency Economy and Human Development*. Bangkok: United Nations Development Programme.

————. 2010. *Human Security, Today and Tomorrow: Thailand Human Development Report 2009*. Bangkok: United Nations Development Programme.

United States, Department of State, Division of Biographic Information, Office of Libraries and Intelligence Acquisition. 1950. *Far Easterners in the Comintern Structure*. Washington, DC: (OIR Report No. 5226), December 7.

United States. International Development Cooperation Agency, Agency for International Development. 1980. *Thailand: Country Development Strategy Statement FY 82*. Washington, DC.

Usher, Ann Danaiya. 2009. *Thai Forestry: A Critical History*. Chiang Mai: Silkworm Books.

Vail, Peter. 2007. "Thailand's Khmer as 'Invisible Minority': Language, Ethnicity and Cultural Politics in North-Eastern Thailand." *Asian Ethnicity* 8 (2): 111–30.

Vandergeest, Peter, and Nancy Lee Peluso. 1995. "Territorialization and State Power in Thailand." *Theory and Society* 24:385–426.

Vella, Walter F. 1955. *The Impact of the West on the Government in Thailand*. Berkeley and Los Angeles: University of California Press (University of California Publications in Political Science, vol. 4, no. 31).

————. 1957. *Siam Under Rama III*. Locust Valley, NY: J. J. Augustin (Association for Asian Studies, Monograph 4).

————, assisted by Dorothy Vella. 1978. *Chaiyo! King Vajiravudh and the Development of Thai Nationalism*. Honolulu: University of Hawaii Press.

Vietnam Information Service, Paris, 1947.

Voranai Vanijaka. 2010. "Amart and Prai." *Bangkok Post*, July 18.

Walker, Andrew. 2010. "Royal Sufficiency and Elite Misrepresentation of Rural Livelihoods." In *Saying the Unsayable: Monarchy and Democracy in Thailand*, edited by Søren Ivarsson and Lotte Isager, 241–65. Copenhagen: Nordic Institute of Asian Studies, NIAS Studies in Asian Topics 47.

———. 2012. *Thailand's Political Peasants: Exploring Power in a Modern Rural Economy*. Madison: University of Wisconsin Press.

Ward, Barbara. 1965. "Varieties of the Conscious Model: Fishermen of South China." In *The Relevance of Models for Social Anthropology* (Association of Social Anthropologists, Monographs 1), 113–37. London: Tavistock Publications.

Warner, Roger. 1996. *Shooting at the Moon: The Story of America's Clandestine War in Laos*. South Royalton VE: Steerforth Press.

Watson, Keith. 1982. *Educational Development in Thailand*. Hong Kong: Heinemann Asia.

Weber, M. 1958 [1946]. *From Max Weber*. Translated and edited by H. H. Gerth and C. W. Mills. New York: Oxford University Press.

———. 1978 [1968]. *Economy and Society: An Outline of Interpretive Sociology*, edited by G. Roth and C. Wittich. Berkeley/Los Angeles: University of California Press.

Wedel, Yuangrat Pattanapongse. 1981. "The Communist Party of Thailand and Thai Radical Thought." In *Southeast Asian Affairs 1981*, 325–39. Singapore: Institute of Southeast Asian Studies.

Wedel, Yuangrat, and Paul Wedel. 1987. *Radical Thought, Thai Mind: The Development of Revolutionary Ideas in Thailand*. Bangkok: Assumption Business Administration College.

Weisman, Jan. 1997. "Rice Outside the Paddy: The Form and Function of Hybridity in a Thai Novel." *Crossroads* 11 (1): 51–78.

———. 2000. "Tropes and Traces: Hybridity, Race, Sex, and Responses to Modernity in Thailand." Unpublished PhD dissertation, University of Washington.

Wenk, Klaus. 1968. *The Restoration of Thailand under Rama I, 1782–1809*. Translated from the German by Greely Stahl. Tucson: University of Arizona Press (Association for Asia Studies, Monograph 24).

White, Joyce. 1995. "Modeling the Development of Early Rice Agriculture: Ethnoecological Perspectives from Northeast Thailand." *Asian Perspectives* 34 (1): 37–68.

Wilson, Constance M. 1997. "The Holy Man in the History of Thailand and Laos." *Journal of Southeast Asian Studies* 28 (2): 345–64.

Wilson, David A. 1959. "Thailand and Marxism." In *Marxism in Southeast Asia*, edited by F. N. Trager. Stanford: Stanford University Press.

———. 1961. "Bangkok's Dim View to the East." *Asian Survey* 1 (4): 13–17.

———. 1962. *Politics in Thailand*. Ithaca, New York: Cornell University Press.

Wimonphan Pitthawatchai. 1973. *Hit sipsong* [The twelve customs]. Bangkok: Mahachon.

Wolf, Eric R. 1956. "Aspects of Group Relations in a Complex Society." *American Anthropologist* 58: 1065–78.

———. 1966. *Peasants*. Englewood Cliffs, New Jersey: Prentice-Hall, Inc.

————. 1969. *Peasant Wars of the Twentieth Century*. New York, Evanston, and London: Harper and Row.

Wolters, O. W. 1966. "A Western Teacher and the History of Early Ayudya." *Social Science Review* (Bangkok), Special Issue on Thai history (Special Issue No. 3): 88–97.

————. 1982. *History, Culture, and Region in Southeast Asian Perspectives*. Singapore: Institute of Southeast Asian Studies.

Wood, W. A. R. 1924. *A History of Siam*. London: Fisher Unwin.

World Bank (International Bank for Reconstruction and Development). 1959. *A Public Development Program for Thailand*. Baltimore: Johns Hopkins Press.

Worsley, Peter. 1968. *The Trumpet Shall Sound*. 2nd rev. ed. New York: Schocken Books.

Wyatt, David K. 1963. "Siam and Laos, 1767–1827." *Journal of Southeast Asian History* 4 (2): 13–32.

————. 1966. "The Buddhist Monkhood as an Avenue of Social Mobility in Traditional Thai Society." *Silapakorn* [Fine Arts] 10:41–52.

————. 1969. *The Politics of Reform in Thailand: Education in the Reign of King Chulalongkorn*. New Haven: Yale University Press.

————. 1984. *Thailand. A Short History*. New Haven: Yale University Press.

Yatsushiro, Toshio, et al. 1964. *The Village Organizer in Thailand: A Study of His Needs and Problems*. Bangkok: Department of Community Development, Ministry of Interior and United States Operations Mission to Thailand.

Yatsushiro, Toshio, ed. 1968. *Studies of Northeast Villages in Thailand*. Bangkok: United States Agency for International Development, September.

INDEX